I Love you!
From: Ashley
To: Somebody

FOREWORD

The Revenue Reconciliation Act of 1993 affects taxpayers in all income brackets. Many new law changes either are currently in effect or will go into effect within a matter of months. You will find references many of these changes and to Internal Revenue Code Sections, Revenue Rulings, court cases, etc. throughout. Quotations of important portions of tax law and regulations are scattered throughout the text to give you confidence in what you learn.

Therefore it is necessary each year to update "Income Tax Guide for Ministers and Religious Workers." So we must strongly encourage you to READ EACH NEW EDITION carefully, in order for you to be able to apply the law changes to your situation. Keeping detailed records has become more important as the IRS has become more demanding. **We publish a "Professional Tax Record Book," that we feel is a very useful tool to meet this need.**

Ministers quite often have difficulty teaching and communicating to the church officials how they, the employer, can assist him in paying the least amount of tax legally possible. They, too, will benefit if they will carefully read each new edition. A **one hour tape presentation** of "Minister's Compensation Package, Tax & Financial Planning," is available to share the basic information with your financial committee. After you have read the text, we encourage you to **take advantage of our** "Tax Preparation by Mail" service. Detailed information is given at the end of the book.

You have no doubt experienced frustrations in the past when you sought professional help or purchased a tax guide, and found your questions unanswered. Even calls to the IRS Taxpayer Service are often fruitless and confusing. Many tax guides for ministers contain much information about itemized deductions, rentals, dividends, etc., and not enough about your particular tax problems. You will not find information concerning all aspects of income, deductions, and tax in this book. Information for these general subjects is available from the IRS. Call your toll-free number for your state IRS office and ask for Publication 17, and they will send it to you free. From the list of publications in your 1040 Package, order any topic you need in the general areas that apply to your tax circumstance. There are many good commercial tax guides at your newsstand that can help in other areas. You are a busy professional person and this book is designed to give you in a compact nutshell all you must know as a minister not to OVERPAY UNCLE SAM!!

Our duty as individual Christians is to use wisely that which the Lord gives us. The success or failure you, as a servant of God, have with the money God gives you greatly affects your testimony for Jesus Christ. Ministers and religious workers in the church should then be the most successful people on earth. There is no question as to your ability to make better use of the money for the Lord's work rather than letting the government waste it.

Share the information on the following pages with your friends in the ministry. We are available to conduct seminars on ministers' tax law. It is our prayer that your mind will be freed from financial burdens by applying the facts in the book to your situation; then with zeal share Christ with the world.

- B.J. Worth, EA, ATA, CPT

Table of Contents

Chapter One - INCOME 7
  Where to Report Income 7
    Dual-Status Minister 7
    Lay Employees 7
    Employed Ministers Are Not to Use Sch C For Reporting Salary 8
    Self-Employed 10
  Taxable Sources Of Income 11
    Professional Income 11
    Gift or Bonus From Employer 11
    Social Security Paid By the Employer 12
    Moving Reimbursement 12
    Insurance 13
    Housing 13
    Non-Accountable Allowances 13
    Personal Use of Auto Provided by Employer 13
  Non-Taxable Sources of Income---Exclusions 14
    Fringe Benefits 14
      Qualified Retirement Plan Contributions 14
      Group Term Life Insurance 16
      Accident And Health Insurance 16
      Self-Insured Medical Reimbursement Plans 17
      Disability Insurance 17
      Qualified Educational Assistance 17
      Qualified Tuition Reduction 17
      Qualified Scholarships 18
      Cafeteria Plans 18
    Voluntary Tax Shelter Plans 18
      Tax Sheltered Accounts - (TSA) 19
      Individual Retirement Accounts - (IRA) 19
      Self-Employed Keogh Plans (H.R. 10) 20
    Housing Exclusion 21
      Dual-Status Minister - Sec. 107 21
      Lay Employees - Sec. 119 21
    Gifts 21
    Accountable Reimbursement Plan for Professional Expenses 22
    Deferred Compensation Plans 22
    Gratuity Payments to a Retired Minister 22

Chapter Two - PARSONAGE ALLOWANCE 23
  Are You Entitled to the Parsonage Allowance Exclusion? 23
  Are You Employed by a Church or An Integral Agency of a Church? 23
    Definition of Church 24
    Integral Agency of a Church 24
  Are You Performing Ministerial Services? 25
    Qualifying Services Include 25
    Non-Qualifying Duties Include 26
  Are You Ordained By A Church Or "The Equivalent Thereof?" 26
    What about equal treatment of male & female religious workers? 27
  Parsonage Allowance Exclusion Rules 28
    What Does the Parsonage Allowance Exclusion Include? 28
    How much of a Minister's Salary Can Be Designated? 29
    What is Meant By "Official Designation"? 31
      Ministers Who Own 32
      Ministers Who Rent 32
      Church Owns The Parsonage 32
      Evangelists 32
      Missionaries 33
      Retired Ministers 33
    Steps in Designating & Deducting Parsonage Allowance 33
    Suggested Wording of the Official Designation 34
    Computation of Parsonage Allowance -"Worksheet For Form 2106" 35
    Computation of Social Security -"Worksheet For Form 2106" 36

Chapter Three - PROFESSIONAL EXPENSES 37
   Recordkeeping a Must!! 38
   Unreimbursed Professional Expenses 38
      If You Do Not Adequately Account To Your Employer 39
      Dalan Case - Proration of Unreimbursed Expenses 39
   Reimbursed Professional Expenses 40
      Tax Law & Regulations 41
         Business Connection 41
         Adequate Accounting 43
            Definition Of Adequate Accounting 43
            If You Do Adequately Account To Your Employer 44
            Adequate Accounting Requirement Is Satisfied by Mileage Allowance & Per Diem . . 44
            When Actual Auto Expenses Exceed The Cents Per Mile Computation 45
         Return of Amounts Exceeding Expenses 45
      Adopt One of the Following Reimbursement Plans 46
         Salary Plus Unlimited Reimbursement 46
         Salary Plus Fixed Limit Reimbursement 46
   Typical Professional Expenses for a Minister 47
      Auto Expense 47
         Log Your Business Miles 47
         Sale Or Trade Of Business Auto 48
         Auto Interest & Personal Property Tax 49
         Lease or Own 49
         Choose the Best Method of Deducting Auto Expenses 49
         Mileage Allowance Method 49
         Actual Method 50
         How To Compute Auto Depreciation 50
         Leased Automobiles 51
         Employer Provided Autos 52
      Travel 55
         Lodging, Meal, And Incidental Expense Per Diem Rates 56
      Entertainment 57
      Educational Expenses 58
      Library & Equipment Depreciation 58
      Office Supplies And Postage 60
      Religious Materials 61
      Seminars And Dues 61
      Subscriptions, Paperbacks And Tapes 61
      Business Telephone 61
   Moving Expenses - Form 3903 61
   Earned Income Credit 62

Chapter Four - SOCIAL SECURITY AND RETIREMENT PLANNING 63
   Social Security for Religious Workers 63
      Dual-Status Minister 63
         Computation Of Social Security Base - "Worksheet for Form 2106" 63
         Social Security Exemption 64
            What Happens To What I Have Already Paid In? 64
            Disability Coverage 65
            Irrevocable 65
            When To File Form 4361 65
            Opportunity for Minister of New Faith 65
            How To File Form 4361 66
            You Must Establish That the Church is a Church 66
            How To Send Your Form 4361 67
            How It Gets Processed 68
            Put Your Approved Copy In Several Safe Places 68
      Social Security & the Religious Sects Under Vow of Poverty 68
      Social Security and the Lay Employee 68
         Electing Churches—Form 8274 68
         How To Do Correction For Wrong Treatment 69
      Should the Minister's Spouse be on the Payroll? 70
   Estimated Tax, Form 1040ES 70
      Underpayment Penalties 71
      Waiver of Penalty 71

Optional Withholding Agreement	71
Retirement Planning For Religious Workers	71
Mutual Funds	72
Life Insurance	73
Annuities	73
Unqualified and Qualified Plans	73
Qualified Retirement Plan (QRP)	73
Tax Sheltered Account or Sec. 403(b) Plan	74
Individual Retirement Account	74
When You Should Have A Qualified Plan?	74
Tax Planning for the Retired or Semi-retired Minister	74
Definition of Earned Income	75
Social Security Benefits are Sometimes Taxed	75
Is Your Social Security Earnings Record Correct?	75
Chapter Five - OVERSEAS MISSIONARIES AND RELIGIOUS ORDERS	76
Missionaries Serving Overseas	76
Bona Fide Residency and Physical Presence Rules	76
Discussion of Form 2555	77
Foreign Earned Income Exclusion	77
Foreign Housing Exclusion	77
Vacation Computation	77
Moving Expense—Overseas	78
Foreign Moves - Form 3903F	78
Non-Foreign Move—Form 3903	78
When and Where To File As An Overseas Missionary	78
Special Extensions Of Time For Filing	79
Independent Missionaries	79
Religious Orders — Two Types	79
Protestant Religious Orders Described in Sec. 1402(c)(4)	79
Information Returns and Proper Tax Treatment for Sec. 1402(c)(4) Religious Orders	80
Religious Orders Described in Sec. 1402(g)	80
Information Returns and Proper Tax Treatment for Sec. 1402(g) Religious Orders	81
Chapter Six - COMPLETED PAYROLL REPORTS	82
Steps in Establishing a Compensation Package	82
Dual-Status Minister - Rev. Snodgrass' Compensation Package	83
Lay Employee - Joseph Mop's Compensation Package	83
Organizations Must File Information Returns!	84
Who is An Employer?	84
Who Is An Employee?	84
Who Is An Independent Contractor?	84
Informational Return Penalties	85
Willful Or Intentional Disregard	85
Attitude Towards the IRS Should Be One of Cooperation	85
How To Prepare Information Returns	86
Obtain A Federal Identification Number	86
Withhold Required Taxes	86
Lay Employees	86
Dual-Status Ministers	87
Independent Religious Workers	87
Prepare a Payroll Sheet for each Employee	88
Chart of Where to Show Income	89
Make Payroll Tax Deposits as Required	89
Prepare Quarterly Reports	90
Prepare Year End Reports	91
Chart of Where to Show Income	93
Completed Payroll Reports	94
Chapter Seven - COMPLETED INCOME TAX RETURN	100
CHECKLIST	113
SERVICES	125
Information for Ordering Supplies	125
Consultation and Seminar Registration Information	126
Seminar Location and Dates	127
Tax Preparation by Mail Information	128

CHAPTER ONE

INCOME

Employees of churches and integral agencies of churches are divided into two classifications; the dual-status minister and the lay employee. **Dual-status means** that the minister is an **employee** for income reporting, fringe benefit and expense deducting purposes and **self-employed** for social security purposes. A dual-status minister is one who has been given the authority by a church to perform substantially all of the ministerial duties. These duties include preaching, teaching, evangelism, conduct of worship, administration, baptisms, weddings, funerals and communions. Commissioned, licensed or employed ministers of a church or an integral agency of a church that provides for ordination of ministers are considered **as if** they were ordained or "the equivalent thereof" if they are performing ministerial duties. Employees of churches and integral agencies of churches who do not perform ministerial duties are lay employees. Generally, employees of non-integral agencies are lay employees, even if they are officially ordained. There are definite tax advantages to being a dual-status minister. It is important to determine the proper status of each employee when they are employed. Recent court cases and letter rulings have caused major changes in the definition of who is a dual-status minister. Chapter Two gives full discussion concerning these changes.

Where to Report Income

Dual-Status Minister

Ministers employed by churches and integral agencies of churches have a dual-status treatment in the Internal Revenue Code. They are to be treated as employees for income tax reporting according to "common law rules" in Reg.31.3401(c)-1; and as self-employed for social security reporting Sec. 1402(a)(8). On a dual-status minister's Form W-2, Box 3 for social security wages and Box 5 for medicare wages should be left blank. The chart shown in Chapter Six gives specific directions as to what is considered taxable income and what is to be entered in Box 1 and what is not to be shown. Withholding of income tax for the dual-status minister is not required according to Sec. 3401(a)(9), it is optional. If the dual-status minister did not file Form 4361, it is necessary for social security to be computed on Schedule SE. If a minister has filed Form 4361, "Application for Exemption from Self-Employment Tax for Ministers", and has received an approved copy, he is exempt from social security on earnings from the ministry, and needs only to indicate that by writing "Exempt---Form 4361" on the self-employment line of Form 1040, page 2.

Ministers are considered employees for income reporting, expense deducting and fringe benefit eligibility. Since 1987, unreimbursed or reimbursed without "an accountable plan," automobile, travel and professional expenses are allowed only as miscellaneous itemized deductions on Schedule A. They are also subject to limitations: meals & entertainment are reduced by 20%, then combined with other miscellaneous deductions, and further reduced by 2% of the Adjusted Gross Income.

Lay Employees

Lay Employees are employees for both income and social security purposes. On a lay employee's Form W-2, Box 1 will show his salary, Box 3 will show the social security wage, and Box 5 will show the medicare wage. Until the end of 1983, a not-for-profit organization or church was exempt from withholding and matching social security on their lay employees, unless they chose to cover them by filing Form SS-15. As a part of the Social Security

Amendments Act of 1983, social security coverage was extended on a **mandatory** basis to all lay employees of not-for-profit organizations as of January 1, 1984. The Tax Reform Act of 1984 provided for an election by a church or qualified church-controlled organization that is opposed for religious reasons to the payment of social security taxes, not to be subject to such taxes. (Form 8274) Lay employees of churches that make the election **are liable for paying social security** on their personal returns on Schedule SE, Section B. Electing church employers are responsible for withholding income tax and filing Form 941E and a W-2 for each employee. (See complete discussion in Chapter Four.)

Since 1987, unreimbursed or reimbursed without "an accountable plan," automobile, travel and professional expenses are allowed only as miscellaneous itemized deductions on Schedule A. They are also subject to limitations: meals & entertainment are reduced by 20%, then combined with other miscellaneous deductions, and further reduced by 2% of the Adjusted Gross Income.

Employed Ministers Are Not to Use Sch C For Reporting Salary

Before 1980 the IRS allowed ministers to use Schedule C to report income and expenses which basically ignored the dual-status treatment. The dual-status treatment of the minister has always been a part of tax law. To ignore the historic IRS position and report a minister's salary and deduct their professional expenses on Sch C, will often cause an audit and an assessment of additional tax liability. Hundreds of clergy have suffered this traumatic experience in the past three years.

The IRS's position that an employed minister is an employee for income reporting purposes is well defined in the following quote from Publication 517, page 1:

> "EMPLOYMENT STATUS FOR OTHER TAX PURPOSES
>
> Because of statutory law, you are considered a self-employed individual in performing your ministerial services for social security tax purposes. However, because of common law rules (discussed next), you may be considered an employee for income or retirement plan tax purposes.
>
> **Common law rules.** Under these nonstatutory rules, you are considered an employee or a self-employed person depending on all the facts and circumstances. Generally, you are an employee if your employer has the legal right to control both what you do and how you do it, even if you have considerable discretion and freedom of action.
>
> **Example**. A church hires and pays you to perform ministerial services for it, subject to its control. Under the common law rules, you are an employee of the church while performing those services. Your wages are reported on Form W-2, Wage and Tax Statement, for income tax purposes, but no social security taxes are withheld. However, you are treated as self-employed for social security purposes. Therefore, you must pay self-employment tax on those wages yourself unless you request and receive an exemption from self-employment tax. **On your Form W-2, Box 3 for social security wages and Box 5 for medicare wages should have been left blank.**
>
> To find out if you are an employee or a self-employed person, you may get a determination from the IRS by filing Form SS-8."

Before requesting a determination from the IRS, get and study a copy of the full text of Revenue Ruling 87-41. It states, "If the relationship of employer and employee exists, the designation or description of the relationship by the parties as anything other than that of employer and employee **is immaterial**."

As an aid to determining whether an individual is an employee under the common law rules, twenty factors have been developed based on an examination of cases and rulings considering whether an individual is an employee. Some of the factors, such as "subject to control," weigh more in importance on the scale of determining if an employer/employee

INCOME

relationship exists. If enough of the factors indicate there is an employer/employee relationship, and the employer does not treat the employee correctly, the IRS penalties are substantial. According to Rev. Ruling 87-41,CB 1987-1, 296, a brief listing of **THE TWENTY FACTORS ARE:**

(1) Compliance with instructions;
(2) Training required;
(3) Integration of services into business operations;
(4) Services rendered personally;
(5) Hiring, supervising, and paying assistants;
(6) Continuing relationship;
(7) Set hours of work;
(8) Full time required;
(9) Doing work on employer's premises;
(10) Services performed in order or sequence set;
(11) Oral or written reports;
(12) Payment by hour, week, month;
(13) Payment of business and/or traveling expenses;
(14) Furnishing of tools and materials;
(15) Significant investment;
(16) Realization of profit or loss;
(17) Working for more than one firm at a time;
(18) Making service available to general public;
(19) Right to discharge;
(20) Right to terminate relationship without incurring liability.

Dual-status ministers are definitely self-employed for social security purposes. However, for income reporting, expense deducting, fringe benefit provision purposes, the Internal Revenue Code speaks clearly about their status being that of an employee. IRS publications on the issue have historically presented the dual-status treatment for ministers performing services for a church or an integral agency of a church.

When the source of income is from individuals for whom a service was performed, reporting the income on Schedule C is correct. Honorariums received for performing weddings, funerals, baptisms and counseling are correctly reported as self-employment income on Sch C.

To be eligible to make contributions to a Sec. 403(b) Tax Sheltered Account, an individual must be a common law employee of a not-for-profit organization according to Rev. Ruling 66-274. This limitation would also apply to other excludable fringe benefits such as medical insurance, group term life insurance, etc. **If** a minister could be considered as an independent contractor and use Sch C for reporting income and expenses, **he would have to report as taxable income** any amounts the congregation pays for employee fringe benefits.

When the source of income is from a not-for-profit corporation under Sec. 501(c)(3), it is not independent contractor income, but rather wages or salary. Even a person who creates a for-profit corporation becomes it's employee and receives a salary and/or dividend income. Rev. Ruling 71-86 states that a president, sole shareholder, who sets his own hours, duties, salary and wasn't responsible to anyone else, was an employee for income tax withholding, social security and federal unemployment tax purposes. Similarly, Rev. Ruling 78-361 treats an officer performing substantial services as an employee. In Harris Inc. v. U.S., May 7, 1991, only officers who perform no services or perform only minor services and who are not entitled to receive direct or indirect remuneration are exempted from employee tax status.

Establishing a written accountable reimbursement plan is the legal way to reduce your taxable income as an employee. Chapter Three discusses how to establish an accountable reimbursement plan and adequately account to your employer for your professional expenses. If, as an employee of a church, all professional expenses are adequately accounted to an employer and reimbursed, the end tax liability will be similar to that of a self-employed evangelist able to report his income and expenses on Schedule C.

Preparer penalties: Tax preparers are subject to negligence penalties if they knowingly prepare a return incorrectly. After a careful study of the citations just presented, a tax preparer who disregards the position of the IRS by not preparing an employed minister's tax return as dual-status would be guilty of negligently understating the minister's tax liability. Sec. 6694 provides for a penalty of $1,000 per return prepared with an intentional disregard of rules or regulations ($500 for returns prepared before 1990).

Churches who fail to prepare W-2's for their employees are subject to severe penalties. Providing a Form 1099 to an employed minister rather than a W-2 can result in a $50 penalty, as **it is necessary to prepare "correct" informational returns to avoid penalties**. It is very important to learn what the law requires and carefully meet those obligations. Chapter Six discusses the rules and shows filled out examples of payroll reporting and informational returns.

Some clergy tax advisors and publications insist on continuing to use Schedule C for **employed ministers**. We feel it is unfortunate that much confusion has resulted from the issue. The "fight for the right to use Sch C" that causes ministers to be audited and assessed tax liabilities is inexcusable.

In denominations where the local church does not have a choice as to whom the superintendent or bishop appoints to be the minister of their congregation, **we feel that a co-employer relationship exists**. The regional church representative **controls and appoints** the minister and the local congregation **pays the salary**.

- *What to do if your employer gives you the wrong informational return*
    1. Have your employer prepare a corrected Form 1099 with -0- income shown. Then prepare a Form W-2 correctly reporting the taxable salary in Box 1. This correction may prevent an audit.
    2. When an employed dual-status minister, paid by a church or church controlled organization, receives Form 1099 rather than a Form W-2, **and the employer will not prepare corrected forms,** we recommend the following procedure for preparing Form 1040: enter the amount shown as income on the Form 1099 on Sch C as gross income because IRS computers will scan the tax return and expect it to be there. Then subtract the same amount as "expense" on Sch C to have a net result of zero on Sch C to the extent of the salary. Then enter the amount as income on Form 1040, line 7 as though it were wages on a W-2. IRS computers will accept an amount on line 7 that is greater than the total of other W-2's attached to the return. Use Form 2106 and Sch A to deduct any unreimbursed employee business expenses. Even though IRS has conducted many audits for taxpayers who entered income from one Form 1099 on Sch C, there will be no additional tax assessed for a correctly prepared Form 1040.

Self-Employed

Some ministers are self-employed as evangelists and are not common-law employees of a church or an organization, and it is correct for them to use Schedule C. Honorariums received from speaking, evangelism, weddings, funerals, counseling, and writing are to be entered on Schedule C as self-employed earnings by all ministers.

When an independent religious worker personally receives his support from individual contributions, it becomes necessary to show these amounts on Schedule C and to deduct the expenses of doing ministry to arrive at net income. If large amounts of money for work projects are received, it becomes difficult to prove they are legitimate ordinary and necessary ministry expenses to the IRS in an audit. **The ideal solution to the Sch C problem is for the independent religious worker to establish an employer/employee relationship with a church.** (See complete discussion in Chapter Six.)

INCOME

Taxable Sources Of Income

Gross income, according to Sec. 61, includes all income (cash, value of property, or value of services) from whatever source, unless it is specifically excluded by a section in the Internal Revenue Code. It is important to understand that regardless of what a payor or payee calls a sum of money, property or value of service; facts and circumstances will determine whether it is taxable or not. **Any income that is received because you performed a service is taxable**. Generally, the employee will be taxed on all remuneration that is not a qualified fringe benefit (Chapter One), housing allowance (Chapter Two), or reimbursed professional expenses (Chapter Three).

Professional Income

Fees, offerings, or gifts for speaking, performing weddings, funerals or baptisms are considered professional income. An evangelist receives professional income from the churches to which he ministers. When as a minister you have provided a service and the person receiving the benefit of your ministry gives you money, it should be considered as earned professional income.

Income received from writing, lecturing, radio or television appearances, etc., are additional types of professional income. The income or royalties and expenses of selling religious tapes and books are to be shown on Schedule C as professional income, according to Rev. Ruling 59-50. For ministers not exempt from social security, the net profit will be subject to social security.

Professional income and any expenses incurred in connection with earning the professional income are to be shown on Schedule C.

If honorariums and fees for weddings, funerals, etc., are paid directly to his employer, they are not taxable to the individual minister. (CCH, Standard Federal Tax Reports ¶5507.015)

Gift or Bonus From Employer

When an employer gives a bonus or "love gift" to an employee it is simply additional salary, and should be included in the W-2, Box 1. When the donors have been given receipts for deductible contributions to the church and the church pays the gift or bonus to the employee, it is taxable compensation. Gifts of other than cash should be considered at their fair market value; and, if from the employer, included in the W-2. A common occurrence involves a contributor giving an auto to the church. The church then "pays" or transfers the auto to their pastor. The contributor should be given a statement that the auto was given to the church, then it is a Schedule A contribution at the FMV (donor must determine FMV). The church then must include in the pastor's income the FMV of the auto given as extra compensation.

Small or nominal non-cash gifts at special occasions (birthdays, anniversaries, or holidays) should not be considered taxable according to Rev. Ruling 59-58. Since in Sec. 162, "business gifts" are limited to $25, it would seem appropriate to use the same guideline for "small or nominal gifts."

When an employer sells at a bargain price or transfers without payment any property, such as the parsonage, it results in taxable compensation. The difference between the amount paid and the amount of its fair market value at the time of the transfer is taxable according to Reg. 1.61-2(d)(2). To avoid an excessive tax burden in the year of transfer we suggest the following: The employer should loan the employee the amount of the difference between the FMV and the amount paid by the employee and over a period of time, forgive a portion of the loan each year. The annual income would be the amount of forgiveness and if the loan is secured by a home, it would be principal payment that can be parsonage allowance.

When an employer helps an employee or a member of an employee's family with crisis needs it will result in taxable compensation. We recommend that a local non-employer,

Social Security Paid By the Employer

When an employer agrees to provide extra payment to a dual-status minister to pay all or part of his social security tax, **it must be shown as taxable salary** according to Rev. Ruling 68-507. Dual-status ministers are treated as self-employed taxpayers when computing their social security on Schedule SE. Their combined rate of social security tax and medicare tax is 15.3% (less adjustments of approximately 2%) for 1993 and 1994. It may be convenient to have the employer pay this amount to the minister on a quarterly basis, to coincide with the due dates of his estimated tax payments.

The Social Security Amendments Act of 1983 (H.R. 1900) increased the rates of social security and the maximum wage on which each taxpayer pays. Self-employed persons had always paid less than the total rate that employees and employers paid. H.R. 1900 began a gradual closing of the difference until 1990, at which time the self-employed are paying the same rate as the employer/employee. By giving credits, the increased cost of social security for those who were self-employed was phased in gradually. Employees have never included as gross income the amount of their employer's matching portion of social security. As a part of the original H. R. 1900, deductions are now available for the self-employed to take the place of the 2% credit. Otherwise, the self-employed would be paying more than the employee. On Schedule SE the gross social security base is adjusted to allow ½ of social security as a deduction. On Form 1040, page 1, an adjustment for ½ of the social security paid by the self-employed taxpayer is allowed.

For a taxpayer in the 15% tax bracket, the deductions result in nearly the same social security cost as the 2% credit did. For a taxpayer in the 28% tax bracket, the deductions are better!

Since 1-1-1991: The wage base for the two parts of the social security tax (social security and medicare) are different. **The 7.65% combined rate** is made up of 6.2% rate for social security and 1.45% rate for medicare.

Here's the schedule of what has happened since 1983:

YEAR	SOC SECURITY WAGE BASE	MEDICARE WAGE BASE	EMPLOYEE RATE	SELF-EMPLOYED RATE	LESS CREDIT	NET SE RATE
1983	$35,700		6.70%	9.35%		9.35%
1984	$37,800		6.70%	14.00%	2.7%	11.30%
1985	$39,600		7.05%	14.10%	2.3%	11.80%
1986	$42,000		7.15%	14.30%	2.0%	12.30%
1987	$43,800		7.15%	14.30%	2.0%	12.30%
1988	$45,000		7.51%	15.02%	2.0%	13.02%
1989	$48,000		7.51%	15.02%	2.0%	13.02%
1990	$51,300		7.65%	15.30%	0	15.30%
1991	$53,400	$125,000	7.65%	15.30%	0	15.30%
1992	$55,500	$130,200	7.65%	15.30%	0	15.30%
1993	$57,600	$135,000	7.65%	15.30%	0	15.30%
1994	$60,600	No limit	7.65%	15.30%	0	15.30%

Moving Reimbursement

Dual-status ministers are employees for moving expense purposes. Moving reimbursements cannot be "above the line" reimbursed employee business expense deductions, according to Revenue Ruling 75-362. Moving expenses are unique and must be treated according to their own special set of rules.

According to Sec. 82, any reimbursement received from an employer, directly or indirectly, by an individual, for expenses of moving from one residence to another, which is

(continued from previous page: not-for-profit organization (such as Red Cross) be utilized to solicit help for an employee with crisis needs.)

INCOME

attributable to employment, **must be shown as income on the W-2, Box 1.** Employers are to prepare Form 4782 or a similar statement, showing the details of the moving reimbursement, and give it to the employee. If the move meets the requirements of Sec. 217, (35 mile distance and 39 weeks of work), the allowable expenses are to be entered on Form 3903 and subtracted as a "below the line" itemized deduction on Sch A, line 19.

If the employer expects the employee to satisfy the 35 mile and 39 weeks of work requirements for deduction, the moving reimbursement is not subject to income tax withholding or social security, according to Revenue Ruling 70-482. **Dual-status ministers and lay employees do not pay social security on deductible moving reimbursements.**

If the employer knows that the requirements of Sec. 217 **will not be met**, the moving reimbursement is subject to both income tax and social security tax withholding for the lay employee. Nondeductible moving expense reimbursement paid to a dual-status minister is subject to income tax and social security tax and the additional tax liability should be included in his estimate or optional withholding.

New Moving Deduction Rules for 1994: The Revenue Reconciliation Act of 1993 contains many changes for moving expense deductions effective 1-1-94. Reimbursements of deductible moving expenses will not be included in the W-2. The distance test will be 50 miles and many deductible expenses have been eliminated. The deduction will move from Schedule A to page 1, Form 1040, where it will become an above-the-line deduction.

Insurance

The cost of regular term and permanent life insurance (whole, universal, etc.) paid by the employer is a taxable fringe benefit if the minister names the beneficiary of his choosing. Any premium paid for group term life insurance **over $50,000** coverage is also taxable. The Table in Reg. 1.79-3(d)(2) is to be used to compute the amount to be included in an employee's income, even though the employer's actual premium may be more or less.

Housing

We recommend that the dual-status minister "over estimate" his parsonage allowance that is required to be designated in advance by his employer. When filing the tax return, any unused parsonage allowance becomes taxable income, and is to be entered on Form 1040, line 22 as "excess parsonage allowance."

The lay employee who is provided living quarters that are not on the premises of the employer, nor for the convenience of the employer, nor a requirement of the job, must show as taxable income the value of the living quarters provided. This value is also subject to social security tax. (Sec. 119 qualifications are not met.)

Non-Accountable Allowances

If you are paid a non-accountable expense allowance or reimbursement and you are not required to submit your records and receipts to your employer, the income has to be shown on your Form W-2. When an employee receives $300 a month for his auto expenses and is not required by a written accountable plan to submit a mileage log to his employer as substantiation, the auto allowance must be reported on Form W-2, box 1.

It is very important to establish a written accountable reimbursement plan and "adequately account" to your employer in order not to lose some or all of the deduction for your professional expenses. A complete discussion of how to comply with **the change that took effect on 1-1-91** is in Chapter Three.

Personal Use of Auto Provided by Employer

Strict regulations require the value of personal auto use of an employer owned auto to be included in the W-2 as a taxable fringe benefit. The amount to be included in income is to be reduced by any amount the employee pays the employer for the taxable fringe benefit. (See complete discussion in Chapter Three.)

Non-Taxable Sources of Income---Exclusions
Fringe Benefits

Gross income, for tax purposes, includes all income from whatever source, unless specifically excluded by an Internal Revenue Code Section. Certain fringe benefits are tax-free if they meet the qualification rules provided in the Internal Revenue Code.

The fringe benefits we will briefly discuss are available for either dual-status or lay employees of not-for-profit employers and employees of for-profit employers. As long as the employer follows the strict requirements, fringe benefits are not taxed to the employees. Providing fringe benefits in an employee's "pay package" reduces the base upon which both income tax and social security tax are paid.

To keep abuse out of fringe benefit plans, Congress has enacted a series of statutes that are overwhelming, time consuming and costly to the employer. It is beyond the scope of this publication to discuss in detail the many Internal Revenue Code Sections that deal with all fringe benefits. **Before establishing employee fringe benefits, seek the assistance of an expert attorney and/or benefits consultant.** With congressional changes happening two or three times a year, existing plans must be continually examined and revised to meet new requirements. It is important to follow the rules in the Internal Revenue Code and establish qualified tax-free fringe benefits. **Any non-qualified benefits provided are simply taxable fringes.**

Nondiscrimination rules apply to most fringe benefits. An exemption from the nondiscrimination rules of Sec. 79 applies to certain church plans providing group-term life insurance to employees. Providing accident & health insurance coverage to employees is also a fringe benefit that does not have to meet discrimination rules.

Qualified Retirement Plan Contributions

For retirement plans, the Internal Revenue Code considers the salaried minister as an "employee." When the employer pays the premium for a qualified retirement plan under Sec. 401(a), 403(b), 408(k), or 414(e), it is not taxable income to an employee during his working years. At retirement or at the time of any withdrawals from an employer's qualified retirement plan, the benefits are taxable. (See exception below for retired ministers.)

Plans may be available through your denominational headquarters. Several brokers and insurance companies specialize in plans for the not-for-profit organizations and their employees.

- *Sec. 401(a)*

    For-profit employers must establish their qualified retirement plans according to Sec. 401(a) rules. Many technical requirements must be met for a plan to be qualified under Sec. 401(a). These rules prohibit discrimination and plans must be established for the benefit of the employer's employees in general. The cost of administration of a qualified 401(a) retirement plan is great. Not-for-profit organizations generally establish retirement plans according to Sec. 403(b) or Sec. 414(e) rules because they are less strict. Annual contributions to a qualified retirement plan cannot exceed the lesser of (1) $30,000 or (2) 25% of the employee's compensation for the year.

- *Sec. 403(b) Tax Sheltered Account (TSA)*

    A not-for-profit employer can establish a Sec. 403(b) plan that functions like Sec. 401(a) qualified employer plan. If an employer makes **forfeitable** (employee loses if not vested) contributions to a Sec. 403(b) account on the behalf of its employees, the maximum limit for a defined contribution plans applies (lesser of $30,000 or 25% of pay). The cost to establish and administrate this type of Sec. 403(b) employer plan does not make it a good choice for an employer with few employees. An employer's plan can be established to accept forfeitable contributions by the employer and also accept **non-forfeitable** (employee is always 100% vested) voluntary contributions by the employee.

INCOME 15

A Sec. 403(b) retirement plan can be established to accept only non-forfeitable voluntary contributions from one or several employees. Many employers establish Sec. 403(b) plans that only allow salary reduction non-forfeitable voluntary contributions because they are quick to establish and involve very little cost of administration. Employees of not-for-profit organizations who change employers from time to time like the "portability" of a Sec. 403(b) non-forfeitable type of plan. (Also see "TSA" under "Voluntary Tax Shelter Plans".)

- **Sec. 408(k) - Simplified Employee Pension (SEP)**

The employer can make contributions directly to a SEP-IRA account or annuity that has been set up for each employee with a broker, bank, or insurance company qualified to sponsor an IRA under Sec. 408(k). Contributions are limited to $30,000 or 15% of an employee's compensation, whichever is less. Employer contributions must be made to a SEP for each employee age 21 or over who has worked for the employer for at least 3 of the last 5 years and received annual compensation of $385 or more. Contributions to SEPs must not discriminate in favor of highly compensated employees. Employer contributions must be determined under a definite written allocation formula and withdrawals must be allowed.

Employees of tax-exempt organizations and state or local governments **may not** make additional voluntary salary reduction contributions to a Sec. 408(k) SEP. They are eligible for Sec. 403(b) salary reduction plans instead.

- **Sec. 414(e) - Church plans**

A plan established and maintained for its employees by a church or by a convention or association of churches exempt from tax under Sec. 501, is excluded from minimum participation, vesting, and funding rules. These rules may be elected. A church plan may be administered by an independent organization, such as a retirement board or a bank. Amounts contributed are limited according to Sec. 415(c). Contribution allowed is the least of: 25% of includable compensation plus $4,000; the exclusion allowance; or $15,000 according to Sec. 415(c)(4)(B).

- **Distributions from Employer Qualified Retirement Plans (QRP)**

Upon retiring, resigning or disability an employee usually has a choice of receiving their employer's qualified retirement all at once as a lump-sum distribution, or as an annuitized monthly income distribution.

Lump Sum Distributions have a special 5 or 10 year averaging available if you do not "roll-over" any portion of the lump-sum distribution. It is a computation that often results in a lesser tax liability. If you choose to "roll-over" a lump-sum distribution into a tax-sheltered IRA account within a 60 day period, you will avoid tax in the year of distribution and the 10% early withdrawal penalty assessed if you are not age 59½ or disabled. However, you will not be able to designate the distributions from the IRA account as tax-free parsonage allowance.

Beginning 1-1-93, new rules require the payor of a lump-sum distribution from a QRP to withhold 20% of the distribution for income tax, unless you ask for a transfer from trustee to trustee.

Periodic income distribution: The choice of monthly income from a qualified plan is more attractive to dual-status ministers because of the ability to designate it as tax-free parsonage allowance.

- **Penalties**

Early distributions are generally subject to 10% early withdrawal penalties if received before age 59½ or disability. However, early distributions which are rolled over to another sheltered account or are a part of a series of substantially equal periodic payments received at least once a year for the life or life expectancy of the taxpayer or for joint lives of taxpayer and beneficiary will not be subject to 10% penalty regardless of taxpayer's age, according to Sec. 72(T)(2)(A)(iv).

- **Retired Ministers**

A **retired minister** receiving a taxable annuity from an employer funded qualified Sec. 401(a), Sec. 403(b), Sec. 408(k) or Sec. 414(e) plan **may have a "parsonage allowance" designated** by the former employer or denominational headquarters. The total cost of his living quarters can be treated as a non-taxable retirement to the extent used for parsonage expenses. (Rev. Ruling 63-156 and CCH, Standard Federal Tax Reports ¶6852.34). The payor of the retirement plan is not required to include the retirement distributions on a Form 1099-R to the extent they have been designated as "parsonage allowance". If they are included by the payor on a 1099-R in error, the taxpayer must enter the amount on Form 1040, line 17a. After computing the amount of housing actually spent, enter either a -0- or the unused portion on line 17b as taxable. It is the responsibility of the taxpayer to show as taxable on Form 1040, line 17b, any designated distributions not spent for parsonage expenses.

- **Tax Planning Is Important**

Information about the rate of return, survivor benefits, etc. are going to enter into the decision you must make at retirement time. Every taxpayer's circumstances are different. So **ask your tax advisor** which choice of distribution provided by your plan will have the least tax liability.

Group Term Life Insurance

Premiums paid by an employer for group term life insurance on the first $50,000 coverage are not to be included in income according to Sec. 79. An exemption from the nondiscrimination rules of Sec. 79 applies to certain church plans providing group-term life insurance to employees. Any coverage for group term life insurance **over $50,000** is taxable. Use the Table from Reg. 1.79-3(d)(2) to compute the amount to be included in an employee's income, even though the employer's actual premium may be more or less.

The only time premiums paid by the employer for regular term or permanent life insurance are not taxable is when the employer is named as beneficiary.

Cost Per $1,000 of Protection for 1-Month Period [Sec. 1.79-3(d)(2)]

Age	Cost	Age	Cost
Under 30	8¢	50 through 54	48¢
30 through 34	9¢	55 through 59	75¢
35 through 39	11¢	60 through 64	$1.17
40 through 44	17¢	65 through 69	$2.10
45 through 49	29¢	70 and above	$3.76

Accident And Health Insurance

Premiums paid for accident and health insurance by an employer are not taxable income according to Sec. 106. Premiums for accident and health plans are able to be a "tax free" fringe benefit whether the policy or plan is individual, group or fraternal. **There are no discrimination rules that apply to insured health and accident plans.** A plan underwritten by an insurance policy or a prepaid health care plan must involve the shifting of risk to an unrelated third party to be considered an insured plan.

Whenever possible, have the premium notice of an individual policy billed to the employer and have them pay it directly. Reimbursement by an employer to employees for premiums for accident and medical insurance may be considered as employer contributions and result in exclusion of payments from employees' income, according to Rev. Ruling 61-146. Sometimes the medical insurance company will only allow payment as a debit

INCOME 17

payment from the employee's checking account. In this situation, we recommend that the employer reimburse the employee with a separate check, specifically for the purpose of accident and health premium reimbursement.

Brotherhood Newsletter is a Fraternal form of insurance carrier. Fraternals are not normally incorporated under state insurance laws as are insurance companies. Fraternities were popular at the close of the Civil War. Lutheran Brotherhood, Woodmen of the World and others have existed for a long time. We feel that monthly payments to a fraternal form of medical insurance qualifies for "tax free" fringe benefit treatment.

If an employee were to receive taxable salary and pay their own medical insurance premiums, two costly things happen:
1. Because of the 7.5% limitation on Sch A or not having enough to itemize, the premium may not be deductible, and
2. Social security tax will be paid on that portion of the salary.

Self-Insured Medical Reimbursement Plans

There are strict discrimination rules in Sec. 105(h) that apply to self-insured plans and **it is wise to seek the assistance of an expert attorney and/or benefits consultant to draft a qualified self-insured plan.** A medical expense reimbursement plan is a plan or arrangement under which an employer pays the medical expenses incurred by its eligible employees, their spouses and dependents and is non-taxable according to Sec 105(b). The employer may make direct payments to the provider of the service (the physician, hospital, or insurer) or it may reimburse the employees.

Often a self-insured medical reimbursement plan is established as a supplement to a group health insurance program. The upper limit or cap, for example, $500 or $1,000, must be uniform for all employees eligible for the plan. As a fringe benefit, available amounts not used for medical expenses can not be paid as additional compensation. It is a "use it or lose it" fringe benefit.

Disability Insurance

Premiums for disability insurance paid by the employer are not taxable income according to Sec. 105(e). The income from a disability plan provided by the employer is taxable as sick pay.

However, if the employee pays the premium for a private disability insurance policy, the cost of the premiums is not deductible, and the income from the plan is not taxable.

Qualified Educational Assistance

The tax-free status of qualified educational assistance provided according to Sec. 127 has been restored retroactive to July 1, 1992. However, the exclusion is slated to terminate for tax years beginning after 1994. Taxpayers who paid tax on assistance received between July 1, 1992 and December 31, 1992 should file amended returns to claim a refund.

The annual excludable educational assistance is $5,250. A qualified educational assistance program is a plan established and maintained by an employer under which the employer provides educational assistance to employees. Education expenses that improve or develop the capabilities of an individual, not limited to courses that are job related or part of a degree program, qualify under Sec. 127.

Notice in **Chapter Three that educational expenses that are job related** can be reimbursed by an employer as business expenses or deductible on Sch A if unreimbursed.

Qualified Tuition Reduction

A not-for-profit organization that is **not a school cannot provide** this fringe benefit according to Revenue Ruling 78-184. A church that provides tuition payments for employee's children must treat the payments as a taxable fringe benefit, as payment for services. (Private Letter Ruling 9226008)

Effective for education furnished after 6-30-85, employees of qualified educational organizations described in **Sec. 170(b)(1)(A)(ii)** can exclude from gross income qualified tuition reduction, including cash grants.

An educational organization is described in Sec. 170(b)(1)(A)(ii) if it has as its primary function the presentation of formal instruction, and it normally maintains a regular faculty and curriculum and normally has a regularly enrolled body of pupils or students in attendance at the place where its educational activities are regularly carried on.

According to Sec. 117(d)(2), the exclusion applies to tuition for education provided at the employer's school as well as at any educational institution. The exclusion is limited to education below graduate level. A special rule applies to graduate students at eligible educational institutions who are engaged in teaching or research activities for the institution.

Qualified tuition reduction applies to: (1) an individual currently employed by the educational institution; (2) a person separated from service with the institution due to retirement or disability; (3) a widow or widower of an employee who died while employed by the institution, (4) spouses and dependent children of the above.

Effective 1-1-88, the nondiscrimination rules under Sec. 414(q) apply to a qualified tuition reduction plan.

Qualified Scholarships

Sec. 117(a) provides for qualified scholarships given to degree candidates to be excluded from income to the extent amounts are used for "qualified tuition and related expenses". Related expenses include fees, books, supplies, and equipment required for courses of instruction. Additional amounts for room, board, or incidental expenses are not excludable. So that recipients understand their tax liabilities, they should be formally advised in writing that amounts granted for expenses incurred are taxable income if the total amount exceeds tuition and fees required for enrollment and related expenses. (Notice 87-31, IRB 1987-17,13)

To establish a private foundation that can grant qualified scholarships, requires legal assistance. Revenue Procedure 76-47, clarified by Revenue Procedure 85-51 establishes seven conditions and a percentage test or a facts and circumstances test for a qualified scholarship program. The program must impose minimum eligibility requirements that limit the independent selection committee's consideration to those children of employees who meet the minimum standards for admission to an educational institution. No more than 10% of the program's recipients can be employee's children.

Notice in **Chapter Three that educational expenses that are job related** can be reimbursed by an employer as business expenses or deductible on Sch A if unreimbursed.

Cafeteria Plans

A cafeteria plan is a separate, written benefit plan maintained by an employer under which all participants are employees and each participant has the opportunity to select the particular benefits that he desires according to Sec. 125. A plan must offer both a cash benefit and at least one statutory nontaxable benefit. Nontaxable benefits include group-term life insurance up to $50,000 coverage, dependent care assistance, disability benefits, accident and health benefits, self-insured medical reimbursement benefits and group legal services.

Salary reduction agreements under which participants elect to reduce their compensation or to forgo increases in compensation can be utilized to begin a cafeteria plan. Benefits are of the "use it or lose it" nature and therefore should be set conservatively.

Voluntary Tax Shelter Plans

The following "sheltered" retirement plans are those to which a taxpayer can contribute on a voluntary basis and reduce their taxable earnings by the amount of the contribution. When a taxpayer has an income tax liability, it is good tax planning to consider making

INCOME 19

contributions to a "sheltered" retirement plan. **Even when a minister has no income tax liability, he may wish to contribute to a Sec. 403(b) Tax Sheltered Account and reduce his social security base.**

Employees of not-for-profit organizations can contribute to Sec. 403(b) voluntary salary reduction plans and to Sec. 408 IRA accounts. After July 2, 1986, a not-for-profit organization can not establish a Sec. 401(k). Contributions to self-employed Keogh Plans can be made to the extent of Sch C honorariums and professional income.

Tax Sheltered Accounts - (TSA)

TSA's are available for employees of tax exempt organizations or public schools according to Sec. 403(b). An employee of a qualified organization can make an election to reduce their taxable salary and request that the employer make non-forfeitable (employee is always 100% vested) contributions to a Sec. 403(b) plan. Salary reduction contributions to a TSA are not to be shown on the W-2 as income in Box 1. They **are subject** to social security tax and medicare tax for the lay employee, according to Rev. Ruling 65-208, and must be shown on the W-2, Box 3 and Box 5. However, contributions to a TSA by a dual-status minister **are not subject** to social security according to Rev. Ruling 68-395. If you have paid social security on contributions to a TSA as a dual-status minister you should file amended returns for the open years and request a refund.

An employee can exclude up to 20% of includable compensation multiplied by the number of years of service, less amounts contributed in prior years. Includable compensation is defined in Reg. 1.403(b)-1(e) as the amount of compensation earned, less any forfeitable employer contributions to a 403(b) plan. The regulation further states that includable compensation shall be computed without regard to the exclusions for Sec. 105(d) and Sec. 911. Although Sec. 107 is not mentioned in the regulations for Sec. 403(b), we find in Reg. 1.401-1(b)(1)(i) and Rev. Ruling 73-258 that a minister's housing allowance, although excludable from income, is compensation for purposes of determining benefits under an employer's qualified retirement plan. The nature of Sec. 105(d), wage continuation plans (repealed); and Sec. 911, exclusion for foreign earned income; is that of an exclusion that is subject to social security, but free from income tax. Companies who offer Sec. 403(b) annuities or accounts differ on their position on whether the parsonage allowance and/or value is includable compensation. Our position is that parsonage allowance does qualify as includable compensation.

For tax years beginning after 12-31-86, the maximum amount of such deferrals cannot exceed $9,500. If a taxpayer can participate in a Sec. 401(k) plan with another for-profit employer, the combined limit for both plans will be $9,500. There is an exception to the annual limit on contributions to Sec. 403(b) accounts. Any "qualified" employee who has completed 15 years of service with a qualified organization can make additional salary reduction contributions. An additional contribution of up to $3,000 can be made in any one year. An aggregate or total limit of $15,000 applies to additional contributions. Additional contributions are not available if a taxpayer's lifetime elective deferrals top his lifetime limit ($5,000 X years of service performed by the individual with the employer). The above limit of $9,500 and this additional $3,000 can be combined for a total limit of $12,500.

Individual Retirement Accounts - (IRA)

You may also contribute, and possibly deduct, up to $2,000 annually to an IRA, described in Sec. 408. If both you and your spouse work, you may each contribute up to $2,000. You may set up an IRA for a nonworking spouse and make contributions of up to $2,250 on a joint return. A spousal IRA can be divided between the spouses in any manner, as long as the amount contributed to either IRA is not more than $2,000. Contributions for 1993 must be made by April 15th, 1994.

You will receive a Form 5498 by May 31, from the trustee of your account each year stating the amount you have contributed for the current year and the value of your account. The earnings of an IRA accrue tax-free as long as you do not withdraw them.

Payments to an Individual Retirement Account (IRA) are to remain shown as salary, are subject to social security and subtracted as an adjustment on Form 1040, line 24, if allowed as deductible contributions.

For those who are active participants in an employer retirement plan, SEP, 403(b), or a Keogh; contributions to an IRA can still be made but may not be deductible contributions. When one spouse is an active participant, it affects the deductibility of contributions for both spouses. If the Adjusted Gross Income (before IRA's) is over $25,000 for single, $40,000 for married joint, or $0 for married separate the deduction is reduced or eliminated by phase-out rules.

If you and/or your spouse are an active participant and your AGI is within the phaseout range, figure your reduced deduction as follows:
1. From the amount of $35,000 for single, $50,000 for married joint, $10,000 for married separate, subtract the AGI before IRA deductions.
2. Multiply Step 1 by .20 if your contribution limit is $2,000; .225 if $2,250 for spousal account. This is your deductible contribution. If the result is not a multiple of $10, the allowable deduction is increased to the next highest $10. A special rule gives a $200 deduction if your AGI falls within the last $1,000 of the phaseout range.

There is a provision that allows you to designate contributions as non-deductible, even though you are not required to by the above limitations. **This prevents "wasted" deductions when there is no tax liability.** It allows the combination of "sheltered" and "non-sheltered" contributions to the same plan. Contributions that you choose to designate as non-deductible can be changed to deductible on an amended return for three open years.

Recordkeeping for non-deductible contributions to an IRA is the responsibility of the taxpayer!! Form 8606 is necessary to be completed and attached to your Form 1040. The non-deductible basis in your IRA and the **value at year end** is to be shown. Your non-deductible contributions will be returned to you in retirement as non-taxable. If a taxpayer fails to keep record of the basis of his IRA account, the IRS can treat it as fully taxable upon withdrawal. Keeping copies of your tax returns in a safe place for your total working lifetime is your responsibility. The earnings of non-deductible or designated contributions are sheltered from tax until withdrawal.

Self-Employed Keogh Plans (H.R. 10)

Salaries received as "employees" are not eligible for making contributions to self-employed Keogh plans. Only income from honorariums or true self-employment qualify as income from which Keogh contributions can be made under Sec. 401(c). Annual contributions cannot exceed the lesser of (1) $30,000 or (2) 25% of the Sch C income.

- **Distributions and Penalties**

Early distributions of voluntary plans before age 59½ or disability are subject to the 10% early withdrawal penalty. To transfer or "roll-over" distributions within 60 days to another qualified tax shelter plan will prevent tax in the year of distribution and the 10% penalty. However, early distributions which are part of a series of substantially equal periodic payments received at least once a year for the life or life expectancy of the taxpayer or for joint lives of taxpayer and beneficiary will not be subject to the 10% penalty regardless of taxpayer's age, according to Sec. 72(T)(2)(A)(iv).

- **Retired Ministers**

Distributions from qualified voluntary plans, such as salary reduction 403(b), an IRA, or a self-employed Keogh plan are fully taxable. They are not eligible for tax free parsonage allowance.

INCOME

Housing Exclusion
Dual-Status Minister - Sec. 107

Dual-status ministers are not taxed on the parsonage provided them and/or the parsonage allowance paid to them as a part of their compensation. Chapter Two gives full detailed discussion on how to designate in advance and compute tax-free parsonage allowance.

It is necessary to compute and pay social security tax on the value of the parsonage provided and/or the parsonage allowance for the dual-status minister, unless Form 4361 has been timely filed. Do not misapply the Rowan Case (Sec. 119) discussed below to Sec. 107 housing for ministers.

Lay Employees - Sec. 119

For the lay employee (janitor, dorm parents, managers, caretakers, etc.) the value of employer-furnished lodging and utilities is not taxable if:
1. Furnished on your employer's business premises;
2. For your employer's convenience;
3. And as a condition of your employment. Regular and emergency duties must be continuous, on constant 24-hour call.

All three conditions must be met, or the value of housing provided is taxable. The exclusion does not apply if an employee can take cash instead of the housing.

Employees furnished lodging in a camp located in a foreign country by or on behalf of his employer, such camp shall be considered to be the business premises of the employer according to Sec. 119(c).

Employees of colleges, universities, and other educational institutions described in Sec. 170(b)(1)(A)(ii), can exclude the value of qualified campus lodging, provided they satisfy a rent-payment requirement. The rent must be at least equal to:
1. 5% of the appraised value of the lodging, determined at close of year or
2. the average of rentals paid to the educational institution for comparable housing during such calendar year, whichever is the lesser figure.

If the rent paid equals the lesser of (1) or (2), the employee gets to exclude the entire lodging's value according to Sec. 119(d) and IRS Pub 525.

In the past, Sec. 119 housing was subject to social security. A Supreme Court Decision (Rowan Companies, Inc. v. United States) and Revenue Ruling 81-222 states that the IRS can't have a different definition for wages for the lay employee for income and social security purposes. Therefore, the value of the meals and lodging that was subject to social security in the past became exempt retroactively. For the three years during which claims can be filed, (1990, 1991, and 1992), any employer that withheld and matched social security on Sec. 119 housing or meals, can file Form 843 and claim a refund for the social security paid on the meals and lodging.

Unfortunately, the Rowan court case has no effect on the Sec. 107 for the dual-status minister. Parsonage provided and/or parsonage allowance paid are still subject to social security, unless Form 4361 has been timely filed. Some tax advisors have applied the Rowan case to Sec. 107 out of context, and the IRS has assessed the preparer a penalty for each return filed in error. If you have failed to pay social security on your housing under Sec. 107, we would advise you to amend your returns and pay the correct amount of social security.

Gifts

When you **have not performed a service** and someone gives you a gift for which they cannot deduct a charitable deduction on their Schedule A, (gifts to individuals are not deductible), **and it does not come from an employer**, the gift can be considered non-taxable according to Sec. 102. Gifts received directly from relatives and personal friends for personal reasons are not taxable.

Often a church is asked to "funnel" a designated contribution to a specific individual. If that individual is involved in a ministry or missionary endeavor and the church finance committee chooses to honor the request, it should be treated as compensation to the individual receiving it, and included in the church's payroll reports. When the gift can be forwarded to a mission organization with which the individual is affiliated, they will include the amount in their payroll reports. If the individual to whom the gift is designated is not involved in a ministry, extreme caution must be exercised by the church. **Deductible contribution receipts should not be issued when the church does not have the right to control the monies.** Deductible contribution receipts should not be issued when the donor and the designated recipient are related, (if the recipient is not involved in a ministry).

Scholarship funds, permanently and formally established, should be used to assist students attending qualified schools. The church must have the control to determine who receives the benefit based on the criteria established in the scholarship.

Deacon's Fund or Benevolence Fund: Churches should never hesitate to help people in need in the community. Such gifts to those in need are non-taxable to all non-employees. Churches should be actively serving their community in a charitable manner. Benevolent gifts to non-employees are never to be reported on an information return (Form 1099).

Accountable Reimbursement Plan for Professional Expenses

Auto, travel, and professional expenses are able to be deducted from gross income if they are reimbursed by the employer according to Sec. 62(2)(A). You must "adequately account" to your employer. Several beneficial reasons will be given in Chapter Three for establishing an accountable reimbursement plan with your employer. A complete discussion of how to comply with the change that took effect on 1-1-91 is in Chapter Three.

Deferred Compensation Plans

Employees who have fully funded qualified tax shelter retirement plans may be able to defer additonal taxable income through a "non-qualified deferred compensation plan." These plans, which frequently use a trust arrangement known as a "rabbi trust," may be adopted with a model rabbi trust published by the IRS in Rev. Proc. 92-64.

To successfully defer taxes under a "nonqualified plan," the compensation deferred must, until actual payment, continue to be owned by the employer and be available to the employer's creditors if the employer becomes bankrupt or insolvent.

Before establishing a non-qualified deferred compensation plan, an employer must seek the assistance of an expert attorney and/or benefits consultant.

Prizes and Awards

Prizes and awards received in recognition of past accomplishments, even if you are selected without action on your part and you are not expected to render any future services are taxable, according to Sec. 102(c). They can be non-taxable if you "designate" the prize to charity according to Sec. 74.

Gratuity Payments to a Retired Minister

Payments made to a retired minister (because of age or disability), if he is not expected to perform any further services, are non-taxable. Such non-taxable gifts based on gratitude and appreciation can be given after a minister retires in addition to his receiving taxable pension from an established plan. It is also necessary that the payments not be required by an established plan or agreement and that they are based on his needs and the ability of the congregation to pay. (Rev. Ruling 55-422; CCH, Standard Federal Tax Reports ¶5507.1401).

This special provision for retired ministers is an exception to the general rule. Such payments made in all other careers or employer/employee relationships are considered taxable compensation or taxable pension.

CHAPTER TWO

PARSONAGE ALLOWANCE

The understanding of this chapter will result in tremendous income tax savings. Some dual-status ministers have spent many years in the ministry and have not been aware of how to "designate" their expenses of providing a home as non-taxable parsonage allowance. Internal Revenue Code Sec. 107 says:

"In the case of a minister of the Gospel, gross income does not include---
1. The rental value of a home furnished to him as part of his compensation; or
2. The rental allowance paid to him as part of his compensation, to the extent used by him to rent or provide a home."

Are You Entitled to the Parsonage Allowance Exclusion?

The answer to the question, "Are you entitled to parsonage allowance?" is also going to answer another question, "Are you considered Self-employed for social security purposes?" **Sec. 107's** regulations refers us to **Sec. 1402(c)'s** regulations for the definition of some important terms. When we determine that an you are entitled to tax-free parsonage allowance, we will have also determined that you are is to be considered self-employed for social security purposes. **Dual-status means** that the you are an **employee** for income reporting, fringe benefit and expense deducting purposes and **self-employed** for social security purposes.

If we determine that an you are not entitled to tax-free parsonage allowance, we will have also determined that you are to be considered as a lay employee for income tax and social security withholding purposes.

Generally, there are three circumstances to be considered. (1) Are you employed by a church or an integral agency of a church? (2) Are you performing ministerial services? and (3) Are you ordained by a church or "the equivalent thereof?" While all three tests must be satisfied for you to be treated as a dual-status minister for tax purposes, recent court cases reflect a very liberal definition of circumstance #3.

Are You Employed by a Church or An Integral Agency of a Church?

To be entitled to tax-free parsonage allowance you must be employed by a church or an integral agency of a church. **An exception** to this requirement is provided if you are assigned or appointed to a position by your denomination or church. **Another exception** is provided when the services you are performing is that of conducting religious worship or ministering sacerdotal functions. (See conditions in Reg. 1.1402(c)-5(b) below.)

You must establish that your employer is exempt from federal income tax under Sec. 501(a) as a religious organization described in Sec. 501(c)(3). You must also establish that your employer is a church (or convention or association of churches) described in Sec. 170(b)(1)(A)**(i)**. If you are employed by a 501(c)(3) organization that is described in Sec. 170(b)(1)(A)**(vi)**, it must meet most of the requirements of Rev. Ruling 72-606 to be considered an integral agency of a church. If you are considering becoming employed by an organization that is not an integral agency, have your church assign you to the position **before** you accept the position. The following definitions will help you determine your correct status:

Definition of Church

The regulations for Sec. 107 state:
> "The term, religious organization, has the same meaning and application as is given to the term for income tax purposes."

The scope of what organizations are included in the definition of "churches" is found in the instructions of **Pub. 557, page 17.** Because beliefs and practices vary so widely, there is no single definition of the word "church" for tax purposes. The Internal Revenue Service considers the facts and circumstances of each organization applying for church status. A separate organization affiliated with a church will be considered an integrated auxiliary if the principal activity of the organization is exclusively religious. Examples of organizations considered to be integrated auxiliaries of a church are a men's or women's organization, a religious school (such as a seminary), a mission society, or a youth group.

The following list of organizations that are not required to file an annual information return (Form 990) gives us an **"expanded definition"** of what the IRS deems to be a church to satisfy Sec. 107 and Sec. 1402(c). *(Summary from Pub. 557, page 6:)*

1. A church, an interchurch organization of local units of a church, a convention or association of churches, an integrated auxiliary of a church, or an internally supported, church-affiliated, organization.
2. An exclusively religious activity of any religious order. Specifically a religious order that is not opposed to insurance.
3. A mission society sponsored by or affiliated with one or more churches or church denominations, more than one-half of the activities of which society are conducted in or directed at persons in foreign countries.
4. A school below college level affiliated with a church or operated by a religious order even though it is not an integrated auxiliary of a church.

Integral Agency of a Church

A not-for-profit organization with a determination letter showing it is not a church but is described as an organization for charitable, educational, or other purposes in Sec. 170(b)(1)(A)**(vi)**, would be **unable** to treat an employee as a dual-status minister for tax purposes **unless** it meets **most** of the following requirements as an integral agency of a church.

Rev. Ruling 70-549 and Rev. Ruling 72-606 clearly state what is required for a school, mission, or other religious organization to be treated as an integral agency of a church. The eight criteria listed in Rev. Ruling 72-606 are:

1. whether the religious organization incorporated the institution;
2. whether the corporate name of the institution indicates a church relationship;
3. whether the religious organization continuously controls, manages, and maintains the institution;
4. whether the trustees or directors of the institution are approved by or must be approved by the religious organization or church;
5. whether trustees or directors may be removed by the religious organization or church;
6. whether annual reports of finances and general operations are required to be made to the religious organization or church;
7. whether the religious organization or church contributes to the support of the institution; and
8. whether, in the event of dissolution of the institution, its assets would be turned over to the religious organization or church.

In the court case, Flowers v. U.S. CA 4-79-376-E, 11/25/81, it was found that Texas Christian University only met two of the possible eight tests of Rev. Ruling 72-606. Therefore, an ordained employee could not have a parsonage allowance as allowed by Sec.

PARSONAGE ALLOWANCE 25

107. The case stated that schools and colleges can satisfy the IRS criteria to become an integral agency of a church. That, in fact, Rev. Ruling 70-549 was specifically written to give advice to them in meeting the requirements of Sec. 107.

In Private Letter Ruling, 9144047, the teaching staff of a college was allowed to be dual-status, because their employing college was deemed to be an integral agency of a church.

We advise any organization that is unsure of their standing to examine their determination letter from the IRS and their bylaws. If it is determined that your organization is not an integral agency of a church, consider taking action to change your bylaws to comply with those areas of control and become an integral agency.

Another possible action to take, would be to resubmit Form 1023 and ask for your organization's exempt status to be changed from the **(vi) to the (i)**.

Are You Performing Ministerial Services?

The salary or honorarium you receive for services which are ordinarily the duties of a minister of the gospel is eligible for the housing allowance exclusion. As a minister you are not required to be performing or even able to perform all of the duties to be a dual-status minister for tax purposes.

Regulations describe the types of services that a minister in the exercise of his ministry performs. These services include:
1. the ministration of sacerdotal functions,
2. the conduct of religious worship,
3. service in the administration, control, conduct, and maintenance of religious organizations, including integral agencies, under the authority of a church or church denomination, and
4. the performance of teaching and administrative duties at theological seminaries.

- **Qualifying Services Include** *(Summary from Reg. 1.1402(c)-5(b).)*
    1. A minister employed as pastor of a church is eligible for parsonage allowance. If more than one minister is on the staff, they may all exclude their parsonage allowance as long as their duties are those of ministers of the gospel.
    2. Conducting religious worship services or ministering sacerdotal functions are ministerial services whether or not performed for a church or integral agency of a church. This provision makes it possible for a chaplain to qualify for dual-status treatment, even though he may be employed by a secular organization.
    3. Service performed by a chaplain at either a church-related hospital or health and welfare institution, or a private nonprofit hospital is considered to be in the exercise of his ministry according to Rev. Ruling 71-258. The parsonage designation should be done by the church that ordained the minister.
    4. A minister engaged in the control, conduct, and maintenance of an integral agency of a religious organization or church. Service includes directing, managing, or promoting the activities of such organization.
    5. A minister **assigned or designated by a church to perform services for an organization that is not a church,** even though such service may not involve the conduct of religious worship or the ministration of sacerdotal functions, is in the exercise of his ministry. **Example:** A minister assigned to perform advisory service to a printing company in connection with the publication of a book dealing with the history of his church denomination. (Reg. 1.1402(c)-5(b)(v)) Your services are ordinarily not considered to have been assigned or designated by your church if any of the following is true:
        A. The organization for which you perform the services did not arrange with your church for your services.

B. You perform the same services for the organization as those performed by its other employees who were not designated as you were.
C. You perform the same services before and after the designation.
6. A rabbi is a minister of the gospel and qualifies for the parsonage allowance. Cantors also qualify. (Rev. Ruling 78-301)
7. A minister who performs evangelistic services at churches away from his permanent home may exclude parsonage allowance paid to him by the churches. (Rev. Ruling 64-326)
8. Income from religious books or articles is considered to be in the exercise of ministry and subject to social security.

- **Non-Qualifying Duties Include** *(Summary from Reg. 1.1402(c)-5(c).)*
    1. Ministers as administrators of non-profit nursing homes. They were not a religious organization nor an integral agency of a church. No support was provided by a church, and directors were not required to be ministers or affiliated with a church. (Jesse A. Toavs et al., 67 TC 897)
    2. If a minister is performing service for an organization which is neither a religious organization nor operated as an integral agency of a religious organization and the service is not performed following an assignment or designation by his ecclesiastical superiors, then the service performed is not in the exercise of his ministry. **Example**: Minister is employed by a university to teach mathematics and history. The university is not a church nor an integral agency of a church. He receives honorariums from time to time performing wedding and funerals for friends. The honorariums are his only ministerial income.
    3. Services as secretaries, stenographers, mail clerks, file clerks, doctors, nurses, auto mechanics, pilots, carpenters, cooks and janitors are not in exercise of ministry according to Rev. Ruling 57-129.
    4. A chaplain in the armed forces is specifically denied this exclusion since he is considered to be a commissioned officer, and as such is not a minister in the exercise of his ministry. Military officers are given a tax-free parsonage, therefore, Sec. 107 is not needed.
    5. Similarly, service performed by an employee of a State as a chaplain in a State prison is considered to be performed by a civil servant of the State and not by a minister in the exercise of his ministry.

If you remain uncertain whether you are entitled to claim parsonage allowance and be self-employed for social security purposes, you may request an IRS ruling on whether you perform qualifying duties.

Are You Ordained By A Church Or "The Equivalent Thereof?"

If you are employed by a church or an integral agency of a church and are performing ministerial services, you are considered to be "the equivalent of" ordained at the time you begin your employment. When a church calls or hires a person to be their minister, they have informally given him the authority to conduct religious worship and to administer ordinances at the time of employment. A minister satisfies the ability to perform services in control, conduct and maintenance of the church merely by being employed by the church as their minister. In Salkov v. Commissioner, supra, 46 TC at 190 (1966) it was concluded that the congregation's formal selection of the taxpayer as their cantor constituted commissioning him as their minister. In J.M. Ballinger, U.S. Court of Appeals, 10th Circuit, No. 82-1928, 3/7/84, it was stated, "Not all churches or religions have a formally ordained ministry, whether because of the nature of their beliefs, the lack of a denominational structure or a variety of other reasons. Courts are not in a position to determine the merits of various churches... We interpret Congress' language providing an exemption for any individual who is 'a duly ordained, commissioned, or licensed minister of a church' to mean that **the triggering event is the assumption of the duties and functions of a minister.**"

It is very important for a minister who wishes to become exempt from social security to be aware of the date his/her ministry begins. The deadline for a timely filed Form 4361 is the due date of the tax return (including extensions) for the second year in which he/she earns more than $400 from the ministry. The minister who is formally ordained, licensed, or commissioned by his church or denomination experiences a very important and meaningful event. However if it takes place after the date of hiring, it is not an important event for tax purposes. There is less confusion when the formal recognition of a minister's status can be accomplished before the assumption of the duties and functions.

A "non-integral agency of a church" **can not** give the authority to do the duties of the ministry. It is necessary for a church to have formally ordained, licensed or commissioned a minister, before they can "assign or designate" him to a position at a "non-integral agency" and thus qualify him for dual-status treatment. It is also necessary for a church to have formally ordained, licensed or commissioned a minister who conducts worship and administers ordinances or sacraments, but is not employed by a church or an integral agency of a church.

Prior to 1978, Rev. Ruling 65-124 was very strict in stating that a minister had to be able to perform "all" the religious functions of the church to be defined as "ordained" for tax purposes.

Since 1978, Rev. Ruling 78-301 added the word "substantially" to the definition in order to allow Jewish cantors to qualify for parsonage allowance. Until 1989, everyone remained conservative as to the meaning of the word "substantially." Two tax court cases decided in **1989**, involved ministers with limited authority who waited until formal ordination to file Form 4361 to become exempt from social security. IRS denied both applications as being untimely filed.

James S. Wingo, 89 TC No. 64, Docket No. 8613-85: Taxpayer was an ordained "deacon" and licensed as a probationary pastor of the United Methodist Church beginning in 1980. He became an ordained "elder" in 1984 and wished to become exempt from social security. The United Methodist Church considers both "deacons" and "elders" as ordained ministers of the Church, and as an appointed full-time pastor Rev. Wingo was permitted to administer the Sacraments, provide for the organizational concerns of the local church, conduct divine worship, preach the Word, perform marriage ceremonies and bury the dead. IRS determined that for purposes of applying for the exemption from self-employment tax **under Sec. 1402** or for obtaining the parsonage exclusion **under Sec. 107**, Rev. Wingo was a minister.

John G. Knight, 92 TC No. 12, Docket Nos. 45505-86, 27182-87: Taxpayer was a licentiate of the Cumberland Presbyterian Church and served as a supply pastor. He preached, conducted the worship service, visited the sick, performed funerals, and ministered to the needy. Because he was not ordained, he could not moderate the session, administer sacraments, or solemnize marriages. Duties and functions were considered by the court to be appropriate for a "duly ordained, commissioned or licensed minister."

- *What about equal treatment of male & female religious workers?*

Because some churches allow both genders to be given full authority in the ministry and others extended full authority only to the men, an unequal tax advantage resulted for some women in the ministry. On February 20, 1992, Private Letter Ruling 9221025, gave a positive answer to a major denomination concerning their "commissioned" female teachers being eligible for dual-status treatment. The female staff performed full-time public ministry functions including: classroom teaching; evangelizing; counseling individuals; leading Bible study groups, devotions, worship services for youth and a congregation's music ministry;

giving the children's sermon at the regular Sunday worship service, coordinating lay church workers; caring spiritually for the sick and imprisoned and their families; etc. **It is important to understand** that Sec. 6110(j)(3) of the Code provides that a letter ruling may not be used or cited as precedent.

The impact of a church or an integral agency of a church making the switch to dual-status tax treatment for their female staff should be carefully administered with good communication and instruction. **An additional salary factor equal to the matching portion of social security should be paid to each staff member affected.** Otherwise, an employee with little or no parsonage expense would experience a loss in net salary. Whether or not an employee has an opportunity to elect to become exempt from Social Security will depend on the date they were hired or assumed the duties and functions of a minister.

Parsonage Allowance Exclusion Rules

What Does the Parsonage Allowance Exclusion Include?

It includes anything spent to provide a home for the dual-status minister and his family. Regulations for Sec. 107 state that the parsonage allowance does not include food or a maid. Parsonage allowance is the tax-free treatment of a ministers **personal** home expenses on a **cash basis**. Do not use business capital asset rules. Do not depreciate home capital expenses. Parsonage allowance expenses include those for the house, its contents, the garage and the yard.

The following list shows typical expenses that are to be considered in computing the amount of parsonage allowance:
1. Rent or principal payments, cost of buying a home and down payments. (See limitations below)
2. Real estate taxes and mortgage interest for the home. These expenses are deductible again as itemized deductions. **A DOUBLE DEDUCTION**, but allowable by IRS!! (Rev. Ruling 62-212 and Sec. 265(a)(6)) **An amazing "tax shelter"!**
3. Insurance on the home and/or contents.
4. Improvements, repairs and upkeep of the home and/or contents. Such as a new roof, room addition, garage, patio, fence, pool, appliance repair, etc.
5. Furnishings and appliances: dish washer, vacuum sweeper, TV, VCR, stereo, piano, computer (personal use), washer, dryer, beds, small kitchen appliances, cookware, dishes, sewing machine, garage door opener, lawnmower, hedge trimmer, etc.
6. Decorator items: drapes, throw rugs, pictures, knick knacks, painting, wallpapering, bedspreads, sheets, towels, etc.
7. Utilities - heat, electric, non-business telephone, water, cable TV, sewer charge, garbage removal, etc. (Show business telephone expense as a professional expense. It will result in less social security tax.)
8. Miscellaneous - any thing that maintains the home and its contents that you haven't included in repairs or decorator items: cleaning supplies for the home, brooms, lightbulbs, dry cleaning of drapes, shampooing carpet, expense to run lawnmower, tools for landscaping, garden hose to water lawn, etc.

The expenses in item No. 8 are often purchased at the grocery or variety store. It is a good practice to buy a supply of household cleaning supplies separately and save the receipt. An easy way to keep record of them is to use the "Housing Expense" section of our **"Professional Tax Record Book."**

Do Not Include the following: Maid (or hired lawn care), groceries, personal toiletries such as toothpaste, shampoo, deodorant, laundry and dish soap, paper products; personal clothing, coats, shoes, jewelry; toys, bicycles, hobby items, cassette tapes, CD's, computer games, personal computer software, VCR movies, etc.

PARSONAGE ALLOWANCE 29

- **Double Deduction of Interest & Taxes**

  Sec. 265(a)(6) provides for the deduction of home mortgage interest and property taxes on Sch A even though all or part of the mortgage is paid with funds you get through a nontaxable parsonage allowance. In 1983 Congress attempted to end the "double deduction", but Rev. Ruling 83-3 was revoked by Sec. 265(a)(6). This "double deduction" has been available since 1962. Rev. Ruling 62-212 provided for this amazing "tax shelter" and it has been strengthened with an addition to Sec. 265.

- **Interest Rules**

  Interest for the purchase of a home and furnishings can be used for parsonage allowance exclusion. However non-mortgage interest for home purchases will not be allowable on Sch A as "personal interest." Mortgage and home equity loan interest will qualify as Sch A "mortgage interest" deduction because the home is used as collateral. Mortgage and home equity loan interest for the purchase of and improvement of the parsonage can also be used for parsonage allowance exclusion. Mortgage and home equity loan interest for any other purpose will not be allowable as parsonage allowance exclusion. If a home equity loan is used for home improvements and the purchase of an auto, only the home improvement portion of the interest can be used as parsonage allowance exclusion.

- **Cash Basis**

  Since capital expenditures for home principal, improvements, furniture and appliances are on a cash basis, it is important to understand when to deduct them if the purchase involves borrowed funds. Any purchases with bank charge cards are treated the same as if you paid cash for the item. Any purchases for the home that involves a loan from a bank, store, or individual are treated as not paid for in full. Loan payments for home purchases are to be deducted as they are paid.

- **Transition Periods**

  Generally, a minister can use the expenses of one home for his parsonage allowance exclusion. When he owns a vacation or second home on a permanent basis, he can only use the expenses for the "main" home as parsonage allowance exclusion.

  During a temporary period of changing employers, changing parsonages, or building a parsonage; expenses for two parsonages is allowable according to a tax court case, Fred B. Marine, 47 TC 609. The temporary period would continue as long as both homes remained personal use. If before a sale, the previous home is rented, the rental income and expenses will generally be reportable on Schedule E.

How much of a Minister's Salary Can Be Designated?

Nothing in the Internal Revenue code or regulations establish a "flat" dollar limitation or a percentage of income limitation for the parsonage allowance exclusion. The amount designated as parsonage allowance must be a specific dollar amount or a specific % of salary. Employers can designate a blanket % of their staff's salaries as parsonage allowance. Individuals on their staff who anticipate incurring a greater amount for parsonage expenses should be allowed to ask for a higher amount to be designated.

Publication 517, page 7, gives a very clear explanation of how much the parsonage allowance can be:

> "If you own your home and you receive as part of your pay a housing or rental allowance, you may exclude from gross income the lowest of the following amounts:
> 1. The amount actually used to provide a home,
> 2. The amount officially designated as a rental allowance, or
> 3. The fair rental value of the home, including furnishings, utilities, garage, etc.

You must include in gross income any rental allowance that is more than the lowest of your reasonable compensation, the fair rental value of the home plus utilities, or the amount actually used to provide a home."

The **"top" limit** that can be claimed by a minister as parsonage allowance exclusion is based on his furnished home's fair rental value, cost of utilities and cost of etc. Actual expenses incurred up to this top limit can be used as parsonage allowance exclusion. In the year of purchase, or a year a major payment of principal is made or a large outlay is made for improvements or furniture, it is important to carefully compute the "top" limit. **The computation of the "fair rental value" should be based on a professional appraisal of your home in your location and neighborhood.** Fair rental value is what it would cost to rent a comparable home in your neighborhood. The fair rental value of furniture can be estimated with the help of a local furniture rental store. A "rule of thumb" among realtors nationwide is that the fair rental value of a home (without furnishings) amounts to 1% of the appraised value per month.

For example, if your home is appraised at $115,000, the monthly FRV could be $1,150. Annual FRV could be $13,800 ($1,150 X 12). This formula is only the beginning point of determining the FRV of your home; **the condition, location, local market demand and local economic conditions will cause quite a variation of FRV nationwide.** It is necessary to consider the facts and circumstance of your individual location.

We have included space on the "Worksheet for Form 2106" to compute the limitation in a year of major expense. FRV of the home would take the place of principal, interest, taxes, insurance and major repairs (line 2 through line 6). FRV of the furniture would take the place of actual furniture purchases (line 7). Actual costs of decorator items (line 8), utilities (line 9), and miscellaneous items (line 10) are to be used.

When actual expenses exceed the fair rental value limitation (FRV of house + FRV of furniture + decorator items + utilities + miscellaneous), they are lost. There are no provisions for carryover of unused portions. Rather than lose the ability to exclude major home expenses, consider obtaining a second mortgage and spreading the cost over a few years and keep within the "top" limit each year.

Loans from employers can be used to accomplish the above suggestion to avoid "wasting" parsonage allowance expenses. It is important that interest be charged if the loan exceeds $10,000 and that the loan is secured by the home. Sec. 483 rules concerning "below market" interest loans require that the Applicable Federal Rate (published monthly by the IRS) be charged for loans over $10,000. If the loan is secured by the home, the interest will qualify for fully deductible "home interest" on Sch A and also as a part of parsonage allowance.

Reasonable compensation means that a minister should not be over-compensated for the amount of time spent and amount of work accomplished. Usually the opposite is true, a minister is under-compensated. In Rev. Ruling 78-448, a minister was considered to have been over-compensated and was not allowed to have 100% of his compensation be tax-free housing allowance **because he didn't perform any services to earn it**. The Rev. Ruling deals with a tax protest situation, and has no application to a legitimate church/minister employment relationship. Some IRS auditors have used Rev. Ruling 78-448 out of context and wrongly denied a minister the tax-free treatment of parsonage allowance that he was entitled to.

- *Tax Plan*

Good tax planning for a minister is to **"over designate"** his parsonage allowance and allow for unexpected expenses and increases in utility costs to be covered. The "unused parsonage allowance" will be shown as income on Form 1040, line 22.

PARSONAGE ALLOWANCE 31

- **Part-Time Ministers**

For a minister who is serving part-time and is not fully supported by the employer, it is possible to designate all or 100% of his salary as parsonage allowance. When a minister is employed outside the church and a new or small congregation cannot fully support him, it is good tax-planning for the minister to make substantial Sch A contributions to the church. The church will then have the funds to pay an adequate salary, designate it as parsonage allowance, and allow him to take full advantage of Sec. 107. The minister who is not exempt from social security, will have to pay social security taxes on the parsonage allowance.

- **What If Home Is Debt Free?**

For the minister whose home is paid for or nearly so, the amount of actual expenses for taxes, insurance, upkeep, utilities, etc. does not allow much tax-free parsonage allowance. In Swaggart v. Commissioner, TC Memo 1984-409, the taxpayer argued that rental allowance was fully excludable from gross income regardless of how the funds were spent....In rejecting such argument, the court concluded that Congress intended to exclude from the minister's gross income only that portion of his compensation paid by the church which was ACTUALLY used by the minister for providing a home for himself. In a previous case, Reed et al, 82 TC 208, the court had also restricted tax-free parsonage to out-of-pocket expenses.

In Private Letter Ruling 9115051, the IRS tells us their position in regards to "refinancing the debt-free parsonage." It is important to understand that Sec. 6110(j)(3) of the Code provides that a letter ruling may not be used or cited as precedent.

The IRS was asked to respond to these questions: "Are payments made on a home equity line of credit (secured by the debt-free home) expenses for which a parsonage allowance may be granted by the church? Would taking out a loan secured by a mortgage on the home result in expenses for which a parsonage allowance may be granted by the church?"

The response of IRS was: "Neither payments made on the home equity line of credit nor on the mortgage secured by the house are being used to rent or provide a home as required by Sec. 107 and the regulations. Therefore, amounts designated by the church to pay for these expenditures are not excludable from the minister's gross income as a parsonage allowance under Sec. 107."

What is Meant By "Official Designation"?

"Official designation" means that the employer designates, by official action, **IN ADVANCE**, the amount the dual-status minister expects to spend for all the expenses of his home. The designation can be done by the official board or the congregation, and should be recorded in their minutes. Internal Revenue Bulletin 1957-27, 40 requires the advance designation of amounts paid as parsonage allowance. Reg. 1.107-1(b) says:

> "The designation of an amount as rental allowance may be evidenced in an employment contract, in minutes of or in a resolution by a church or other qualified organization or in its budget, or in any other appropriate instrument evidencing such official action. The designation referred to in this paragraph is a sufficient designation if it permits a payment or a part thereof to be identified as a payment of rental allowance as distinguished from salary or other remuneration."

The designation of an amount as parsonage allowance should be done before the minister begins his duties. Although the IRS will accept **a perpetually worded designation**, we recommend that a minister consider a new estimate annually and "officially designate" an adequate amount each calendar year. **As a safety net**, our suggested wordings include a perpetual clause.

If you were not aware of how to designate your parsonage allowance or you have had an inadequate amount designated, there is no way to fix the problem for the past. **Now** is the time to designate an adequate parsonage allowance for the rest of the year. In advance of a major unexpected expense, or a change from a parsonage provided to buying your own home, don't hesitate to **amend and increase** your designation for the balance of the year.

During the time you did not have enough parsonage allowance designated, you may be able to compute a percentage of the home expenses as an "office-in-the-home" deduction, if you are not provided office space in the church. If the entire cost of providing a home for your family is tax-free as parsonage allowance, do not deduct an "office-in-the-home" expense.

- **Ministers Who Own**

Ministers who own their homes will want to designate an amount to cover the total cost of owning, cost of their furnishings, cost of decorating, utilities and etc.

When the title to the home and the real estate mortgage is in the minister's name, the employer should not make the payments for him. Pay the minister enough salary to pay all the home expenses, and designate an adequate amount as parsonage allowance. The minister who owns his own home should pay his payment and all of the home expenses himself. **Keep it simple.** Hybrid arrangements where the employer pays some of the expenses and the minister pays others, causes confusion and may result in an inadequate designation of parsonage allowance.

- **Ministers Who Rent**

Ministers who rent their homes will want to designate an amount to cover the actual rent paid, cost of their furnishings, cost of decorating, insurance, utilities, and etc.

- **Church Owns The Parsonage**

If the employer provides the home and/or pays the utilities, it's value is income tax-free automatically. The minister then needs to estimate how much he expects to spend in all of the other categories of home expenses and have that amount of his cash salary designated. It is important to understand that the minister living in a church-owned parsonage has "two pieces" to his parsonage allowance:
  1. a value provided and
  2. a designated portion of his cash salary for the additional home expenses.

- **Evangelists**

According to Rev. Ruling 64-326, a traveling evangelist may exclude amounts he receives from various churches as tax-free parsonage allowance by having the churches designate a portion of his honorariums as parsonage allowance. This involves communicating with the various churches in advance and sending them a statement requesting that they take action to "designate" a portion of your honorarium as parsonage allowance. We recommend that you get duplicate non-carbon copies of the "Statement of Parsonage for An Evangelist" printed. Each church on your itinerary can keep a copy and easily provide you a copy.

A traveling evangelist or conference speaker with a permanent home, will incur deductible travel expenses for lodging and meals while on the road and use parsonage allowance exclusion for his permanent home. If he lives in a motor home or travel trailer and does not have a permanent home, his lodging and meal expenses will not be deductible as business expenses. His tax home for tax purposes is wherever he "hangs his hat." He may treat the motor home as his parsonage, but his meals would not be deductible.

It would be advisable for an independent evangelist to funnel all offerings received from churches through his "home" church and for that church to designate an annual amount as parsonage allowance, include the evangelist on their payroll and issue a W-2 for taxable salary. Travel and ministry expenses could be "adequately accounted" and treated as reimbursed expenses.

An evangelist who forms his own not-for-profit corporation, will be its employee. If such a corporation is established as an integral agency of a church as discussed earlier in this chapter, it can designate parsonage allowance for him and treat him as a dual-status minister. If it is not an integral agency of a church, it can not designate parsonage for him and he does not qualify for dual-status treatment. His employing corporation would be required to withhold and match social security and medicare tax on your salary, even if he has an approved exemption from social security.

- **Missionaries**

Missionaries serving outside of the United States may be able to earn as much as $70,000 and pay no income tax. If they do not qualify to use the $70,000 exclusion, the mission should definitely designate the parsonage allowance for the dual-status missionary. Missionaries who are dual-status ministers should always designate a parsonage allowance so that their home expenses will be excluded while on furlough or sick leave. Chapter Five contains a detailed discussion of the special tax situation for missionaries serving outside of the United States.

- **Retired Ministers**

Pension distributions or retirement allowances paid from a Qualified Employer's Plan (Sec. 401(a), forfeitable contributions to Sec. 403(b), Sec. 408(k) or Sec. 414(e)) are fully taxable as a pension. However, according to Rev. Ruling 63-156, the former employing church or denomination of a retired minister can "officially designate" the estimated cost of the retiree's home expenses as tax-free parsonage allowance. If the entire pension income is designated as parsonage allowance, a Form 1099R would not be required. The retired minister would be responsible to report any "unused parsonage" as taxable. Most payors of qualified pension plans do include the total distribution on a Form 1099R. It is important to include on Form 1040, line 17a, all amounts reported on a Form 1099R. On Form 1040, line 17b, enter the unused portion of the distribution as taxable or -0- if it was all spent for parsonage expenses.

Pension distributions are not subject to social security. A surviving spouse receiving benefits from a Qualified Employer's Plan after a minister's death is not able to designate any of it as parsonage allowance.

Distributions from voluntary non-forfeitable Sec. 403(b) or IRA retirement plans are not able to be designated as tax-free parsonage allowance.

Steps in Designating & Deducting Parsonage Allowance

1. The dual-status minister is to estimate the amount he expects to spend for the coming year and present this to his employer. It is good to over estimate and allow for unexpected expenses and utility cost increases. In advance of a major unexpected expense, or a change from a parsonage provided to buying your own home, don't hesitate to "amend" and increase your designation for the balance of the year.
2. The employer then makes an official written designation based on the dual-status minister's estimate. You may use the suggested wordings we provide.
3. At the close of the tax year, the dual-status minister then compares his actual expenses with the amount designated. If he has incurred any major expenses he will compute the FRV limit. The lowest amount is allowed as his parsonage allowance exclusion.

Parsonage expense details, receipts and records are **not to be submitted to the employer.** They are handled differently than the professional business expenses we will discuss in Chapter Three. The personal home expenses can remain confidential. If the designated amount is greater than the amount substantiated, it is the responsibility of the individual minister to show the "excess parsonage allowance" as income on Form 1040, line 22. Use the "Worksheet for Form 2106" provided in this publication to compute taxable parsonage allowance, if any.

A minister who moves and/or changes amounts of parsonage allowance during the year should allocate the annual designations by the week. For example: You were at ABC Church for 17 weeks and your annual parsonage allowance was $5,200. You were at XYZ Church for 35 weeks and your annual parsonage allowance was $13,000. Compute as follows:

$$\$ 5,200 \div 52 = \$100 \times 17 \text{ weeks} = \$1,700$$
$$\$13,000 \div 52 = \$250 \times 35 \text{ weeks} = \$8,750$$

Total parsonage allowance for the two positions would be:
$$\$1,700 + \$8,750 = \$10,450.$$

Once the parsonage allowance has been timely designated, there is no need to attach a copy of the official designation to the tax return itself. Merely show the amount properly designated on the "Worksheet for Form 2106." In the event you are chosen for an audit, the IRS will ask for a verification of the timely official designation from the church records.

We recommend that the "Worksheet for Form 2106" be attached to Form 1040 to explain how you arrived at amount of "excess parsonage allowance" entered on Form 1040, line 22.

Suggested Wording of the Official Designation

When The Church Owns The Parsonage

The chairman informed the meeting that under the tax law, a minister of the Gospel is not subject to federal income tax on "the parsonage allowance paid to him as a part of his compensation to the extent used by him to rent or provide a home."

The parsonage is owned by the church and the actual utility expenses will be paid by the church.

After considering the estimate of Rev. _____ of his additional home expenses, a motion was made by _____, seconded by _____ and passed to adopt the following resolution:

Resolved that of the total cash salary for the year 19___, $_____ is hereby designated as parsonage allowance.

Resolved that as long as Rev. _____ is our employee the above amount of designated parsonage allowance shall apply to all future years until modified.

When A Minister Owns Or Rents His/Her Own Home

The chairman informed the meeting that under the tax law, a minister of the Gospel is not subject to federal income tax on "the parsonage allowance paid to him as part of his compensation to the extent used by him to rent or provide a home."

After considering the estimate of Rev._____ of his home expenses, a motion was made by _____, seconded by _____ and passed to adopt the following resolution:

Resolved that of the total cash salary for the year 19____, $_____ is hereby designated as parsonage allowance.

Resolved that as long as Rev. _____ is our employee the above amount of designated parsonage allowance shall apply to all future years until modified.

When A Minister Is Employed By A School, College, Or Mission

Most teachers and administrators working for a church or integral agency of a church have an annual contract of employment with that organization. It is convenient to include the

PARSONAGE ALLOWANCE

necessary written designation within the contract itself. An annual "Agreement for the Designation of the Parsonage Allowance" could be worded as follows:

According to the provisions in income tax law, a minister of the Gospel is not subject to federal income tax on the "parsonage allowance paid to him as part of his compensation to the extent used by him to rent or provide a home."

Based on Rev._____'s estimate of his home expenses, it is agreed to officially designate $_____ of his total cash salary as parsonage allowance.

Resolved that as long as Rev. _____ is our employee the above amount of designated parsonage allowance shall apply to all future years until modified.

Statement Of Parsonage For An Evangelist

As evangelists travel from church to church, they can send a statement to churches on their itinerary and have a portion or all of the honorarium designated as parsonage allowance, in advance of the engagement. **Get duplicate non-carbon sets printed of the following statement:**

According to the provisions in income tax law, a minister of the Gospel is not subject to federal income tax on the "parsonage allowance paid to him as a part of his compensation to the extent used by him to rent or provide a home."

After considering the request of Rev._____, our evangelist, to designate $_____ of his honorarium as parsonage, a motion was made by _____, seconded by _____ and passed to adopt the following resolution:

Resolved that of the total cash honorarium paid to our evangelist, we hereby designate $_____ or _____% as parsonage allowance.

   Name of Church _____
   Signature _____
   Title _____
   Date _____

Computation of Parsonage Allowance -"Worksheet For Form 2106"

- **Column A**

Enter the value of a home and utilities provided by the employer in this column. It is subject to social security tax. Though it seems to be contradictory, we do not have to use the same formula we used earlier in the chapter for computing the "top" limit for the minister who owns his own home. The fair rental value of the parsonage provided should be reasonable, but has histroically been allowed to be a conservative amount in audits. **Do not be guilty of understating your rental value** below a reasonable amount and thereby understating your social security liability.

You may wish to consult a local realtor for an appraisal, or make inquiries of local landlords.**The condition, location, local market demand and local economic conditions will help you to determine a reasonable value.** The fact that you must live in a particular home, as a part of your employment gives reason for a more conservative estimate of the value of a parsonage provided.

We would recommend that the guidelines in Sec. 119 for qualified campus lodging could be followed. The guidelines for Sec. 119 are not necessarily applicable to Sec. 107, but they do represent a parallel to go by. **The minimum rental value** should be at least 5% x the appraised value of the home provided. Example: 5% x $115,000 = $5,750 annual FRV of home including utilities. A more realistic rental value of a $115,000 home including utilities, considering all the facts and circumstances, might be $10,000 to $12,000 a year. The guidelines for Sec. 119 further require that the appraised value be determined at the end of each year by an independent appraiser, not the employer. However, it is intended that the appraisal be reviewed annually without undue cost to the employer.

- **Column B**

Enter amounts for all parsonage allowance expenses the minister pays or provides for himself on a cash basis in this column. The actual expenses of the home, furniture, utilities, decorating and miscellaneous expenses, are to be shown in Column B. Enter their total on line 11 of the worksheet.

In a year of incurring major expenses, show the computation of fair rental value of furnished home, utilities, etc. on line 12. Examine the sample computation we have shown on Rev. Snodgrass's return in Chapter Seven. Enter the lesser of line 11 or line 12 on line 13.

Show the amount that has been officially designated as parsonage allowance by the employer on line 14. If line 14 is greater than line 13, enter the "excess parsonage allowance" on line 15 and as income on Form 1040, line 22.

Parsonage allowance, as an exclusion, **is not to be included on Form W-2, Box 1!!** When the parsonage allowance is included in error on Form W-2, Box 1, we recommend that a corrected Form W-2c be prepared. When it becomes necessary to deduct a large negative parsonage allowance amount on Form 1040, line 22, it can cause an IRS audit. Though not required, we recommend using Form W-2, Box 14, to show a memo of the amount designated as parsonage allowance.

Computation of Social Security -"Worksheet For Form 2106"

Parsonage allowance is free from income tax, but subject to social security tax. Enter Column A, line 11 and/or Column B, line 14 amounts on the lines provided. A minister who has elected to be exempt from social security and has an approved Form 4361 does not have to compute this value for Sch SE. A minister who qualifies for earned income credit must include the value of a parsonage provided and/or a parsonage allowance on Schedule EIC.

CHAPTER THREE

PROFESSIONAL EXPENSES

In any profession, the ordinary and necessary expenses incurred in order to be able to earn income are deductible according to Sec. 162. In this Chapter we will explain how to have an accountable reimbursement plan. The IRS issued permanent regulations on how to handle reimbursed employee business expenses in December, 1990. **Regulation 1.62.2, (TD 8324) required employers to modify their reimbursement policies for 1991 and future years.**

- *Contributions ARE NOT allowable as Professional Expenses*

Contributions, tithes or offerings paid to a not-for-profit organization are **always Sch A, itemized deductions**. Some tax advisors suggest that you reduce your salary by the amount you would tithe and thereby save tax if you are unable to itemize. In Sec. 61, the assignment of income rule says, "Income received for personal services is taxable to the person who earns it, even though he assigns it to another."

Other tax avoidance suggestions include renaming tithes as "dues" and treating them as a professional expense. Reasonable professional dues might be a few hundred dollars not a few thousand dollars. Even if a contract or other arrangement states that dues must be paid by the employee to retain their position, facts and circumstances will not change compensation from taxable to non-taxable. Regardless of what a contract or other arrangement calls a sum of money, facts and circumstances will determine whether it is taxable compensation.

The business expense code Sec. 162(b) specifically states:

"No deductions shall be allowed under subsection 162(a) for any contribution or gift which would be allowable as a deduction under section 170 (Schedule A) were it not for the percentage limitations, the dollar limitations or the requirements as to the time of payment, set forth in such section."

- *Difference Between Parsonage Allowance and Professional Expenses*

It is important to separate in our thinking the parsonage allowance from professional expenses since their tax treatment is so different. Parsonage allowance is designated in advance and the details of expenses are not turned in to the employer; they are accounted for on the Form 1040 at the end of the year.

Professional expenses must be turned in to the employer and be reimbursed for the best tax treatment. An IRS regulation requires a written reimbursement plan. Be sure to read this chapter carefully for information about Sec. 62(c).

- *Professional Expense Rules are not Unique to Ministers*

The professional expenses discussed in this chapter are available to all religious workers — both the dual-status minister and lay employee. All of the information in this chapter about auto, travel and professional expenses is also applicable to for-profit employers and their employees. Independent contractors or evangelists can adequately account their expenses to a payor.

- *Volunteer Workers*

When a religious worker receives no income as a volunteer, but incurs out-of-pocket expenses, they are contribution deductions on Sch A. Any miles driven for charitable work are deductible at the rate of 12¢ per mile, or actual cost of gas and oil. Do not deduct the miles driven for personal worship to regular church services. Do not deduct any value for your time given, it is not allowable.

Volunteer workers who are reimbursed for travel and ministry expenses must adequately account to the organization making the reimbursement. If the receipts and diaries are not submitted to the organization, the organization will be required to treat the payments as compensation, prepare Form W-2 and withhold taxes.

Recordkeeping a Must!!

We recommend a careful reading of **IRS Publication 463**, "Travel, Entertainment, and Gift Expenses." Recordkeeping rules have always existed, adequate records or sufficient evidence must be available to support deductions for auto and professional expenses. A record of the elements of an expense made at or near the time of the expense, supported by sufficient documentary evidence, has more value than a statement prepared later when generally there is a lack of accurate recall. A log maintained on a **weekly basis** is considered a record made at or near the time of the expense. If you charge business expense items on your employer's credit card or otherwise, you must make a record of the details for the amounts you spend. It cannot be stressed enough — **adequate records and receipts must be kept to substantiate all expenses.** Good stewardship means keeping good records!

IRS regulations require that careful and adequate records be kept for submitting to the employer for reimbursement. "Adequate accounting" means you will give your employer the same type of records and supporting information that you would be required to show to the IRS if they questioned a deduction on your return. **There is no relief from keeping adequate records!**

We have available a **"Professional Tax Record Book"** for ministers, religious workers and professional individuals. It is designed to provide a convenient and efficient way to keep the auto, travel, and professional expense record details required by the IRS. Monthly summary pages are provided. You can easily photocopy the pages and receipts and submit them to your employer for reimbursement. Information for ordering this book is given in the back of this publication.

Unreimbursed Professional Expenses

There is no dispute that adopting a written accountable reimbursement plan is an overwhelming task. Therefore, the following results of not establishing such a plan will hopefully give the motivation to do so and save tax dollars legally. It is good stewardship to take the time to learn the rules and **legally reduce income tax** by adopting a written accountable plan for professional expenses!

Unreimbursed professional expenses, other than auto and travel, carry the extra burden of being "required by your employer" and as "a condition of your employment". Having them reimbursed by your employer is a good way to show they meet these requirements.

If an employer chooses to provide an expense allowance arrangement that **does not meet** the accountable plan requirements, **the employer must report all amounts paid under the plan as wages or other compensation on the employee's Form W-2, Box 1**, even though an employee might voluntarily substantiate expenses to the employer and return any excess amounts to the employer. All amounts paid under a non-accountable plan are wages. Such wages paid to lay employees are subject to withholding of income tax and social security withholding and matching. The dual-status minister will incur the additional income tax and social security tax for estimated tax purposes.

Our sample return for Rev. Snodgrass in Chapter Seven is computed "without reimbursement" and "with accountable reimbursement plan." The difference in tax liability illustrates the value of establishing an accountable reimbursement plan.

PROFESSIONAL EXPENSES

If You Do Not Adequately Account To Your Employer

Reg. 1.274-5(e)(3) says, **"Reporting of expenses for which the employee is not required to make an adequate accounting to his employer. If the employee is not required to make an adequate accounting to his employer for his business expenses or, though required, fails to make an adequate accounting for such expenses, he must submit, as a part of his tax return, a statement showing. . ."** all amounts received as advances or reimbursements from his employer. He must complete Form 2106 based on records and supporting evidence. His employer must show amounts not adequately accounted for on Form W-2, Box 1. **The following consequences will happen:**

1. The expenses become "below the line" deductions on Form 2106 and Sch A. Meals and entertainment are first reduced by 20%, then combined with other miscellaneous expenses, and further reduced by 2% of the employee's Adjusted Gross Income. With higher standard deductions, many taxpayers don't have enough deductions to itemize. **UNLESS** — they adopt a written reimbursement plan and adequately account to their employer and become reimbursed for all their professional expenses they may lose the income tax deduction entirely. The standard deduction for 1993 is $6,200 for a joint return and $3,700 for a single return. Reimbursed auto, travel and professional expenses are not reduced by 2% of AGI. Employees can be 100% reimbursed for meals. Employers deduct only 80% of reimbursed meals & entertainment as a business expense. Not-for-profit employers are not affected, since they have no tax liability.

    New Meal and Entertainment Rules for 1994: The deductible portion of meal and entertainment expenses is reduced from 80% to 50%, effective 1-1-94.

2. A large amount of unreimbursed professional expenses deducted on Schedule A causes many employees to be audited. It is a high "dif" score area of a tax return. Establishing an accountable reimbursement plan with your employer could prevent the time consuming trauma of proving your expenses to an IRS auditor.
3. Many states do not allow itemized deductions; therefore unreimbursed professional expenses cause additional state income tax.
4. Items such as earned income credit, deductible IRA's, % of medical deduction limitation, % of child care credit allowable, taxable social security benefits, etc. are all affected by the amount of the Adjusted Gross Income figure. Establishing a written accountable reimbursement plan with your employer may qualify you for other deductions and credits. **Parents of college students may qualify for more financial aid.**
5. For lay employees, the social security base for both the employer and the employee is greater when there are unreimbursed professional expenses. Establishing an accountable reimbursement plan with your employer will allow the employer to compute social security withholding and matching on just the salary. Dual-status ministers have always been able to reduce their social security base by unreimbursed business expenses.
6. Depending on the outcome of the Dalan Case and Sec. 265 problem we will discuss next, dual-status ministers may not be allowed to deduct all of their unreimbursed professional expenses.

Dalan Case - Proration of Unreimbursed Expenses

If you establish a written accountable expense reimbursement plan and are adequately accounting to your employer for your auto, travel and professional expenses, **the following facts WILL NOT affect you.**

A 1988 court case, Melvin H. Dalan & Lillian J. Dalan, Docket No. 8278-87, T.C. Memo 1988-106, filed March 9, 1988, resurrected an old application of Sec. 265. When a minister's income is a combination of taxable salary and Sec. 107 non-taxable parsonage allowance, only the percentage of **unreimbursed** expenses that were spent in earning the taxable salary are allowable. The percentage of expenses spent in earning the non-taxable housing are not allowed. **The official position of the IRS is to follow the Dalan Court Case.**

Example: A minister receives $20,000, including $8,000 housing allowance. His unreimbursed professional expenses amount to $4,500. ($8,000 divided by $20,000 = 40% X $4,000 = $1,600) $1,600 is the amount of the unreimbursed expenses spent to earn the non-taxable housing, that he would not be able to deduct. The proration of unreimbursed expenses is to be computed on Sch A for the employed minister and on Sch C for the self-employed evangelist.

History of the issue goes back to the David E. Deason case, Docket No. 3993-62, January 10, 1964, which was used during the 60's and early 70's to prorate and not allow a minister's expenses spent to earn the non-taxable housing allowance. In 1977, the Internal Revenue Manual — Audit, 45(11)3 said, that the interpretation of the Service was that Sec. 265 should not be applied to a minister's unreimbursed employee business expenses. The promise of a revenue ruling in the 1977 Memo, never happened. Instead, the memo seems to have vanished from current audit manuals. Therefore, several decisions, such as the Dalan case, are being made in certain regions of the country that are contrary to the IRS's 1977 position. A 1992 court case, Robert H McFarland and Georgia W. McFarland, Docket No. 28246-90, T.C. Memo 1992-440, filed August 4, 1992, upholds Deason and Dalan cases.

Congressional intent for Sec. 265 was to disallow deductions spent in earning municipal or exempt interest. It would seem that other "non-taxable" fringe benefits would have to be considered in prorating the allowable unreimbursed employee business expenses for all careers of employees, if this application to minister's unreimbursed expenses were to stand as the Service's position. Another consideration is the language of the regulations for Sec. 162(a), "Business expenses, if otherwise deductible, are deductible in full even though they exceed the business income." It does not seem logical that Sec. 265 should be applied as a limit to Sec. 162 professional business expenses.

We feel Sec. 265 is being wrongly applied, out of context. We submitted a formal request to the IRS for a Rev. Ruling on the issue on November 8, 1988. IRS was unable to act on our request because it was an issue they were already working on. We have been in contact with IRS personnel in Washington, D.C. throughout the **past five years.** We were advised by the IRS to prorate "unreimbursed" expenses on 1988, 1989, 1990 1991 and 1992 returns. **A Rev. Ruling was drafted in December 1990.** As this publication goes to press, it has yet to be finalized! If and when the ruling is finalized, there will be discussion of the position in IRS Publication 517.

Even though the outcome can not be predicted, any return that contained a Sec. 265 allocation deduction for unreimbursed professional expenses for **1990 should have a 1040X amended return filed by April 15th, 1994.** The three year statute of limitations can be extended by filing a claim. If a Rev. Ruling is issued after April 15th, 1994 supporting the court cases, the claims will simply be denied.

Our sample return for Rev. Snodgrass in Chapter Seven shows the computation for prorating unreimbursed expenses and the worksheet we use. **If your expenses have not been reimbursed according to an accountable plan, call us before you file your return to find out if the IRS has published a decision.**

Reimbursed Professional Expenses

An employee may deduct from gross income to arrive at adjusted gross income only those expenses paid or incurred by him in connection with his employment that are reimbursed under a reimbursement or other expense arrangement with his employer.

PROFESSIONAL EXPENSES 41

To be an accountable reimbursement plan, the plan must meet the following three requirements: **(1)** business connection **(2)** adequate accounting, and **(3)** return of any excess reimbursement.

Reg. 1.62-2(d)(1) requires evidence of an obligation by the employee to make an adequate accounting to the employer for the employee's business expense. **Therefore a written reimbursement plan is REQUIRED.** The regulation also requires that the payment for an "adequately accounted reimbursement" be identified either by making a separate payment or by specifically indicating the separate amount if both wages and the reimbursement are combined in a single payment. If you pay salary, housing and professional expense reimbursement to your employees with one check, identify the different amounts on their checks and in your accounting. **We recommend separate checks to be written for reimbursement of employee business expenses.**

We recommend that an employee submit his substantiation of employee business expenses for reimbursement no less often than **monthly.** If an employee has a cash flow problem and needs to be reimbursed more often, allow him to submit his records on a **weekly** basis.

CAUTION: When an employer and employee have established an accountable reimbursement plan, it is important to be careful to submit all allowable expenses. An employee cannot deduct expenses on his tax return that he failed to submit to the employer for reimbursement. (CCH, Standard Federal Tax Reports ¶8474.2538)

Tax Law & Regulations

Sec. 62(a)(2)(A) says, "**General Rule.**—. . .the term 'adjusted gross income' means, in the case of an individual, gross income minus the following deductions: . . .(A) Reimbursed expenses of employees.—The deductions allowed by part VI (section 161 and following) which consist of expenses paid or incurred by the taxpayer, in connection with the performance by him of services as an employee, under a reimbursement or other expense allowance arrangement with his employer....."

Sec. 62(c) says, "**Certain Arrangements Not Treated as Reimbursement Arrangements:**—For purposes of subsection (a)(2)(A), an arrangement shall in no event be treated as a reimbursement or other expense allowance arrangement if:

(1) such arrangement does not require the employee to substantiate the expenses covered by the arrangement to the person providing the reimbursement, or

(2) such arrangement provides the employee the right to retain any amount in excess of the substantiated expenses covered under the arrangement. The substantiation requirements of the preceding sentence shall not apply to any expense to the extent that substantiation is not required under section 274(d) for such expense by reason of the regulations prescribed under the 2nd sentence thereof."

Regulation 1.62-2(d)(3) says: "**Reimbursement requirement**— (i) In general. If a payor arranges to pay an amount to an employee regardless of whether the employee incurs (or is reasonably expected to incur) business expenses of a type described in paragraph (d)(1) or (d)(2) of this section, the arrangement does not satisfy this paragraph (d) and all amounts paid under the arrangement are treated as paid under a nonaccountable plan."

Business Connection

No part of an employee's salary may be **recharacterized** as being paid under a reimbursement arrangement or other expense allowance arrangement. This narrow definition of "business connection" was not included in previous temporary regulations before 1-1-91.

This permanent regulation has forced employers to adopt a reimbursement plan that changes the "cash flow."

Is the employer willing to assume the unknown amount of their employee's business expenses? Many employees of not-for-profit organizations have historically absorbed the "cost of doing ministry business." The tax benefits to be gained by establishing an accountable reimbursement plan should convince employers to bear the burden of the "cost of doing ministry business."

Ideally, to begin an accountable plan, the employer can initially adjust the cash salary and **be willing to reimburse their employees for their actual allowable business expenses** as they are incurred regardless of the amount they total at year end. However, when a medium to small employer feels that they can not assume the unknown amount of employee business expenses, they can set a fixed limit or cap. To pay an initially adjusted cash salary, plus agree to reimburse their employees for all adequately accounted business expenses up to a fixed limit amount will not be the best plan to adopt because:
1. If the employee's expenses end up being greater than the fixed amount, they will be treated as "below the line" Sch A itemized deductions subject to limitations.
2. If the employee's expenses end up being less than the fixed amount, the employer can not pay the difference as additional salary or bonus.

This **"use it or lose it"** nature of an accountable reimbursement plan is similar to the tax treatment that applies to self-insured medical reimbursement and cafeteria fringe benefit plans. An initial adjustment to the salary to begin an accountable reimbursement plan should be **conservative**, carefully planned and based on previous years' actual expense amounts.

The adjusted salary and the new accountable reimbursement plan will be two completely separate budget amounts **forever.** After an accountable plan has been established the employer should not adjust the salary to increase the amount available for reimbursement. An employer who chooses to use an accountable reimbursement plan with a fixed limit can fund an increase from their own resources. Visualize your hands fully extended. Your right hand represents the "salary" and your left hand represents the "accountable reimbursement plan." The two budget categories can independently be given increases, but they should always remain separate budget items.

- *Examples*

    Example (1). Community Church pays its pastor $500 per week or $26,000 annually. $10,400 has been designated as parsonage allowance. At the end of the month he adequately accounts his employee business expenses of $265 for the month. Community Church designates $265 of the $500 as paid to reimburse the pastor's employee business expenses. Because Community Church would pay the pastor $500 a week regardless of whether the pastor incurred employee business expenses, the arrangement **does not satisfy** the reimbursement requirement of Reg. 1.62-2(d)(3)(i). Community Church must report ($26,000 - $10,400) $15,600 as wages on Form W-2. (This plan would have been an accountable plan for years ending before 1-1-1991.)

    Example (2). Community Church pays its pastor $500 per week or $26,000 annually. Community Church initially adjusts its pastor's salary to $23,000, designates parsonage allowance of $10,400 and adopts a fixed limit reimbursement plan of $3,000. Each month the pastor received an expense reimbursement check for the amount of employee business expenses he adequately accounted to his employer. At the end of the year, Community Church had paid their pastor expense reimbursements of only $2,400. They decided that they would give him a bonus of $600. The entire $3,000 must be included on Form W-2. Community Church must report ($26,000 - $10,400) $15,600 as wages on Form W-2. The plan **does not satisfy** the reimbursement requirement of Reg. 1.62-2(d)(3)(i)

    Example (3). Community Church pays its pastor $500 per week or $26,000 annually. Community Church initially adjusts its pastor's salary to $23,000, designates parsonage

PROFESSIONAL EXPENSES

allowance of $10,400 and adopts a fixed limit reimbursement plan of $3,000. Each month the pastor received an expense reimbursement check for the amount of employee business expenses he adequately accounted to his employer. At the end of the year, Community Church had paid their pastor expense reimbursements of $2,400. Community Church correctly included ($23,000 - $10,400) $12,600 on Form W-2 for their pastor. Their reimbursement plan **does satisfy** all the conditions of an "accountable plan."

Example (4). Community Church pays its pastor $500 per week or $26,000 annually. Community Church initially adjusts its pastor's salary to $23,000, designates parsonage allowance of $10,400 and adopts an unlimited reimbursement plan for employee business expenses. Each month the pastor received an expense reimbursement check for the amount of employee business expenses he adequately accounted to his employer. At the end of the year, Community Church had paid their pastor expense reimbursements of $3,600. Community Church correctly included ($23,000 - $10,400) $12,600 on Form W-2 for their pastor. Their reimbursement plan **does satisfy** all the conditions of an "accountable plan."

Adequate Accounting

- **Definition Of Adequate Accounting**

    Reg. 1.274-5(e)(4) says, **"Definition of an 'adequate accounting' to the employer . . .means the submission to the employer of an account book, diary, statement of expense, or similar record maintained by the employee in which the information as to each element of an expenditure is recorded at or near the time of the expenditure, together with supporting documentary evidence, in a manner which conforms to all the 'adequate records' requirements of paragraph (c)(2) of this section."**

Regulations further instruct us that a responsible person other than the employee must verify and approve the records and amounts of expense. Such a person should be careful not to allow personal expenses to be submitted. Employers are to maintain or keep records of reimbursed business expenses for at least three years after the due date of the employee's tax return. Even though it is not required, we would recommend that the records and receipts be photocopied and that both the employee and the employer keep the records. Our **"Professional Tax Record Book"** contains monthly summary pages, is easily photocopied and has been designed to make it easy to adequately account to your employer. **The instructions for each section of the record book outline the requirements of Sec. 274 and the necessary details to record for each category of expense.**

The details of time, place, destination, business purpose, business discussion, etc. are very important details to record at or near the time of the business expense or trip. Each type of business expense and Sec. 274 requirements that apply to it are discussed in more detail later in this chapter. A record of the elements of an expense made at or near the time of the expense, supported by sufficient documentary evidence, has more value than a statement prepared later when generally there is a lack of accurate recall. A log maintained on a **weekly basis** is considered a record made at or near the time of the expense. If you charge business expense items on your employer's credit card or otherwise, you must make a record of the above details for the amounts you spend.

You must have actual receipts for lodging and any other professional expense of $25.00 or more. Ask for and get receipts and pay by check when possible. Both forms of proof will be strong substantiation. Canceled checks alone may not provide adequate record. **You must maintain an account book or diary for any expense under $25.00.**

It is not sufficient if an employee merely groups expenses into broad categories such as "travel" or reports individual expenses through the use of vague, nondescriptive terms such as "miscellaneous business expenses", according to Reg. 1.162-2(e)(3).

- **If You Do Adequately Account To Your Employer**

    Reg. 1.274-5(e)(2) says, **"Reporting of expenses for which the employee is required to make an adequate accounting to his employer—(i) Reimbursements equal to expenses. For purposes of computing tax liability, an employee need not report on his tax return business expenses for travel, transportation, entertainment, gifts, and similar purposes, paid or incurred by him solely for the benefit of his employer for which he is required to, and does make an adequate accounting to his employer and which are charged directly or indirectly to the employer or for which the employee is paid through advances, reimbursements, or otherwise, provided that the total amount of such advances, reimbursements and charges is equal to such expenses."**
    1. You do not report on your tax return the reimbursement for professional business expenses when you establish an accountable reimbursement plan with your employer.
    2. You do not have to keep records for possible IRS audit. You do not have to substantiate your expense account for the IRS auditor as you have already done so with your employer. The employer must retain the records and receipts submitted by you. If your return is audited, show the IRS auditor a copy of the written accountable reimbursement plan you established with your employer.
    3. The employer does not include the reimbursements on the W-2, Box 1.

    Other references to support the above discussion of reimbursement policies are Reg. 1.62-2 and Reg. 1.162-17.

    If you are reimbursed more than your allowable expenses, you must return the excess reimbursement to your employer. If your employer has an "accountable plan" and you fail to either adequately account or return excess reimbursement, it will be deemed to be a "non-accountable" plan for you and your employer is required to report all of your reimbursements as salary on Form W-2. You will then be required to treat such non-accountable expenses as "below the line" deductions on Form 2106 and Sch A, subject to the limitations.

- **Adequate Accounting Requirement Is Satisfied by Mileage Allowance & Per Diem**

    Adequate accounting requirement is satisfied when the amount of reimbursement is based on the auto mileage allowance of **28¢** per mile and the employee's log of business miles, date, place and purpose. Likewise, when the amount of reimbursement for travel away from home is based on the per diem allowance of **$150 or $94** (see IRS list of eligible high cost cities later in the chapter) per day and the employee's record of number of days, place and purpose of travel. Likewise, when the amount of reimbursement for meals away from home (incurred without cost of lodging) is based on **$36 or $28** (see IRS list of eligible high cost cities later in the chapter) per day and the employee's record of number of days, place and purpose. (CCH, Standard Federal Tax Reports ¶14,417.625 and Rev Proc 93-21)

    Per diem rates were adjusted for inflation on **March 12, 1993**. The high-low per diem rate for **January 1 to March 11, 1993**, remain at **$147 or $93** and meals away from home remain at **$34 or $26**.

    It was not until early 1990 that the high-low per diem and meal rates were published by the IRS. However, they were able to be applied to 1989's expenses. Employee mileage allowances and per diem travel subsistence allowances that are not in excess of IRS-set maximums may relieve difficulty of substantiation and generate a deduction that is greater than actual travel expenses. The previous meal per diem of $14 and $9 were skimpy and actual expenses generally were greater. The new meal and/or travel per diem are much more realistic. You must use the same method of accounting for the whole year. We will

PROFESSIONAL EXPENSES 45

give more detailed discussion under "travel" later in this chapter. Compare the options shown in our discussion of "travel," and use the method that allows the greater deduction.

Rev. Proc. 92-104 announced the **28¢ mileage allowance rate** for **1993** on **January 1, 1993.** IRS will announce the 1994 mileage allowance rate in December, 1993 or January, 1994. Now that IRS announces the mileage allowance rate near the beginning of the year, retroactive application of an increase is no longer necessary.

For years after 1989, the mileage allowance rate is available for all business miles (even in excess of 15,000). With or without a reimbursement plan taxpayers are allowed **28¢** per mile for all of their business miles.

- *When Actual Auto Expenses Exceed The Cents Per Mile Computation*

If you are incurring more than **28¢** per mile to operate your auto, it may be beneficial to submit your business % of actual expenses to your employer. Otherwise, any unreimbursed excess expense becomes a Schedule A deduction subject to the 2% of AGI limitation and the Sec. 265 limitation. **Annually** choose to become reimbursed for actual expenses **or** mileage allowance. Rev. Proc. 92-104, Sec. 8, describes a fixed and variable rate (FAVR) allowance that is acceptable to the IRS. However, we recommend the following procedure of computing actual:

1. Compute auto depreciation for year and divide by 12.
2. Total actual monthly expenses for gas, oil, repairs, etc. (omit principal portion of auto payment).
3. Estimate what your annual % of business use will be, or use the business % that you recorded for previous year.
4. Multiply business % by the total of depreciation and expenses for the month and submit to your employer for reimbursement.
5. At the end of the year: Divide business miles by total miles for the year to know what your ACTUAL business % is.
6. Multiply actual business % by the total of depreciation and expenses for the full year.
7. Submit the difference between the annual auto expense computed and what has been reimbursed during the other 11 months of the year to your employer for December's reimbursement.

Return of Amounts Exceeding Expenses

If you are advanced more than your allowable expenses, you must return the excess reimbursement to your employer within a reasonable time. Committee reports for Sec. 62(c)(2) state: In cases where an employee is reimbursed by the employer on **the basis of a per diem or auto mileage allowance up to the IRS-specified rates,** there is deemed to be **no excess retained** by the employee. An "above the line" deduction is allowed up to the IRS-specified rate. Any reimbursement to an employee in excess of the IRS-specified rates can be treated by the employer as "above the line" deductions when the employee submits proof of actual expenses that equal the amount of reimbursement.

An accountable plan must generally require the employee to return any amount paid under the arrangement over and above substantiated expenses within a reasonable period of time. Advances for expenses must be reasonably calculated to not exceed anticipated expenses and any excess must be returned to the employer within a reasonable period of time after receipt. Under the "fixed date method," the following are treated as having occurred within a reasonable period of time:

1. An advance made within 30 days of when an expense is paid or incurred,
2. an expense substantiated to the payor within 60 days after it's paid or incurred, or
3. an amount returned to the employer within 120 days after an expense is paid or incurred.

We recommend that not-for-profit employers avoid adopting a plan that allows for payment of "advances." If an "advance" is not paid to an employee this more complex bookkeeping procedure is automatically satisfied. Employers who have volunteer treasurers should chose the **simplicity** of periodically reimbursing their employees for actual expenses and/or IRS specified rates as they are submitted.

Although the "reasonable time" periods do not specifically apply to plans without "advances," we do recommend that an employee account for his expenses within the guidelines. We also recommend that an employee submit his substantiation of employee business expenses for reimbursement no less often than **monthly**. If the employee has a cash flow problem and needs to be reimbursed more often, allow him to submit his records on a **weekly** basis.

Adopt One of the Following Reimbursement Plans

One of the following plans should be adopted for each employee. An employer does not have to have the same plan for all employees. An accountable reimbursement plan is very important to your employees' economic health!

If you and your employer have not adopted a written reimbursement plan, you must report your expenses as "unreimbursed" on Form 2106 and Sch A. A plan is not able to be retroactive, it becomes effective for the future at the time it is adopted.

You may customize one of the following policies to clearly state the agreement between the employer and the employee. For example, if you wish to state that the amount of reimbursement will be the government mileage allowance and/or per-diem allowances for travel, add a sentence that clearly states that agreement.

Salary Plus Unlimited Reimbursement

The chairman informed the meeting that according to Sec. 62(a)(2)(A), an employee that adequately accounts to the employer the details of their professional expenses, is allowed a deduction from gross income. Sec. 62(c) further requires an employee to return any excess reimbursement or advance to the employer within a reasonable time. Reg. 1.62-2(d)(3) further requires that no part of our employee's salary be recharacterized as being paid under this reimbursement arrangement.

A motion was made by_____, seconded by_____and passed to adopt the following resolution:

Resolved that in addition to the salary provided our employee, we will reimburse him/her for auto, travel and professional expenses considered ordinary and necessary for him/her to carry out his/her duties. **(Add special modifications here.)**

It is further understood that a person other than the employee will examine the adequately accounted records and that the records will be kept for at least four years by the employer.

Salary Plus Fixed Limit Reimbursement

The chairman informed the meeting that according to Sec. 62(a)(2)(A), an employee that adequately accounts to the employer the details of their professional expenses, is allowed a deduction from gross income. Sec. 62(c) further requires an employee to return any excess reimbursement or advance to the employer within a reasonable time. Reg. 1.62-2(d)(3) further requires that no part of our employee's salary be recharacterized as being paid under this reimbursement arrangement.

A motion was made by_____, seconded by_____and passed to adopt the following resolution:

Resolved that in addition to the salary provided our employee, we will reimburse him/her for auto, travel and professional expenses considered ordinary and necessary for him/her to carry out his/her duties up to a fixed limit of $_____. **(Add special modifications here.)** If his/her actual expenses are less than this fixed limit, he/she cannot be given the

PROFESSIONAL EXPENSES 47

difference as bonus or salary. If his/her actual expenses are greater than this fixed limit, he/she will be required to deduct the extra expenses on Form 2106 and Sch A.

It is further understood that a person other than the employee will examine the adequately accounted records and that the records will be kept for at least four years by the employer.

Typical Professional Expenses for a Minister
Auto Expense

Though Congress has successfully complicated the tax laws regarding autos, it is important to apply the complex laws in such a way as to arrive at the "largest" deduction or reimbursement. We encourage you to read **IRS Publication 917**, "Business Use of a Car."

- **Effect of Employer Reimbursement Plans**

When you **lease an auto and you adequately account to your employer** for your business mileage, you do have the **choice** of being reimbursed at the mileage allowance rate. If the business % of the cost of your lease (reduced by inclusion factor discussed later), combined with other operating expenses, is greater than the mileage allowance rate, you will want to adequately account to your employer the business % of your actual expenses.

When you **own an auto and you adequately account to your employer** for your business mileage, you have the **choice** of being reimbursed at the mileage allowance rate or the business % of your actual expenses.

Log Your Business Miles

Dedicate one auto for business use: Because of the limits placed on less than 50% business use autos, it is very advisable to concentrate business use and use one auto at a time and to keep the % of business use as high as possible. Usually an auto is part business use and part personal use. **A mileage log is the only possible way to prove the business % of use.** It is important to keep separate mileage logs for each auto used for business. The only way to accurately compute each auto's deduction is to keep separate records for each auto. It is not easy to **keep a consistent record of miles traveled** for business, **but you must.** When you realize the amount of tax saved by being able to fully deduct your "business" mileage, it is more than worthwhile.

Commuting: If you live a distance from the office be careful **not to include personal commuting** miles in your log. They are not considered "business miles." **Multiple trips between home and office during the day are all non-deductible commuting miles.** However, trips from home to first business stop and from last business stop to home are non-deductible commuting according to T.W. McDougal, TC Memo 1980-289. If your employer does not provide an office for you, and your business tax home is an office in your home, you will have -0- commuting miles.

How to Log Business Miles: Only one entry is needed in your business log to record use consisting of a round trip or a period of uninterrupted business use. Use of a passenger automobile for a trip away from home over a period of several days may be accounted for by a single entry. De minimis personal use, such as a lunch stop between two business stops, is not an interruption in business use. Our **"Professional Tax Record Book"** has been designed to make it easy to record all the details necessary for your mileage log and actual auto expenses. Your mileage log should contain the following information:

1. Date
2. Odometer reading at beginning of trip
3. Odometer reading at end of trip
4. Business miles driven for the day
5. Place and purpose of the trip

Sale Or Trade Of Business Auto

One of the most difficult computations to do correctly is that of the sale or trade of an auto used partly for business and partly for personal. It is very important that you keep a record of your auto's basis because, upon trade or sale, you must properly compute the gain or loss. The only way to accurately compute each auto's basis is to keep separate records for each auto used.

Regardless of whether you have used optional mileage allowance or actual expense method, the sale of a part-business auto results in a reportable transaction on Form 4797. Form 8824, Like Kind Exchanges, is required to be attached to your tax return to report a trade transaction. **A trade** will affect the basis of the new auto, according to Sec. 1031. **A sale** will result in **a gain that is taxable** or **a loss that is deductible** on Form 4797. Many taxpayers who have claimed the mileage allowance method have failed to report a gain or claim a loss on the outright sale of their auto. We have included an example of an auto trade and Form 8824 in Chapter Seven for Rev. Snodgrass.

Knowing the basis of your auto makes it possible to tax plan. If the amount of depreciation claimed for your auto would cause a **gain upon sale**, then it would be **best to trade autos.** If the amount of depreciation claimed or computed according to IRS regulations, would cause a **loss upon sale**, then it would be **best to sell the auto outright**, deduct the loss and buy the replacement auto outright. (CCH, Standard Federal Tax Reports ¶31,519.035)

- **Depreciation Adjustment to Basis**

If you choose the mileage allowance method to deduct the business use of your auto for the first year your auto is placed in service an optional depreciation factor reduces the basis of your auto to determine the adjusted basis when you dispose of it. For autos placed in service after 1979 and before 1990, the auto was considered fully depreciated after 60,000 miles of business use at the maximum standard mileage rate. To compute its basis, an auto was considered to have been driven up to 15,000 business miles only each year. As of 12-31-89, the 60,000 mile rule was eliminated. Therefore, an auto treated as fully depreciated in 1989 because of the 60,000 mile rule was able to be treated as having a basis in 1990 under the new rule. Compute **optional depreciation** factor as follows:

1980 thru 1989: Business miles up to but no more than 15,000 per year or 60,000 per auto, multiplied by 7¢ in 1980 and 1981, 7½¢ in 1982, 8¢ in 1983, 1984, and 1985, 9¢ in 1986, 10¢ in 1987, 10½¢ in 1988, 11¢ for 1989.

1990 thru 1993: All business miles multiplied by 11¢ in 1990 and 1991, 11½ in 1992 and 1993. (CCH, Standard Federal Tax Reports ¶8,540.023, ¶31,519.035 and Rev. Proc. 92-104)

Exception: If the actual cost method is used to deduct the business use of your auto for **any year other than the first year**, these rates will not apply to any year the actual cost method is used. You will combine the optional factor for years of mileage allowance method with the actual computation for years of actual expense method.

If the actual cost method is used to deduct the business use of your auto for **the first year** your auto is placed in service, your basis adjustment will be the actual computation of depreciation.

We have designed a **"Worksheet to Compute Auto Basis."** The backside of the worksheet contains the technical rules that we are detailing in this chapter. We advise you to enter your auto information on our worksheet each year, unstaple it each year and bring it forward to the current return. In a year of sale or trade you will have the necessary information to make the required basis calculations. Information for ordering this form is given in the back of this publication. We feel the best way to illustrate the basis computation on the worksheet is to include an auto trade situation in our sample problem for Rev. Snodgrass in Chapter Seven.

PROFESSIONAL EXPENSES 49

If you are sending your information to us for preparation of your return, please give us the type of information you see on the form and **copies of prior year tax returns** showing how your auto basis has been handled. Our **"Checklist"** in the back of the book allows for your auto information to be separated for each auto.

Auto Interest & Personal Property Tax

Auto interest and personal property tax is no longer available as an employee business expense. Do not become reimbursed for the business % of auto interest and personal property tax. Interest on an auto for an employee is considered "personal interest" and no longer deductible on Sch A. Personal property tax can still be deducted on Sch A by employees.

Self-employed business use or farm use have the advantage of being able to deduct the business % of interest and personal property tax on Sch C or F. Based on Rev. Ruling 80-110, Sec. 1402(a) and Sec. 62(1), it is correct to **use the business % of auto interest and personal property tax as a subtraction from a minister's social security base**. Revenue Ruling 92-29 provides for allocation of the fee for tax preparation between business and Schedule A.

Sales tax for the purchase of an auto used in business is to be added to the cost basis as a capital expense.

Lease or Own

Although leasing an auto is subject to luxury limitations, it could be advantageous to lease rather than to own. Lease payments may generate more deduction now that auto interest is considered personal interest for the employee. **The question of whether to lease or own is a difficult question to answer.** Our advice is to shop and negotiate for the least cost of transportation that meets your needs. Be sure to read the "fine print" conditions of the lease. There is usually a limit as to how many miles you can drive the leased auto before an extra charge per mile is assessed.

Spending additional dollars for transportation because it is tax deductible is not sensible. To **spend an additional $500** and be in the 15% tax bracket would only reduce your tax by $75. The difference of **$425 is a real cost** out of your pocket.

Choose the Best Method of Deducting Auto Expenses

There are two methods of computing the deduction for the cost of operating your auto for business. If you have information available to figure your auto expenses both ways, you will want to use the method that results in the largest deduction. There are continual increases in the cost of owning and operating an auto. It is possible that your actual expenses are greater than the mileage allowance method. However, due to the luxury auto limitations on depreciation and the increase of the mileage allowance rate to **28¢**—fewer taxpayers are benefiting from the actual expense computation.

Mileage Allowance Method

IRS allows you to be reimbursed or deduct **28¢** a mile for all business miles driven in 1993. In addition, you may be reimbursed or deduct your actual tolls and parking fees. (Auto interest, personal property tax, and sales tax are not deductible in addition to mileage allowance rate as an employee business expense.) A daily log book of miles driven must be kept in order to use this method.

To use the mileage allowance rate for **unreimbursed** business use you must:
1. Own the auto,
2. Not use the auto for hire, such as for a taxi,
3. Not operate a fleet of autos using two or more at the same time.
4. Not have claimed depreciation using any method other than the straightline method.
5. Not have claimed the Sec. 179 deduction on the auto.

Actual Method

This is an itemized list of your actual auto expenses such as: gas, oil, lubrication, repairs, parts, tires, batteries, tune-ups, auto washes, insurance, auto club dues, licenses, parking fees, tolls, and auto depreciation or auto lease.

Since 1-1-81, if you choose actual expenses as the method of deducting your unreimbursed auto expenses in the **year of purchase**, you must continue to use the actual method as long as you own that car.

- **Deductions Limited For Less Than 50% Business Use**

Tax Reform Act of 1984 began to limit depreciation deductions for autos, computers and other listed property placed in service after June 18, 1984 that are not **predominantly used in business**. When less than 50% use of the property is business use Sec. 179 expensing is not available and the auto's basis must be recovered over five years using the straight-line method and the half-year convention.

Depreciation recapture is to be computed if an auto was more than 50% business use in year of purchase, but drops to 50% or less business use in any future year. Recapture means "pay back". If you used your auto more than 50% in your business in the year you placed it in service, but 50% or less for business in a later year, you must include in gross income the difference between depreciation and Sec. 179 expensing claimed and the amount of depreciation recomputed at the 5 year straight-line method. You must continue using 5 year straight-line even if business use rises back above 50%.

The recapture amount is shown as a memo on Form 4797. Employees enter the income on Form 1040, line 22 and dual-status ministers also include the income on Sch SE.

- **Deductions Limited For Luxury Automobiles**

Yes, if you purchased an auto in 1993 and it **cost $14,300** or more, **you drive a luxury auto!** Even though an automobile is used more than 50% for business purposes, the law placed further limits on the amounts of annual depreciation deductions that could be taken on automobiles. The amount of annual limits are based on 100% business use. If the business use is less than 100%, the maximum annual limits must be reduced to reflect the actual business use percentage. The depreciation limit amounts apply to regular depreciation and Sec. 179 expensing. The limits are indexed for inflation.

For autos purchased after 6-18-84 and before 4-3-85, depreciation limits were $4,000 for the first tax year and $6,000 for each succeeding year. For autos purchased after 4-2-85 and before 1-1-87 depreciation limits were $3,200 for the first tax year and $4,800 for each succeeding year.

- **Luxury Limits for autos purchased after 12-31-86 and before 1-1-94 —**

# of Years Owned	Date Auto Placed in Service				
	1-1-87 thru 12-31-88	1-1-89 thru 12-31-90	1-1-91 thru 12-31-91	1-1-92 thru 12-31-92	after 12-31-92
1st year	$2,560	$2,660	$2,660	$2,760	$2,860
2nd year	$4,100	$4,200	$4,300	$4,400	$4,600
3rd year	$2,450	$2,550	$2,550	$2,650	$2,750
4th - 6th	$1,475	$1,475	$1,575	$1,575	$1,675

How To Compute Auto Depreciation

Methods and limits of depreciation apply to autos according to the date of purchase. Find the paragraph that **matches** your **purchase date** and follow those rules until you change autos.

PROFESSIONAL EXPENSES

- **Autos Purchased After 6-18-84 And Before 1-1-87** —
ACRS (Accelerated Cost Recovery System) allowed for a quick write-off for the cost of an auto. Autos were 3 year Class Property. There were 4 ways to deduct the cost of the business portion of your auto. The percentage method was based on 150% declining balance method.

Year	Percentage
1	25%
2	38%
3	37%

The other three choices were all the straight-line method. You could choose 3 year, 5 year, or 12 year straight-line. When using the straight-line method, you were to use a half-year convention, or 6 months of depreciation in the year of purchase, regardless of what month you purchased the auto. No deduction was allowed in the year of trade or sale. For autos purchased during this period, **Sec. 179 expensing** allowed you to expense up to **$5,000** of the purchase price in the year of purchase until the business % of the luxury limit was reached.

- **Autos Purchased After 12-31-86 and before 1-1-94** —
Under MACRS (Modified ACRS) autos are 5-year Class property. The percentage method is based on 200% declining balance method. The alternative recovery method is 5 year straight-line. **Sec. 179 expensing** of up to $10,000 (1987 to 1992) or **$17,500 (1993)** can very rarely be used within the luxury auto limits. If business use is 50% or less in year of purchase, then the auto's basis must be recovered over five years using the straight-line method and the half-year convention. The most depreciation allowed per year, regardless of your auto's basis is the business % of the luxury auto limits shown above. MACRS allows depreciation deduction in the year of sale. The IRS tables below have computed the mid-year and mid-quarter factors for the year of purchase automatically.

Mid-year convention allows ½ of the annual % available in the year of purchase and in the year of sale.

Mid-quarter convention allows the mid-quarter computation % depending on which quarter the purchase or sale occurs. If more than **40% of the year's** depreciable assets are placed in service in the **final quarter**, then all non-realty assets for that year **must** be depreciated using "mid-quarter" convention instead of the normal mid-year convention.

Here are the percentages for both mid-year and mid-quarter for autos and other 5 year class equipment.

Year	Mid-year	Mid-quarter (1st)	Mid-quarter (2nd)	Mid-quarter (3rd)	Mid-quarter (4th)
1	20.00%	35.00%	25.00%	15.00%	5.00%
2	32.00%	26.00%	30.00%	34.00%	38.00%
3	19.20%	15.60%	18.00%	20.40%	22.80%
4	11.52%	11.01%	11.37%	12.24%	13.68%
5	11.52%	11.01%	11.37%	11.30%	10.94%
6	5.76%	1.38%	4.26%	7.06%	9.58%

Leased Automobiles

If you drive a leased auto for business use and you are not reimbursed by your employer, you must use actual expenses for your deduction on Form 2106. The business % of the actual cost of the lease, gas, oil and any other expense you incur is deductible. You cannot deduct any part of a lease payment that is for commuting or other personal use of the auto. When you lease an auto for business use, the **luxury auto limitations** are applied by the computation of an **income inclusion factor**. IRS Publication 917 contains special tables to compute the income inclusion factor. The inclusion amount is prorated for the number of days of the lease term included in the tax year. The amount computed would be shown on line 24b, Part II, of Form 2106. The net amount of vehicle rental expenses will be shown on line 24c. In determining the inclusion amount, different rules apply depending on when the auto is leased.

- *Autos Leased After 6-18-84 And Before 4-3-85* —
   For each taxable year that a taxpayer leases an auto with a FMV of more than $16,500, you must include in gross income an inclusion amount that represents the depreciation and investment credit limitations that apply to auto owners. There is an additional inclusion amount if you have 50% or less business use.

- *Autos Leased After 4-2-85 And Before 1-1-87* —
   For each taxable year that a taxpayer leases an auto with a FMV of more than $11,250, you must include in gross income an inclusion amount. There is an additional inclusion amount if you have 50% or less business use.

- *Autos Leased After 12-31-86 And Before 1-1-94* —
   For each taxable year that a taxpayer leases an auto with a FMV of more than the amounts listed below, you must include in gross income an inclusion amount. There is **no** additional inclusion amount if you have 50% or less business use for this period. Easy to use tables are in **IRS Publication 917**.

Year	FMV	Table
1987 & 1990	$12,800	Use Table 3 for autos leased after 12-31-86.
1991	$13,400	Use Table 4 for autos leased after 12-31-88.
1992	$13,700	Use Table 5 for autos leased after 12-31-90.
1993	$14,300	Use Rev. Proc. 93-35 Table 2 for autos leased after 12-31-92.

Employer Provided Autos

The value of an employee's personal use of an employer provided vehicle must be included in his income, minus any reimbursement he made to his employer. **Publication 535,** "Business Expenses," contains the valuation table and instructions for the employer providing this "working condition" fringe benefit. **Reg. 1.61-21(c),(d),(e), and (f)** is a thorough presentation of the "working condition" fringe benefit.

In order for an employer to exclude from the employee's gross income the value of an employer-provided vehicle, the employee must substantiate the amount of the exclusion by maintaining and submitting to the employer adequate records of business use.

When an employer **prohibits personal use** by the employee, there will be no taxable income to the employee. All of the following conditions must be met:
1. The vehicle is owned or leased by the employer and is provided to an employee for use in the employer's trade or business.
2. The vehicle is kept on the employer's premises.
3. Only very limited personal use is allowed, such as lunch stops on the road,
4. The vehicle is not being used for personal purposes.
5. No employee using the vehicle lives at the employer's place of business.
6. There must be evidence that the vehicle meets all these conditions.

It is best for the **employer providing the auto** to **pay for all costs or all costs except gasoline.** Hybrid arrangements cause confusion and cause the employee to pay tax on a value he didn't receive. Regulations only allow for a gasoline factor of 5½¢ a mile to be added if the employer pays for the gasoline or omitted if the employee pays for the gasoline.

Whenever an employer does not choose a special valuation method by a timely notification to the employee, the value of the fringe benefit must be determined under **the**

PROFESSIONAL EXPENSES

general valuation method. Under the general valuation method, FMV is the amount that would be paid between unrelated third parties to obtain the particular fringe benefit.

Notification of employee: If you elect to use a special valuation rule, the written notice must generally be given to the employee by **the later of January 31 of the applicable year, or 30 days** after the employer owned auto is provided.

Three special valuation methods are available

1. **The lease valuation method:** The value of availability of an auto to the employee must first be determined. This value of availability is then reduced by the % of business use to determine the value of the employee's personal use of the auto to be treated as compensation.
   A. Employer must request from the employee a statement as to the business mileage and the total mileage driven by the employee. Where the employee supplies such statement or record within a reasonable period of time, the employer must compute personal use percentage and amount to withhold on the basis of such information.
   B. Using the fair market value of the auto, which is determined as of the first date of its availability to the employee, the annual lease value is determined through the use of the table reproduced on the next page. For an auto provided for only part of a year, the value is determined by multiplying the annual lease value by a fraction (days auto is available to the employee divided by 365).
   C. The figures in the annual lease value table are applicable for a four-year period starting on the date on which the special rule is applied and ending on December 31 of the fourth full year following that date. After that period, the annual lease value for each calendar year is based on the fair market value of the auto on January 1 of the applicable year.
   D. If an employer provides fuel; its fair market value or 5½¢ per mile must be an additional computation.

2. **Vehicle cents-per mile method:** The 1993 standard mileage rate of 28¢ may be used to determine the value of personal use for employer-provided autos. All of the following conditions must be met:
   A. Employer must request from the employee a statement as to the business mileage and the total mileage driven by the employee. Where the employee supplies such statement or record within a reasonable period of time, the employer must compute personal use percentage and amount to withhold on the basis of such information.
   B. This method can't be used if the FMV of the auto, as of the first date the auto is made available to any employee for personal use exceeds $14,300 (adjusted for inflation).
   C. It must be reasonably expected that the auto will be regularly used in employer's business, or actually driven primarily by employees at least 10,000 (personal and business) miles during a calendar year.
   D. The cents-per mile method includes all costs of operating the auto. Neither the employer or the employee may adjust the rate for services not provided such as repairs. The only adjustment allowed is that if fuel is not provided by the employer, the cents-per mile value may be reduced by no more than 5½ cents.

3. **Commuting valuation method:** Available for employer-provided vehicles that employees must use for commuting. To qualify for this special $1.50 value per one-way commute valuation ($3.00 for each round-trip), all of the following criteria must be met by employers and employees:
   A. The vehicle must be owned or leased by the employer and is provided to one or more employees for use in connection with the employer's trade or business.

ANNUAL LEASE VALUE TABLE / Reg. 1.61-2(d)(2)(i)(B)(iii)

Automobile Fair Market Value	Annual Lease Value	Automobile Fair Market Value	Annual Lease Value
$ 0 - 999	$ 600	$ 22,000 - 22,999	$ 6,100
1,000 - 1,999	850	23,000 - 23,999	6,350
2,000 - 2,999	1,100	24,000 - 24,999	6,600
3,000 - 3,999	1,350	25,000 - 25,999	6,850
4,000 - 4,999	1,600	26,000 - 27,999	7,250
5,000 - 5,999	1,850	28,000 - 29,999	7,750
6,000 - 6,999	2,100	30,000 - 31,999	8,250
7,000 - 7,999	2,350	32,000 - 33,999	8,750
8,000 - 8,999	2,600	34,000 - 35,999	9,250
9,000 - 9,999	2,850	36,000 - 37,999	9,750
10,000 - 10,999	3,100	38,000 - 39,999	10,250
11,000 - 11,999	3,350	40,000 - 41,999	10,750
12,000 - 12,999	3,600	42,000 - 43,999	11,250
13,000 - 13,999	3,850	44,000 - 45,999	11,750
14,000 - 14,999	4,100	46,000 - 47,999	12,250
15,000 - 15,999	4,350	48,000 - 49,999	12,750
16,000 - 16,999	4,600	50,000 - 51,999	13,250
17,000 - 17,999	4,850	52,000 - 53,999	13,750
18,000 - 18,999	5,100	54,000 - 55,999	14,250
19,000 - 19,999	5,350	56,000 - 57,999	14,750
20,000 - 20,999	5,600	58,000 - 59,999	15,250
21,000 - 21,999	5,850	over $60,000	Auto's FMV X 0.25 + $500

EXAMPLE: *An employer makes an auto available for all of 1993. Its fair market value is $16,000; its annual lease value from the table is $4,600. Employee uses the auto 20% for personal use. Thus, the employer must include in the employee's income 20% of $4,600 or **$920**. If fuel is provided by the employer and personal use of 20% was 4,000 miles, (4,000 X 5½¢) an additional **$220** must be included in income.*

B. The employer must, for genuine, noncompensatory business reasons, require the employee to commute in the automobile.
C. The employer has established a written policy under which neither the employee nor any individual whose use would be taxable to the employee may use the vehicle for personal purposes other than for commuting or *de minimis* personal use (such as a lunch stop between business meetings).
D. The employee required to use the vehicle for commuting must not be a control employee.

A **control employee** of a nongovernmental employer is any employee who (1) is a board-appointed, shareholder-appointed, confirmed or elected officer of the employer whose compensation equals or exceeds $50,000, (2) is the director of the employer, (3) owns a one percent or greater equity, capital or profit interest in the employer, or (4) receives $100,000 or more in compensation.

- *Withholding of Tax*

When an auto is either owned or leased by the employer for an employee's use, the personal portion of the auto's use is a taxable fringe benefit subject to withholding of income tax and social security for the lay employee. The dual-status minister will incur the additional income tax and social security tax for estimated tax purposes.

When an employee pays the employer for personal use, the amount to be included in income can be reduced by what the employee pays. If the proper amount is computed

PROFESSIONAL EXPENSES

(general valuation or one of the three special valuation methods timely chosen), and paid to the employer, nothing would need to be shown on the W-2, nor any taxes withheld for the lay employee.

Travel

Ordinary and necessary travel expenses incurred in order to be able to earn income include: train, airplane, boat, bus fares, auto rental, taxi, hotel, motel, rooming house, meals, gratuities, telephone, telegraph, travel insurance, baggage charges, cleaning and laundry costs. Unreimbursed meals while away from home are subject to the 80% limitation.

To substantiate your travel expenses, you must record the following at or near the time of the travel: the amount spent, the date of the business trip, the place traveled to, and the business reason or purpose of the trip.

"Tax home" is defined as a taxpayer's place of business or employment where he earns most of his income, regardless of where the family residence is maintained. Travel **away from home overnight** is necessary for the above expenses to be deductible. "Overnight" does not necessarily mean a 24-hour period, but there must be enough time allowed for you to be released from activities for 6 hours of sleep, even if it is from noon to 6 p.m.

Meal costs on overnight business trips do not have to satisfy the business discussion test if you eat alone or with your family or personal acquaintances.

A minister may incur away-from-home expenses for the following: attendance at a church convention, speaking engagements, lectures, travel to perform a wedding or a funeral, travel for pulpit supply, evangelistic meetings, deputation for missionaries, travel to youth camps, etc.

DO NOT deduct or adequately account to your employer for travel meal expense when you are not away from home overnight.

Overseas travel has become very limited. The primary purpose of the trip has to be business and your employer has to send or require you to make the trip. Be sure the rules are satisfied before deducting or becoming reimbursed for overseas travel. No deduction is allowed for costs of travel claimed as a **form of education**. For example, a trip to the Holy Land is no longer deductible unless you enroll in a university course of study in the Holy Land, then it could qualify as an education expense.

If a trip is primarily for business and while there you extend your stay for a vacation or have other nonbusiness activities, you may deduct the travel expenses to and from the business destination. You would not be able to deduct side-trip mileage or the extra cost of the meals and lodging for the personal time.

If a trip is primarily for business and while there you have weekend or off duty days, all of the meals and lodging will be deductible. Personal side-trip miles would not be deductible. Saturday lodging and meals is considered an allowable business day when required to obtain a cheaper air fare.

If a trip is primarily for vacation or personal reasons, none of the travel, meals or lodging is deductible except for any expenses directly incurred for the days business is conducted.

Travel expense for business reasons are only allowable for the person earning an income. Expenses for a non-salaried spouse and children to accompany you on a trip are personal and not allowable as business expenses. The single room rate can be used instead of ½ of double room rate. Except for bona fide entertainment the spouse's meals are not deductible. However, if a non-salaried spouse was attending a convention as an official representative of a church or organization, the spouse can be reimbursed for travel expenses. If there is no reimbursement, the travel expenses are allowable as a contribution deduction on Sch A.

New Meal and Entertainment Rules for 1994: The deductible portion of meal and entertainment expenses is reduced from 80% to 50%, effective 1-1-94.

Lodging, Meal, And Incidental Expense Per Diem Rates

Periodically, the IRS publishes per diem rates that may be used by **employers who reimburse employees** for their traveling expenses. The most recent rates are effective for travel on or after March 12, 1993. The IRS tables are not geared to a calendar year. Thus, taxpayers who avail themselves of the per diem method must use two different tables during the course of the same tax year. These per diem rates include an individual's lodging, meals and incidental (M & IE) travel expenses. Incidental expenses covered by a per diem arrangement may include tips, laundry, and cleaning fees, or similar expenses, but do not include cab fares, telephone, or telegraph costs.

The applicable per diem amount depends on the locality of travel. For travel within the continental United States (CONUS) and for foreign and non-foreign travel outside the continental 48 states (OCONUS), separate lodging and M & IE rates are published periodically in the Federal Register, U.S. Government Printing Office. (Sec. 274, CCH, Standard Federal Tax Reports ¶14,417.625.)

M & IE rate must be prorated on partial travel days: For each six-hour period you are away from home overnight, you are allowed one quarter of the allowance. One-fourth of the daily per diem allowances can be calculated for each quarter day (12 to 6 and 6 to 12) that is partially spent away from home on business travel. The entire M & IE rate is subject to the 80% limitation on meal expenses.

Unreimbursed employees and self-employed individuals may only use the per diem rate established for meals and incidental expenses found in the IRS tables. Actual lodging expenses must be substantiated. In addition, the high-low rate available to employers and discussed below may not be used by unreimbursed employees and self-employed individuals.

- *Alternative Method for Employers*

Beginning in 1990, a **high-low per diem method** became available to simplify the administrative burden of sifting through some 10 pages of per diem rates in order to determine the correct rate for an employee's particular areas of travel. Under the high-low method, the IRS publishes a list of localities that are classified as high-cost areas. All other localities within the continental United States are classified as low-cost areas. The IRS then establishes a per diem rate for the two types of localities. For travel on or after March 12, 1993, the per diem rates are **$150** for high-cost localities and **$94** for low-cost localities. The M & IE portion of the alternative method is **$36** for high-cost localities and **$28** for low-cost localities. The remaining **$114 or $66** is the lodging portion of the per diem allowance.

The high-low method may not be used to reimburse an employee for M & IE expenses only. The employer can use the M & IE rate from the IRS tables if the employer: pays for lodging, provides lodging or the employee does not incur lodging.

If an employee is reimbursed under the high-low method during a tax year, that method must be used for all of that employee's travel expenses within the continental United States during the tax year. **Annually compare the three options for computing your best travel reimbursement and use the greater of:**
1. Individual location rates from the Federal Register
2. High-low per diem alternative method
3. Your actual cost of lodging & M & IE

Become reimbursed throughout the year according to the method you expect to be the greater, then at year end, calculate all three. If another method is greater, become reimbursed for the adjusting differential at the end of the year.

High-low Per Diem Rates

Effective Dates	Lodging & Meals	Lodging Only	Meals & Incidentals
3/12/93 -	$150 high/$94 low	$114 high/$66 low	$36 high/$28 low
3/1/92 - 3/11/93	$147 high/$93 low	$113 high/$67 low	$34 high/$26 low
1/1/91 - 2/29/92	$130 high/$88 low	$ 96 high/$62 low	$34 high/$26 low
1/1/90 -12/31/90	$122 high/$85 low	$ 88 high/$59 low	$34 high/$26 low

PROFESSIONAL EXPENSES

The locations listed below are eligible for the high cost rates. Effective date for the list was March 12, 1993. (Rev. Proc. 93-21)

City	County	City	County	City	County
California			and Montgomery and Prince Georges in Maryland.		Hudson, Passaic, and Union
Death Valley	Inyo				
Los Angeles	Los Angeles, Kern, Orange, Ventura, Edwards AFB, China Lake Naval Center	**Florida**		Ocean City/ Cape May	Cape May
		Key West		**New York**	
		Illinois		New York City	The boroughs of Bronx, Brooklyn, Manhattan, Queens, and Staten Island; Nassau and Suffolk Counties
San Francisco	San Francisco	Chicago	DuPage, Cook, and Lake		
Colorado					
Aspen	Pitkin	**Maryland**			
Keystone/ Silverthorne	Summit	Ocean City	Worcester		
		Massachusetts			
Vail	Eagle	Boston	Suffolk	White Plains	Westchester
District of Columbia		Cambridge/Lowell	Middlesex	**Pennsylvania**	
Washington D.C.	Washington DC; the cities of Alexandria, Falls Church, and Fairfax; the counties of Arlington, Loudoun	Martha's Vineyard/ Nantucket	Dukes and Nantucket	Philadelphia	Philadelphia; city of Bala Cynwyd in Montgomery County
		New Jersey			
		Atlantic City	Atlantic	**Rhode Island**	
		Newark	Bergen, Essex,	Newport	Newport

Entertainment

Entertainment expenses and meals for entertainment that are not reimbursed will be subject to the 80% limitation, then combined with other unreimbursed professional expenses and further limited by 2% of AGI and Sec. 265 allocation limitation. An employee can be reimbursed for 100% of meal and entertainment expense. Employers will deduct only 80% of reimbursed meals and entertainment as a business expense. Not-for-profit employers will not be affected, since they have no tax liability.

New Meal and Entertainment Rules for 1994: The deductible portion of meal and entertainment expenses is reduced from 80% to 50%, effective 1-1-94.

Restrictive tests for meals and entertainment require that the event was directly related to the active conduct of your job and directly preceding or following a substantial and bona fide business discussion on a subject associated with the active conduct of your business or ministry.

The record-keeping rules for entertainment, **Sec. 274**, are very strict. The entertainment diary section in our **"Professional Tax Record Book,"** allows you to keep the correct facts easily. **You must have the name of the persons entertained, their title or position, where the entertainment took place, what purpose or discussion took place and the amount.** Receipts are very important. When the entertainment is in the home, keep the receipt from the grocery store for that occasion.

By adopting an accountable reimbursement plan, you will be submitting your expense records to your employer. **Due to the confidential nature of a minister's entertainment activity,** we suggest that the diary showing who was entertained and what business was transacted should be retained by the minister and a dollar amount be submitted to your employer for reimbursement. Reg. 1.274-5T(c)(2)(ii)(C) gives us the authority to be confidential.

Most ministers are required to do substantial entertaining in their home. Since the cost of the home itself is non-taxable as parsonage allowance, the main expense of entertaining is the cost of meals provided. Special speakers, missionaries, board members, prospective faculty, etc., are entertained and a record of the number of meals provided in the home, multiplied by an average cost per meal will result in a sizable deduction. A reasonable amount per meal, depending on your actual circumstances and service practices, might vary between $5.00 to $7.00 per meal. Those afternoon meetings with refreshments, or after evening service snacks for the youth group, etc., might vary between $1.00 to $1.50 per person.

If the meals are eaten outside the home, then the receipt for the actual cost of the meals is deductible. If you entertain business and non-business individuals at the same event, you must divide your entertainment expenses between business and nonbusiness. For example, if you entertain a group of individuals that **includes yourself**, three business prospects, and seven social guests, 4/11 of the expenses qualifies for the deduction.

If your spouse is present during an occasion of entertainment because the spouse of the person being entertained is present, you may deduct the meal cost for both spouses. Meal expenses for your children are never deductible.

Educational Expenses

Educational expenses incurred for the purpose of maintaining or improving present job or professional skills, or meeting the express requirements of an employer to retain the job, are deductible. The deduction will not be allowed if the education qualifies you for a new trade or business, or satisfies the minimum requirements of your present job.

You are unable to be absent from your profession for more than a year. A minister who has not been gainfully employed as a minister will not be able to deduct his seminary education. Most seminary degrees require three or more years. Seminary students who have the opportunity to "part-time" minister while obtaining additional education have an ideal situation. IRS considers you to have changed careers if you work a secular job while obtaining additional education for a period of more than 12 months.

Tuition, fees, books and supplies, any transportation to school away from your hometown, meals and lodging (if necessary to be away from home overnight to attend classes) are typical educational expenses. Unreimbursed meals are only 80% deductible. No deduction is allowed for costs of travel claimed as a **form of education**. For example, a trip to the Holy Land is no longer deductible, unless you enroll in a university course of study in the Holy Land, then it could qualify as an education expense.

Library & Equipment Depreciation

First we will discuss the kinds of capital purchases that are to be depreciated. Usually when a minister begins his career, he already owns a sizable library. Books and equipment that were purchased during college and seminary training were generally not deductible at the time of purchase and were merely for personal use. When a minister begins receiving an income from their use, they become business property and are "placed in service." The **lesser of the cost or fair market value** of items that are converted from personal to business use should be inventoried and placed on the depreciation schedule. Sec. 179 expensing is not available for converted property.

Library, office furniture, typewriters, computers, overhead projectors, VCR or film projectors, cameras, or copiers are examples of items to be depreciated or expensed under Sec. 179. **Tax plan according to your tax liability;** choose to "spread out" or depreciate capital assets in years of no tax liability and choose Sec. 179 expensing during years with tax liability.

If you are fully reimbursed for the purchase of a capital item in the year of purchase, it will be the same as choosing Sec. 179 expensing. We recommend that a depreciation worksheet be completed to show each purchase and any election to expense capital assets.

To be reimbursed by your employer for library and equipment depreciation, compute what this year's depreciation will be for previous assets on your depreciation schedule, divide by 12 and use it as a monthly amount. Then in December, include an extra amount that is the depreciation for the current year's purchases.

PROFESSIONAL EXPENSES 59

- **Computers**

To be excepted from treatment as listed property, a computer must be owned by the business establishment and used exclusively in the establishment. **We strongly recommend that an employer purchase and own the computer.** When you own the computer and less than 50% of computer use is business, you can not choose Sec. 179 expensing. Depreciation is required to be at the rate of 5 years straight line. A log of time must be kept, for a computer that has both personal and business use, to determine % of business use.

When the cost of the computer and software is not separately stated, the software can be depreciated with the computer. Software which may be used for only one year, such as a program for payroll, may be used as a current expense. As listed property (both personal and business use) computers have to qualify as being a **mandatory requirement** of the employer to be allowable.

Example: An insurance agent could not deduct depreciation for a portable computer he used to help develop insurance plans for clients. His employer encouraged him to buy the computer. According to the IRS, it is not enough that the agent's productivity increased or that he used the computer solely for business. Purchasing the computer was optional, not a mandatory job requirement.

However, a later tax court case decided differently **when the computer was 100% business use.** A married couple was allowed to claim a deduction under Sec. 179 for a computer that "substantially aided" the husband as a university professor and enabled the wife to perform her job as a transportation planner properly. The opinion held that both the "convenience of the employer" and the "condition of employment" requirements of Sec. 280F were met **even though the couple's employer did not explicitly require** them to use a computer. (Cadwallader, 1989 TC Memo N0. 356)

Because computers are considered "listed property" depreciation recapture is to be computed if a computer was more than 50% business use in year of purchase, but drops to 50% or less business use in any future year. Recapture means "pay back". If you used your computer more than 50% in your business in the year you placed it in service, but 50% or less for business in a later year, you must include in gross income the difference between depreciation and Sec. 179 expensing claimed and the amount of depreciation recomputed at the 5 year straight-line method. You must continue using 5 year straight-line even if business use rises back above 50%.

- **Equipment Purchased After 12-31-80 And Before 1-1-87** —

Autos are 3-year Class Property and other equipment is 5-year Class Property. ACRS (Accelerated Cost Recovery System) allowed for a quicker write-off for the cost of autos and equipment. The recovery periods were unrelated to and shorter than former useful life determinations. The percentage to apply to the cost is as follows:

Year	Auto	Equipment
1	25%	15%
2	38%	22%
3	37%	21%
4		21%
5		21%

There were 4 ways to depreciate the cost of your business equipment. The percentage method was based on the 150% declining balance method. It was possible to use the straight-line method over either the regular recovery period or a longer recovery period. The alternate recovery periods for 5 Year Class Property were 12 and 25 years. When using the straight-line method, you were to use a half-year convention, or 6 months of depreciation in the year of purchase, regardless of what month you purchased the equipment. There was no deduction allowed in the year of sale or trade.

Sec. 179 expensing allowed you to "expense" up to **$5,000** of the purchase price. Any remaining cost was deducted by one of the 4 ways discussed above.

- **Equipment Purchased After 12-31-86** —

New classes were added to the ACRS rules for equipment. The percentages are based on 200% declining balance method. Under MACRS (Modified ACRS), items still in the 5 year class are computers, typewriters, copiers, and duplicating equipment. In the new 7 year class are library, office furniture and fixtures. **Sec. 179 expensing** allows you to "expense" up to $10,000 (1987 to 1992) or **$17,500 (1993)** of the purchase price. The IRS tables below have computed the mid-year and mid-quarter factors for the year of purchase automatically.

Mid-year convention allows ½ of the annual % available in the year of purchase and in the year of sale.

Mid-quarter convention allows the mid-quarter computation % depending on which quarter the purchase or sale occurs. If more than **40% of the year's** depreciable assets are placed in service in the **final quarter**, then all non-realty assets for that year **must** be depreciated using "mid-quarter" convention instead of the normal mid-year convention.

In our discussion of auto depreciation earlier in this chapter we included the MACRS percentages for 5 year class property. Here are the MACRS percentages for both mid-year and mid-quarter for 7 year class property.

Year	Mid-year	Mid-quarter (1st)	Mid-quarter (2nd)	Mid-quarter (3rd)	Mid-quarter (4th)
1	14.29%	25.00%	17.86%	10.71%	3.57%
2	24.49%	21.43%	23.47%	25.51%	27.55%
3	17.49%	15.31%	16.76%	18.22%	19.68%
4	12.49%	10.93%	11.97%	13.02%	14.06%
5	8.93%	8.75%	8.87%	9.30%	10.04%
6	8.92%	8.74%	8.87%	8.85%	8.73%
7	8.93%	8.75%	8.87%	8.86%	8.73%
8	4.46%	1.09%	3.33%	5.53%	7.64%

Office Supplies And Postage

Typical expenses an employee might have in their ministry are: stationery, carbon paper, erasers, ink, stapler, paper clips, record books, secretarial or typing expenses, postage, copier supplies, computer supplies, etc. Any office equipment or machines that have a useful life of more than one year should be depreciated or Sec. 179 expensed. (See depreciation discussion)

If you are required to provide an office outside of your home, any cost to you would be a deductible expense. Rent, furniture, utilities, etc., would be allowable expenses.

Office-in-the-home deduction is not available if your employer provides an office on their premises. If as a dual-status minister you are required to have your office-in-the-home, and your employer did not designate parsonage allowance in advance for the current year or the amount designated was inadequate; you can deduct a part of your home expenses as an "office-in the-home" deduction. To do this, divide the square footage used as an office by the square footage in your entire home. This % of the whole cost of your home can be used as a deduction.

Generally, it is best for you to have 100% of your home expenses be tax-free under Sec. 107 parsonage allowance. However, a qualified "office-in-home" deduction

PROFESSIONAL EXPENSES 61

would reduce your social security base and if "adequately accounted" to your employer would not increase income tax.

Religious Materials

Many trips to the religious bookstore add up to much expense for most employees in the ministry. Tracts and booklets purchased for distribution in the calling ministry, music and musical supplies for the choir, gifts for presentation at marriages, baptisms, or holidays, teaching aids, including filmstrips, are but a few of the usual expenses a dual-status or lay employee incurs.

Clothing for the minister is usually not deductible. Tax law states that if something is required as a condition of employment and is not adaptable for general wear, it is deductible. Pulpit robes or special shirt collars and their cleaning expense would qualify as a deduction. Suits and shirts that are adaptable for general wear are not deductible for a salesman, businessman nor a minister.

Seminars And Dues

Fees charged to attend seminars or conference meetings that are directly related to your profession are deductible. Dues to professional organizations are deductible.

Subscriptions, Paperbacks And Tapes

A number of periodicals and journals find their way into your mail-box. The cost of the subscriptions that are directly related to your ministry is deductible. Magazines and local newspapers give the current events so necessary for sermon illustrations and provide news of the local community. Except for one subscription to a local newspaper (which IRS claims must be personal), deduct the subscriptions you use directly in your ministry.

Small booklets, paperback books and tapes should be separate from regular library books and the whole cost deducted in full in the year of purchase. **DO NOT deduct** magazines, subscriptions and books that are purchased for **personal reasons and interests.**

Business Telephone

Long distance business calls need to be separated from the personal portion used in the parsonage allowance computation, because as a business expense they will reduce income tax as well as social security and medicare tax.

Moving Expenses - Form 3903

According to **Sec. 217**, the personal cost of moving the family when there is a change of job locations is an itemized deduction. According to **Sec. 82**, if the employer pays for or reimburses an employee for any moving expense, **the amount must be included as income on the W-2, Box 1.** Then if the move meets the distance and time qualifications, the employee can deduct allowable moving expenses on Sch A, line 18. For those unable to itemize, the moving reimbursement becomes taxable. When a state does not allow for itemized deductions, there will be state income tax on the reimbursement.

Two requirements must be met for moving expenses to be deductible on Sch A. The new place of work must be at least **35 miles** farther from the former home than was the former place of work. Employment in the new area must be full-time for **39 weeks** during the 12 month period immediately following the move. Self-employed persons must be employed 78 weeks during a 24-month period immediately following the move. **Employed ministers are subject to the 39 week work requirement.**

Deductible expenses include: the cost of moving household goods and personal effects for the whole family; auto expense at 9¢ per mile and actual cost of meals and lodging enroute for the whole family; temporary living expenses of meals and lodging for up to 30 days and pre-move trips for the purpose of house-hunting if a job is already obtained; expenses of sale or settling a lease; and expenses of purchasing or obtaining a lease.

Meals while enroute, during house hunting trips, and temporary living period, are limited to actual expenses and subject to the 80% meal limitation.

If the employer expects the employee to satisfy the requirements, the moving reimbursement is not subject to income tax withholding or social security. Dual-status ministers can reduce their social security base by moving expense reimbursements that satisfy the distance and time requirements.

If the employer knows that the requirements will not be met, the moving reimbursement is subject to both income tax withholding and social security tax for the lay employee. Moving reimbursements that do not meet the requirements will be subject to income tax and social security and medicare tax for the dual-status minister.

New Moving Deduction Rules for 1994: The Revenue Reconciliation Act of 1993 contains many changes for moving expense deductions effective 1-1-94. Reimbursements of deductible moving expenses will not be included in the W-2. The distance test will be 50 miles and many deductible expenses have been eliminated. The deduction will move from Schedule A to page 1, Form 1040, where it will become an above-the-line deduction.

Earned Income Credit

Earned income credit is available for the low-income taxpayer who maintains a household in the U.S. that is the principal place of abode of the taxpayer and his/her child for more than one-half of the taxable year and has income of **$23,050** or less. It is a refundable credit, and if there is no tax liability, the government "gives" it to the taxpayer.

The amount of the credit for 1993 has been increased and adjustments to the credit have been made to take into account the size of the taxpayer's family. There is a supplemental credit for health insurance premiums. Another supplemental credit is available for taxpayers with a qualifying child who has not attained the age of one at year end. The maximum basic credit for 1993 is **$1,434** for a taxpayer with one qualifying child and **$1,511** for a taxpayer with two or more qualifying children.

Revenue Ruling 79-78 defines "earned income" for the dual-status minister to include parsonage allowance and to include the income of a minister who elected to be exempt from social security. So it is necessary to **add the value of parsonage and/or parsonage allowance to other earnings for computation of earned income credit.**

The credit should be carefully computed on the new Schedule EIC provided in your Form 1040 Instruction Booklet. **If you received nontaxable compensation (housing) from your employer,** complete lines 4 through 7 on page 2 of Schedule EIC. If the amount on line 7 is $23,050 or more, enter "NO" on Form 1040, line 56. Otherwise the IRS computers will not notice the housing amount and may automatically assume you are entitled to earned income credit and send you a check you are not entitled to.

If you receive an unexpected refund check or a larger refund check than you have had computed, don't cash the check. **You have probably received it in error and you will be charged interest for the time you have had the money if you cash the check.** If such a problem arises, call the IRS's Problems Resolution Department. They will give you specific instructions as to the best way to solve the problem.

Schedule EIC should solve some of the problems IRS has historically encountered in processing dual-status minister's earned income credit.

CHAPTER FOUR

SOCIAL SECURITY AND RETIREMENT PLANNING

Dual-status ministers are treated as self-employed individuals in the performance of ministerial services for social security purposes as a result of written law. Sec. 1402(a)(8) is an exception to the "common law" rules for determining whether a person is an employee or self-employed. **Dual-status means** that the minister is an **employee** for income reporting, fringe benefit and expense deducting purposes and **self-employed** for social security purposes.

Social Security for Religious Workers

Dual-Status Minister

We presented detailed information in Chapter Two to help you determine your correct treatment for social security purposes. **Summary:** The same regulations for determining if a minister qualifies for self-employed status for social security purposes are used to determine if a minister is entitled to parsonage allowance. Generally, you must be employed by a church or an integral agency of a church, perform the duties of a minister, and be ordained or "the equivalent thereof" to be treated as if you were self-employed for social security purposes. When, according to the regulations, you are to be treated as self-employed for social security purposes, **it is mandatory**. For your employer to withhold and match social security would be in error.

In the absence of a formal ordination, licensing or commissioning, it is the date a church called or hired you as their pastor and gave you the authority to perform substantially all of the religious duties that your self-employed status begins. It is necessary for a church to have formally ordained, licensed or commissioned a minister before they can "assign or designate" him to a position at a "non-integral agency" and qualify him for dual-status treatment. It is also necessary for a church to have formally ordained, licensed or commissioned a minister who conducts worship and administers ordinances or sacraments, but is not employed by a church or an integral agency of a church.

Before 1968, services performed by ministers were exempt from social security unless they filed a certificate (Form 2031) stating that they wished to be covered by social security. Since 1968, ministers are automatically covered under social security unless they file an application for exemption on the grounds of conscientious or religious opposition to social security and the government's involvement in public insurance. **If you choose to be covered, YOU DO NOTHING**. You are automatically liable for paying social security on Schedule SE.

An individual who had elected to be covered by social security by filing Form 2031 (before 1968) made an irrevocable decision and could not file Form 4361 and elect to be exempt. Anyone engaged in the ministry at the time of the law change in 1968 had until April 15, 1970, to file Form 4361 and continue not being covered by social security. A minister is often unaware of his **opportunity to choose** between paying social security or becoming exempt from paying Social Security. Once a minister begins to pay social security and the time expires for filing Form 4361, **and he does not change faiths**, there is no way for him to become exempt.

Computation Of Social Security Base - "Worksheet for Form 2106"

In Chapter Six we have a chart showing the types of income common to a minister and indicate what is required to be entered as salary on Form 941, line 2 and Form W-2, Box 1. **Parsonage provided and/or parsonage allowance designated is to be omitted from**

Form W-2, Box 1. However, both the parsonage provided and/or the parsonage allowance must be added to the taxable amount of salary for social security and medicare tax purposes. Enter the value of the parsonage provided from Column A, line 11 and the parsonage allowance designated from Column B, line 14.

Because a dual-status minister is treated as "self-employed" for social security purposes, **you can subtract all unreimbursed professional expenses from your income to arrive at the amount of income upon which to compute social security.** Revenue Ruling 80-110 clearly states that unreimbursed auto, travel, and professional expenses can be used to reduce the social security base for the dual-status minister. Based on Rev. Ruling 80-110, Sec. 1402(a) and Sec. 62(1), **it is correct to use the business % of auto interest, personal property tax and business portion of fees paid for tax preparation as a subtraction** from a minister's social security base. Revenue Ruling 92-29 provides for allocation of the fee for tax preparation between business and Schedule A.

Moving expense reimbursements that are correctly included on Form W-2, Box 1, should be subtracted from your social security base. They are not subject to social security if you satisfy the requirements to deduct them on Form 3903. If you do not satisfy the 35 mile and 39 work week requirements, your moving expense reimbursement is subject to social security and medicare tax.

Contributions to a Sec. 403(b) tax sheltered account by a dual-status minister are not subject to social security according to Rev. Ruling 68-395.

If you have filed Form 4361, and are exempt from social security, write "Exempt - Form 4361" on the self-employment line, Form 1040, page 2. If you are exempt from social security on your earnings from the ministry, but have secular self-employment income, use Sch. SE, page 2 to compute social security on your secular earnings.

- *Social Security Deductions For Self-Employed*

The Social Security Amendments Act of 1983 (H.R. 1900) gradually phased in higher rates for the self-employed. As a part of the original H.R. 1900, deductions for the self-employed takes the place of the 2% credit. Otherwise, the self-employed would be paying more than the employee. On Schedule SE the gross social security base is adjusted to allow ½ of social security as a deduction. On Form 1040, page 1, an adjustment for ½ of the social security paid by the self-employed taxpayer is allowed.

For a taxpayer in the 15% tax bracket, the deductions result in nearly the same social security cost as the 2% credit did. For a taxpayer in the 28% tax bracket, the deductions are better!

Social Security Exemption

Form 4361 includes a statement that, because of your religious principles, you are conscientiously opposed to accepting, for services performed as a member of the clergy, any public insurance (governmental insurance that makes payments in the event of death, disability, old age, or retirement). This includes public insurance established by the Social Security Act. Your conscientious opposition must be based on the institutional principles and discipline of your particular religious denomination, **OR** it must be based on **YOUR INDIVIDUAL** religious considerations. Opposition based on the general conscience will not satisfy this requirement.

A dual-status minister must prayerfully make his/her own decision as to whether he/she wants to be covered by social security. It is our purpose here to make you, as a dual-status minister, aware that **you do have a choice in the beginning of your ministry**. If you choose to be exempt, **it must be for the religious and conscientious grounds** stated above. You may not become exempt for solely economic reasons. If you file an application for exemption only for economic reasons, you have not made a valid election.

- *What Happens To What I Have Already Paid In?*

Form 4361 does not cause you to waive the right to receive social security benefits. Any secular employment or work that is **NOT** in the exercise of your ministry will be subject to

SOCIAL SECURITY and RETIREMENT PLANNING

either social security or self-employment tax. You do not have to be opposed to accepting social security benefits that are available as the result of what you have paid on secular earnings.

Any social security you pay on secular earnings will be credited to your account. You will be entitled to the benefits from all mandatory payments, if vested. **Ten years or forty quarters** of social security contributions result in **your being vested** and eligible for benefits based on your lifetime average. You can ask Social Security to give you a record of how **many quarters credit** you have and since secular work is always subject to social security, it would be possible to earn additional quarters after you filed Form 4361. When you retire, you can choose the greater source of benefits, either from your account or your spouse's account.

- **Disability Coverage**

Disability coverage under social security discontinues **five years** after becoming exempt. Overseas missionaries have difficulty obtaining comparable life and disability insurance coverages. If you are considering an overseas ministry, you may wish to choose being covered by social security.

- **Irrevocable**

The exemption, once obtained, is basically irrevocable. However, there have been two periods of time that provisions have been made for revocation. Ministers who revoke their election can never become exempt again. For a short period of time, and if filed by the due date of the 1978 return, Form 4361-A did give opportunity for ministers who were exempt to revoke their election.

The Tax Reform Act of 1986 provided another "window". Application for revocation, Form 2031, had to be filed no later than April 15, 1988 due date (including extensions), but before the applicant became entitled to benefits.

- **When To File Form 4361**

The application for Exemption from Self-Employment Tax, Form 4361, must be filed by the due date (April 15th) of your tax return, including extensions, for the **second tax year in which you had net self-employment earnings of $400 or more** from services as a minister (which includes parsonage allowance and/or parsonage provided). In the absence of a formal ordination, licensing or commissioning, it is the **date a church called or hired** you as their pastor and gave you the authority to perform substantially all of the religious duties, that your self-employed status begins.

Example: you had net earnings of $5,000 in 1992 and $18,000 in 1993, the deadline for filing Form 4361 would be April 15th, 1994. The two years need not be consecutive. If a minister had net earnings of $700 in 1986, less than $400 in 1987 through 1992, and $4,000 in 1993, the deadline for filing Form 4361 would be April 15th, 1994.

An approved Form 4361 is retroactive and exempts ministry income back to the date your ministry began. If you paid social security for the first year of your ministry, and have chosen to file Form 4361 during the second year of your ministry, you can receive a refund of the first year's social security payment. To get a refund file Form 1040X as a claim within the three year statute of limitations. Attach a photocopy of your approved Form 4361 to Form 1040X. **The IRS does not automatically send** social security refunds.

- **Opportunity for Minister of New Faith**

IRS has directed personnel in their departments that approve or disapprove Form 4361 applications to recognize minister's applications after they have changed faiths. This provision **will not** be available to the minister employed by a denomination that appoints a a minister to a different church within the denomination. This provision **will not** be available to a minister who has previously filed an untimely Form 4361 and had his application disapproved.

If a minister changes employment from one autonomous church to another or one denomination to another, he can claim opposition to social security, and timely file Form 4361 by the due date of the second tax year in which he has earnings of $400 or more from the new faith. The date of hiring at the new church begins a new time period of making a choice. No formal re-ordination or re-licensing is necessary.

A three judge panel in J.M. Ballinger, U.S. Court of Appeals, 10th Circuit, No. 82-1928, 3/7/84, said, "The statute makes no distinction between a first ordination and subsequent ordinations. Courts are not in a position to determine the merits of various churches nor an individual's conversion from one church to another. Nor can we hold that an individual who has a change of belief accompanied by a change to another faith is not entitled to the exemption."

- **How To File Form 4361**

It is important in the preparation of your Form 4361 that you give all of the information requested.

Attach a copy of your certificate for ordination, license, or commissioning. If you lack a formal certificate, and qualify to file Form 4361 because you have been hired as a minister of a church, have the church who hired you verify in a letter, on their letterhead, that you are their minister. An important fact to include in the letter is the date you were hired.

If your church or denomination both ordains and licenses ministers, Form 4361, line 6, requires that you attach a copy of the by-laws stating that a licensed minister is invested with the authority to perform substantially all of the duties of the church or denomination. If no such by-laws exist, then type the following statement on your church's letterhead, have a person in authority sign it, and attach it to your application:

"Our church/denomination does not have specific by-laws regarding the powers of ordained, licensed, or commissioned ministers. We do give the same authority to perform all of the ecclesiastical duties to our licensed/commissioned ministers as we do to those who are ordained."

Notify Church: The ordaining, licensing or commissioning body of your church must be informed that you are conscientiously opposed to or because of religious principles, you are opposed to the acceptance of public insurance benefits based on ministerial service. In the absence of a formal ordination, licensing or commissioning, it is the church that hired you that you must notify. When you sign Form 4361 you are certifying (line 7) that you have performed this notification. Individual opposition is sufficient for a minister to be exempt; it does not matter that the position of the employer is different.

Watch For Letter: The Secretary of Health and Human Services has the responsibility of communicating with the applicant to further verify that the applicant understands the grounds (basis) for exemption and is seeking the exemption on those grounds. Discussion in the committee reports suggested that the communication would be in person or by telephone. However, applicants receive a letter instead. The letter asks them to sign again that they understand the grounds under which they filed Form 4361. **The letter must be returned to the IRS within 90 days**, or the effective date of the exemption will not begin until it is received by the IRS.

- **You Must Establish That the Church is a Church**

You must establish that the organization that gave you the authority to do ministerial services **is a church**. A major problem is that the IRS requires the exemption applicant to establish or prove that the church that ordained them or "the equivalent thereof" is a religious organization described in Sec. 501(c)(3) and also in **Sec. 170(b)(1)(A)(i).** IRS Publication 78, published quarterly, lists organizations, denominations or churches that have filed Form 1023 requesting exempt status. If your church is a part of a major denomination, your church will be under the umbrella of its exempt status. If the church that ordained you or "the equivalent thereof" is independent or autonomous and has not requested exempt status, they should do so. **Churches are not required to submit** the information requested

SOCIAL SECURITY and RETIREMENT PLANNING

on Form 8123 or Form 1023. If a minister they have ordained or "the equivalent thereof" wishes to become exempt from social security, **it is important for the church to be willing to submit the information.** You must go ahead and timely file your Form 4361, even if the church's approval has not been received. You will be informed that their records fail to disclose that your church is a "church." Your Form 4361 cannot be approved until your church has been approved. However, even if it takes a long time to establish the church's exempt status, your **timely filed Form 4361** will eventually be able to be approved.

If the church that ordained you or "the equivalent thereof" **has not yet been approved, you have two alternatives:**

    A. File Form 1023—Application for Recognition of Exemption: Once approved, the listing will cover all future ordained or "the equivalent thereof" ministers who wish to become exempt. For this reason, **we recommend that a church choose this method.** Because of several technicalities, we recommend the assistance of an attorney. The IRS charges a fee for filing Form 1023.

    B. File Form 8123—Questions Regarding Status as a Church: Form 8123 is to be submitted by the individual who is filing Form 4361. The church's information will have to be **resubmitted by each minister** who wishes to become exempt. It should be sent to the appropriate EP/EO district office listed in the instructions for Form 1023. The following questions are required to be answered by Form 8123:

1. Full name of organization, address, and Employer Identification Number.
2. What is the legal form of the organization? Attach confirmed copies of the organization's creating instrument.
3. Furnish descriptive and detailed financial statements for the current year and the year immediately before which show the organization's receipts, disbursements, assets and liabilities.
4. Give a narrative description of the activities carried on by the organization. Include a complete description of the characteristics that qualify the organization as a church.
5. List the names, addresses and duties of the officers, directors, trustees, etc., of the organization. State whether any of these individuals receive compensation for their services and, if so, furnish in detail the amount of compensation, duties, the number of hours worked, and the method used to determine the compensation.
6. Do the officers, directors, or trustees have business relationships with the organization or financial interests in other businesses that do business with the organization? If so, please explain.
7. Are any of the officers, directors, or trustees related by blood or marriage to each other? If so, explain.
8. Has the organization received or does it anticipate receiving assigned income, assets, or substantial contributions from officers, directors, trustees, or members? If so, explain in detail and attach an itemized list of the assignments and contributions.
9. List the services, benefits, or products that the organization provides which are related to its religious functions, e.g., religious articles, publications, instruction, or ordination certificates. Explain the qualifications required for ordination.
10. Does the organization engage in activities that attempt to influence legislation or intervene in any way in political campaigns? If yes, please explain.

- *How To Send Your Form 4361*

Make photocopies of the completed Form 4361 for your records and keep in two or three safe places. Send **three** signed copies with the attached documents we have discussed by **Certified Mail** to your **IRS Service Center** so that you can prove that it was timely filed. Send your Form 4361 **separate from your income tax returns.**

- **How It Gets Processed**

  The Service Center will send it to the Social Security department to examine. Then it goes to Washington to see if your church is listed in Publication 78. Eventually it goes back to your Service Center, and they send Copy C back to you marked **"approved"**. The process can take several months. If you fail to get Copy C back in 6 or 8 months, call IRS and ask that they put a tracer on it. Applications sometimes get lost and need to be refiled.

- **Put Your Approved Copy In Several Safe Places**

  Once you receive your **"APPROVED COPY C"** from the IRS—copy it, protect it, and treat it as a valuable document. We recommend making several copies. Give a copy to your tax accountant.

Social Security & the Religious Sects Under Vow of Poverty

A completely different set of rules apply to members of religious orders who are under a vow of poverty. **Sec. 1402(g)** allows any self-employed member of a religious order that opposes both private and public insurance, to file **Form 4029** and be exempt from social security regardless of his work activity (farming, construction, etc.). Beginning on or after 11-10-88, a **Form 4029** can be filed at any time. This exemption is a statement that the individual is opposed to both **public and private insurance,** and **is an actual waiver** of ever receiving any benefits from social security. It is necessary that the religious order has a history and a plan to provide for the members when they become dependent through disability or old age. **It is also necessary that the order was organized before 1950.** New religious orders cannot be formed. If a member ceases to be a member of the order, their exemption is revoked. Members who have filed Form 4029 for exemption from social security and have made contributions to a private retirement annuity, revoke their exemption and will have to pay back-years' social security tax, according to Rev. Ruling 77-88. According to Private Letter Ruling 8741002, funding of an IRA through a CD did not constitute insurance and, thus, did not disqualify the taxpayer from exemption.

Because Rev. Ruling 77-88 has been taken out of context and often thought to apply to Sec. 1402(e) for ministers who have filed Form 4361, we feel it is important for you to know that it does not. Ministers who have filed Form 4361 are opposed to **only public** insurance and must provide their own alternative to social security. They most certainly **can** and **should have a private investment plan for retirement needs**.

Social Security and the Lay Employee

A religious worker who does not qualify for dual-status tax treatment must be treated as a lay employee of the employer for social security and medicare tax purposes. He does not have an individual choice of being exempt or subject to social security. When a dual-status minister is not employed by a church or integral agency of a church or is not doing the duties of the ministry, his employer must treat him as an employee for social security and medicare tax purposes.

Prior to 1984, a not-for-profit religious organization as described in Sec. 501(c)(3), had been automatically exempt from withholding social security from their employees and matching it with their share. So an organization that wished to remain exempt from withholding social security for all its employees did not have to file any form. If an organization and its employees desired to be covered by social security, they had to file Form SS-15.

Since January 1, 1984, the Social Security Amendments Act of 1983 extended social security coverage **on a mandatory** basis to all lay employees of not-for-profit organizations.

Electing Churches—Form 8274

The Tax Reform Act of 1984 provided for an election by a church or qualified church-controlled organization that is **opposed for religious reasons** to the payment of

SOCIAL SECURITY and RETIREMENT PLANNING

social security taxes not to be subject to such taxes, Sec. 3121(w). The election merely **transfers** the social security liability **from the church to the employee**.

The electing church is required to withhold income tax and to report the compensation paid to each employee who earns **more than $108** on Form W-2. The electing church should withhold additional amounts of income tax so their employees will have an adequate amount of tax pre-paid to cover the cost of the social security to be computed on their Schedule SE. Form 941E is the correct quarterly report for an electing church. The electing church **must communicate** to their employees their responsibility to compute and pay their own social security on their Form 1040, Schedule SE. In Chapter Six we show a filled out example of Form 941E and W-2's for an electing church. The memo "Electing church employee to pay S.S. on S.E." is what we recommend to include on Form W-2, Box 14.

- **When To Make The Election—Form 8274**

Churches who desire to be an electing church must file **two copies** of Form 8274 after they hire employees, but before the first date on which a quarterly employment tax return is due. **Example:** a church established on October 1, 1993, with an employee, would need to file Form 8274 by January 31, 1994. Churches with paid staff members, in existance before October 1, 1984, had until October 31, 1984 to file Form 8274.

If an electing church fails to provide the required Form W-2's for two years and fail to furnish the information upon request by the IRS, the IRS will revoke the election. The Tax Reform Act of 1986 **made it easy for electing churches to revoke their election**. By simply filing a Form 941 on or before its due date, for the first quarter for which the revocation is to be effective, accompanied by payment in full of the taxes that would be due for the quarter, the election is revoked.

Employees of "electing churches" do not qualify to claim exemption from paying social security by filing Form 4029. The wages subject to social security on Schedule SE **are the same as** the wage in Box 1 of their Form W-2. Such wages from an electing church can not be reduced by losses from other self-employment activity or unreimbursed employee business expenses. (Sec. 3121(b)(8); 3121(w))

How To Do Correction For Wrong Treatment

Are you a dual-status minister, but your employer **wrongly treated you as an employee for social security purposes**? When, according to the regulations, you are to be treated as self-employed for social security purposes, **dual-status tax treatment is mandatory**. For your employer to withhold and match social security is in error. This can be corrected for all three "open" years that we are allowed to amend returns. The rates for 1990, 1991 and 1992 have been the same: 15.3% withheld and matched for employees and 15.3% for the self-employed.

It is advisable to correct the wrong treatment of the minister's status. The amount of social security matched by the employer is not required to be credited or paid to the employee. The social security withheld from the employee's salary must be paid back to the employee. If the employer chooses to allow their matched portion to be credit for their employee, it must be counted as extra salary on the W-2c in the year of the correction.

Unreimbursed employee business expenses subtracted from the social security base will result in a lower social security cost.

- **Two Ways To Handle The Corrections**
    1. When the employer is willing to count their matching portion as extra salary for the minister:
        A. Prepare 941c and 941 "worksheet" to reflect the changes made. You will not be requesting a refund on the 941c.
        B. Prepare W-2c and W-3c showing matching portion added to "Wages, tips, other compensation" as additional salary.

C. Include total amount of social security withheld and matched as income tax withheld in "Federal income tax withheld.".
   D. Prepare minister's Form 1040X. The minister will have credit on his 1040X for the total social security amount withheld and matched. Depending on the level of his total income, he may have a small refund or owe a small amount of additional tax, plus interest on the balance.
2. When the employer wishes to keep their matching portion:
   A. Prepare 941c and 941 "worksheet" to reflect the changes made and claim a credit on the next quarter's 941 or get a refund for the employer's matching portion.
   B. Prepare W-2c and W-3c showing original salary in "Wages, tips, other compensaton."
   C. Include amount of social security withheld as income tax withholding in "Federal income tax withheld."
   D. Prepare minister's Form 1040X. The minister will have partial credit on his 1040X for social security computed on Sch SE and will incur interest on the balance owed.

It is important when making changes to your federal Form 1040 to remember to amend your state income tax return when it is affected. **Do not hesitate to seek professional accounting help** in preparing corrections to payroll reports. The staff at **Worth Tax & Financial Service** is available to prepare payroll reports, W-2's and corrections for organizations.

Should the Minister's Spouse be on the Payroll?

No one will dispute the fact that a minister's spouse works many hours for the church and usually receives no paycheck. To establish a salary, it is necessary that there is a true employer/employee relationship. The amount of the salary should be reasonable, and paid on the basis of time spent in working for the employer. Ministers **should not personally pay** their spouse a salary. It is not allowed under the "assignment of income" portion of tax law according to Sec. 61. (CCH, Standard Federal Tax Reports ¶5,507.016 and Rev. Ruling 74-32)

- *Benefits* — *When Both Spouses Are Paid*

   When both spouses have income from salaries it qualifies them for claiming Child Care Credit on Form 2441, for babysitting expenses incurred while both are at work. Babysitting expense **is never to be treated as a "professional expense"**. An IRA account can be established for both working spouses. Up to $2,000 for each taxpayer or a total of $4,000 can be contributed, rather than $2,250 for a Spousal IRA. Professional expenses can be justified for both employed spouses. When retirement age approaches there will be the ability to receive two semi-retired salaries and still be within the social security earnings limitation.

Estimated Tax, Form 1040ES

It is necessary for all taxpayers to "prepay" their income tax and their social security tax. An employee has tax withheld from each paycheck and "prepaid" by the employer each quarter. **Withholding by the employer of a dual-status minister is optional.** The dual-status minister is generally required to "prepay" tax by making quarterly payments based on an estimate of the amount of tax he expects to owe for the year. This estimate is to be prepared at the time you prepare the current tax return and the first installment of ¼ of the total is due on **April 15th.** Other due dates are **June 15th, September 15th, and January 15th**. Instead of paying the final January 15th installment, you may elect to file your return early, by January 31st, and pay any tax due with the return.

SOCIAL SECURITY and RETIREMENT PLANNING

If you or your spouse are an employee and earn other wages from which tax is withheld, you may be able to arrange to have enough withheld to cover your combined tax liability. To claim less exemptions or allowances at the other job is usually more convenient than to make quarterly payments. It makes no difference **how you prepay your tax liability,** either **estimated payments** or **adequate withholding** will meet the requirements. An estimate is exactly what the word means. No one can predict the correct amount of tax a year in advance. If you anticipate no tax or **less than $500** for the year, then no estimate is necessary. If circumstances change during the year you may always amend or change your estimate and increase or decrease the quarterly payments.

Underpayment Penalties

You may be charged a penalty for not paying enough estimated tax or for not making the payments on time. The amount of underpayment penalty is the same as the rate of interest the IRS charges on late payments and it is announced each quarter. For individuals (other than high-income individuals) the penalty does not apply if **each required payment is timely** and the total tax paid is based on:
1. 90% of the total tax liability due on the return for the current year (income tax, social security tax, early withdrawal penalties, alternative minimum tax, etc.) or;
2. 100% of the total tax liability shown on the return for the preceding year, commonly referred to as a **safe harbor estimate,** (if your tax liability is expected to increase, you can pre-pay as much as the year before's liability in timely installments and plan to pay any remaining balance with the return on April 15th and not incur a penalty), or
3. 90% of the tax figured by annualizing the taxable income and adjusted self-employment income received for the months ending before the due date of the installment.

New Law: High income individuals with Adjusted Gross income over $150,000 ($75,000 for married separate) for the preceding tax year may avoid estimated tax penalty by basing estimated taxes on 110% of their prior year's tax or 90% of the current year's tax.

File your estimated tax on **Form 1040ES** and keep in mind that the estimate includes both federal income tax and social security tax.

Waiver of Penalty

A waiver of penalty is available if you did not make a payment because of a casualty, disaster, or other unusual circumstance. Also, a waiver may be claimed if you retired (after reaching age 62) or became disabled during the tax year a payment was due or during the preceding tax year and your underpayment was not due to willful neglect. To claim the waiver, follow the instructions given on Form 2210 or in IRS Publication 505, page 34.

Optional Withholding Agreement

A withholding agreement can be made between an employer and a dual-status minister. It is to be a written agreement. A Form W-4 can be prepared with the amount to be withheld each pay period entered on line 6, rather than claiming any allowances on line 5. The employer should withhold enough **income tax** to prepay the minister's total income tax and social security tax liability. Form W-2 will show the amount that has been withheld in Box 2.

Retirement Planning For Religious Workers

All religious workers should establish retirement plans to **supplement** social security income during retirement. Dual-status ministers who have become exempt from social security must have a disciplined savings plan for retirement to take the place of social security. **It would be foolish to become exempt from social security and do nothing to provide for one's needs in retirement.**

We want to present some ideas and information that will make it possible to have the option to retire or semi-retire. Financial planning for retirement has been neglected by many religious workers. We can blame low compensation, busy work schedules, and even a hopeful expectation that the Lord will return before retirement, but the fact is, many ministers and religious workers can not afford to retire. Let us give you an example of **the magic of compounding.** If you began investing at age 25 and invested $150 a month for 40 years and had a 10% rate of return, you would be a millionaire at age 65. If you began investing at age 45 and invested $1,316.88 a month for 20 years and had a 10% rate of return, you would also be a millionaire at age 65.

Investments that are diversified are the best way to plan for meeting your needs during retirement. Through mutual funds it is possible to invest regular amounts in a diversified portfolio. The principle of investing regularly and over a long time horizon results in amazing compound growth. Investments in common stocks or stock funds have historically out performed savings in fixed income investments. **You should never feel it is too late** to begin an investment plan. Most Americans do not begin to save regularly until the children are raised and the mortgage is nearly paid. The increase in life expectancy creates a greater need for investment planning and at the same time allows a longer time for the magic of compounding to function.

Mutual Funds

Over meaningful time spans of 10 years or more, well-managed stock funds have nearly always done better—often much better—than the U.S. market as a whole. The growth of an investment in a mutual fund comes from two sources: income dividends and capital appreciation. While there have been times when the value of an investment in mutual funds have declined, over the years such an investment has produced much better results than savings deposits. There's no doubt that a savings account or certificate of deposit is a good place to put money you want to keep in reserve for short-term needs. Over the long pull they have not been the best place for your **investment** dollars—the larger sums that must be kept hard at work to build for your future and protect you against inflation.

Investing in mutual funds can be confusing if you do not have much time to devote to it. Some publications would encourage you to try to "time" the market and to trade often. Most investors do not have the time to be watching the daily changes in the market place. Even investment professionals cannot always "buy low and sell high." Those who "buy high and sell low" become discouraged and often discontinue investing. A better strategy for investing is to invest regular amounts into a family of mutual funds and let your investment compound over a long period of time. This strategy is often called "dollar cost averaging."

A well managed mutual fund must charge the investors for management costs. Some mutual funds have "loads" or commissions up front or at the time of your investment. Other mutual funds advertised in the Wall Street Journal and financial magazines are "no load" or without a commission at the time of the investment. Generally, the "no load" funds have a higher annual management fee than the "loaded" funds. Some funds have a back end "load" if you do not own the fund long enough. **Before you make any investment in a mutual fund, you will be given a prospectus that fully explains the fees that particular fund will charge.** Choosing a "no load" mutual fund could actually end up costing more over the life of an investment because the annual management fees are charged on the compounded value of the investment. "Loaded" mutual funds, typically have much lower annual management fees. "Loaded" mutual funds are marketed through registered representatives and having received a commission at the time of your investment, they are willing to answer your questions and help you monitor your investments.

Life Insurance

Life insurance is an important part of your portfolio because it provides risk protection for your family. One purpose of life insurance is to replace your earnings should you die prematurely. The amount of your debt, the ability of your spouse to earn a living, the age and number of dependent children are a few of the factors to consider in determining how much life insurance coverage you should have. There is no easy formula to use to decide whether it is best to have a term life policy or a universal life policy or a whole life policy. The facts and circumstances of your individual needs can be evaluated by an insurance professional. It is possible to combine life insurance protection and mutual fund investing within a variable life policy. Upon your death, life insurance benefits are not taxable to your beneficiaries on their Form 1040. However, the amount of benefits are to be included in your taxable estate and could cause estate tax.

Annuities

An annuity is a product of life insurance companies that is a contract which promises to pay you for the rest of your life in exchange for a stated cost of premium. A fixed annuity is invested in interest bearing investments and usually have a better rate of return than a bank certificate of deposit. A variable annuity is invested in the capital market through a group of mutual funds. An annuity's earnings are reinvested and are tax deferred, or not currently taxed. If you are receiving social security benefits, and you have a high adjusted gross income, an annuity is an investment instrument that helps lessen the taxable amount of your social security benefits.

At age 65 you can annuitize the investment through several options. If you annuitize an annuity, and die early, the insurance company wins; if you live beyond life expectancy, you win. The option of choosing joint life is usually a good choice. If your contract allows for the option of a refund feature, to choose it means that your named beneficiary will receive any remainder of principal in your contract upon your death.

An annuity does not have to be annuitized. It is possible to allow the contract to compound and grow and be passed on to your beneficiary. The value will not be subject to probate expense. However, as the contract passes to your appointed beneficiary, the profit or gain in the contract will be taxable on your beneficiary's Form 1040.

Because annuities have an "end load" or cost if you take more than the allowed minimum withdrawal during the first six or seven years of the investment, they should never be used as a short term investment. The taxable portion of withdrawals before age 59½ or disability do incur the 10% penalty assessed by the IRS. The taxable portion of withdrawals are also subject to regular tax.

Unqualified and Qualified Plans

Investments and annuities are available in unqualified plans and qualified plans. An unqualified plan means that the cost or premium is not subtracted from your taxable income. Qualified investment plans have the added advantage of "sheltering" the cost or contribution to the plan from current tax. To establish a qualified investment or annuity, it is usually a simple procedure of signing an extra document that establishes a custodian for the plan.

Qualified Retirement Plan (QRP)

A forfeitable (employee loses if not vested) contribution to a Qualified Retirement Plan (QRP) by your employer is a "tax shelter", that has the added feature of not being subject to social security. Another unique feature of a QRP for a dual-status minister is that all or a portion of its income can be **designated as tax-free housing** according to Rev. Ruling 63-156 and CCH, Standard Federal Tax Reports ¶6852.34. To the extent your income from a designated QRP is spent for housing, it will **not be taxed** even in retirement! The choice of monthly income distribution from a QRP is more attractive to a dual-status minister than a "lump-sum" distribution because of the ability to designate it as tax-free parsonage allowance. Chapter One has additional discussion in this important area of tax planning.

Tax Sheltered Account or Sec. 403(b) Plan

Another qualified tax shelter plan available to employees of non-profit employers is the Tax Sheltered Account, or a Sec. 403(b) plan. Mutual fund companies have qualified Sec. 403(b) plans that allow you to invest in the capital market. Insurance companies have qualified Sec. 403(b) plans that allow you to invest in either a fixed or a variable annuity.

Contributions by a dual-status minister to a Sec. 403(b) plan are not subject to social security tax according to Revenue Ruling 68-395. However, contributions by a lay employee to a Sec. 403(b) plan is subject to social security withholding and matching according to Revenue Ruling 65-208.

Individual Retirement Account

A qualified tax shelter that we are all familiar with is the Individual Retirement Account or the IRA. You can establish an IRA that is invested in mutual funds. You can establish an IRA with an insurance company that is an annuity contract. You can establish an IRA with a bank that is invested in a Certificate of Deposit. **IRA's** are now **flexible** and have the capability of being **qualified or non-qualified.** You can choose to designate contributions to an IRA as "non-deductible" on Form 8606. In a year that you make a contribution to your IRA, not realizing that you will not have an income tax liability, you should choose to designate the contribution as "non-deductible" when you file your tax return.

If you and/or your spouse are an active participant in another plan and your AGI is within the phaseout range, your IRA contribution may be "non-deductible."

When You Should Have A Qualified Plan?

When you have an income tax liability, it is good tax planning to consider making contributions to a sheltered or qualified retirement plan. Even when you have no income tax liability, you may wish to contribute to a Sec. 403(b) retirement plan and reduce your social security base if you are a dual-status minister. When a religious worker has **no income tax** liability, and **no social security** liability (Form 4361), it is best to invest in a non-sheltered investment or retirement plan.

Tax Planning for the Retired or Semi-retired Minister

Between the ages of 62 and 70, every minister considers the possibility of semi-retirement. **Between age 62 and 65,** an employer can pay salary and parsonage value and/or allowance up to the limitation shown below, and the minister will receive all of his social security benefits. If his earned income is more than the limitation, his social security benefits will be reduced by $1 for each $2 of extra earned income. **Between age 65 and 70,** an employer can pay salary and parsonage value and/or allowance up to the limitation shown below, and the minister will receive all of his social security benefits. If his earned income is more than the limitation, his social security benefits will be reduced by $1 for each $3 of extra earned income. **At age 70,** when the earnings limitation ends, you can earn $1,000,000 and still draw your full social security benefits! The amount of the limitation is adjusted for inflation every year and is announced in October.

Sign up, make earnings reports, and receive all benefits available to you. Retired ministers receiving social security benefits while continuing to earn a salary, **must submit an "Annual Report of Earnings"** to their Social Security office if they earn more than the limits shown below. The report is due April 15th, but an extension can be obtained by simply calling your Social Security office. **Failure to file the report can result in the loss of one month's benefits**. If you have submitted an estimate of your earnings for the next year to your Social Security office, you should submit an "Annual Report of Earnings" to show your actual earnings. You may be eligible for additional benefits.

SOCIAL SECURITY and RETIREMENT PLANNING

The amount of earnings a person can receive, before it affects the amount of social security benefits available, are as follows:

1992	- age 62 to 65	$7,440
	- age 65 to 70	$10,200
1993	- age 62 to 65	$7,680
	- age 65 to 70	$10,560
1994	- age 62 to 65	$8,040
	- age 65 to 70	$11,160

Definition of Earned Income

Salary and the value of a home provided and/or the parsonage allowance **ARE** considered "earned income" by social security.

Fringe benefits, an accountable employee business expense reimbursement plan, and non-forfeitable contributions to a salary-reduction TSA **ARE NOT** "earned income" and can be provided in addition to $8,040/$11,160 salary and housing limitation.

Income from pensions, interest, dividends, rents and sale of property **ARE NOT** earned income. You can receive **unlimited** amounts of such **non-earned income** and still receive all of your social security benefits.

Social Security Benefits are Sometimes Taxed

Social security benefits you receive may be taxable in some instances. You will receive Form SSA-1099 showing the total benefits paid to you during the year and the amount of any social security benefits you repaid during the year. The maximum amount of your social security benefits that can be taxable is 50%. The worksheet provided with Form 1040 helps you compute the "modified adjusted gross income", which is 50% of your social security benefits, plus other taxable income, plus tax-exempt interest, less adjustments. If this amount is less than the threshold of $32,000 ($25,000 for single) none of your benefits will be taxed. It is important for married taxpayers to file a joint return. The threshold for married separate returns is -0-, causing 50% of the social security benefits to be included in gross income.

New Rules for 1994: Taxpayers whose incomes fall within current thresholds will still pay tax on up to 50% of their benefits. The new second thresholds above which 85% of the social security benefit is included in gross income are $44,000 ($34,000 for single.)

Is Your Social Security Earnings Record Correct?

It is very important and easy to check your personal social security earnings record. **Get a Form SSA-7004 by calling the "800" number for Social Security in your local phone directory.** By completing, signing and sending the form to the Social Security Administration, you will be sent a printout of your personal earnings record. If there has been a mistake in recording your earnings history, the social security personnel at the "800" number are trained to handle the corrections. They will tell you what documents or information you need to send to them for verification.

Dual-status ministers often experience mistakes in their social security earnings record. The amount of earnings on Form 1040, line 7, is often combined with the social security base on Schedule SE. This mistake can lead to an overstatement of your earnings. If the amount of earnings on Form 1040, line 7, is recorded as your earnings and the parsonage allowance is omitted, your earnings will be understated. Some regional social security personnel are not familiar with the unique tax treatment of a dual-status minister. **Have patience, talk with a supervisor when necessary, but do check your earnings record every three years!** Having a correct social security record will insure that you will receive the benefits you have paid for.

CHAPTER FIVE

OVERSEAS MISSIONARIES AND RELIGIOUS ORDERS

Missionaries Serving Overseas

Missionaries who are U.S. citizens serving overseas in a foreign country are subject to the same U.S. income tax laws as those living in the U.S. However, they may qualify for an exclusion of earned income, according to Sec. 911. An ordained or "the equivalent thereof" minister serving as a missionary overseas is to be treated as a dual-status minister. The qualifications explained in Chapter Two need to be satisfied. On February 20, 1992, Private Letter Ruling 9221025, gave a positive answer to a major denomination concerning their "commissioned" female teachers being eligible for dual-status treatment. (See "What about equal treatment of male & female religious workers?" in Chapter Two)

If a minister serving as a missionary overseas, has an "approved" Form 4361 and is exempt from social security, he is to write "Exempt—Form 4361" on the self-employment line, Form 1040, page 2. Disability coverage under social security discontinues five years after becoming exempt. Overseas missionaries have difficulty obtaining comparable life and disability insurance coverages. If you are considering an overseas ministry, you may wish to choose being covered by social security.

Missionaries who do secular jobs (carpenters, physicians, nurses, pilots, cooks, mechanics, etc.) are regular employees subject to withholding and matching of social security and medicare tax.

Form TD F 90-22.1 "Report of Foreign Bank and Financial Accounts" should be filed for all missionaries who have a savings or checking account overseas which exceeds $10,000 in aggregate value at any time during the calendar year. The Form TD F 90-22.1 is to be filed **separately** from the Form 1040. It is due by June 30th and is to be sent to: Department of the Treasury, P.O. Box 32621, Detroit, MI 48232.

Bona Fide Residency and Physical Presence Rules

To qualify for Sec. 911 foreign earned income exclusion and/or foreign housing exclusion, the missionary must be able to satisfy the requirements of either bona fide residency, or be physically present in a foreign country or countries for a total of at least 330 days during any period of 12 consecutive months.

To be considered a bona fide resident of a foreign country, you must have intentions to remain overseas for an indefinite stay and to give evidence by words and acts as to the length and nature of your stay. You will not be treated as a bona fide resident of a foreign country if you have made a statement to the authorities of that country that you are not a resident of it and have been held not subject to its income tax. To establish your bona fide residency in a foreign country, you must reside there for an uninterrupted period **which includes an entire tax year**. If you use the calendar year as your tax year, your entire tax year is the period beginning January 1 and ending December 31. The term "uninterrupted period" refers to your bona fide residence and not to your physical presence. Temporary absence for vacations or business trips is allowable.

The physical presence test does not apply to the type of residence you establish, to your intentions about returning, or to the nature and purpose of your stay overseas. It is concerned only with how long you stay in a foreign country or countries. If, during a period of 12 consecutive months, you are physically present in a foreign country 330 full days (approximately 11 months), you meet the physical presence test. ANY period of 12 consecutive months may be used. If 12 months during the middle of the overseas stay contains 330 days of physical presence, you will satisfy the requirement and be able to be exempt for the whole stay overseas.

Discussion of Form 2555

The **IRS Publication 54** and **Form 2555 for 1993** returns will be available after the first of the year. Please obtain your copy from IRS and study it carefully.

- *Foreign Earned Income Exclusion*

Exclusion Available Since 1982: For 1982 and later returns, individuals meeting either the bona fide residency test or the physical presence test, could elect to exclude foreign earned income at the following annual rates:

        1982 . . . . $75,000
        1983 through 1986 . . . . $80,000
        1987 and thereafter $70,000

The $70,000 foreign earned income exclusion **is voluntary**, according to Publication 54, page 5. **Basically, your initial choice of the exclusion on Form 2555 must be filed with a timely filed return** (including extensions), a return amending a timely filed return, or a late filed return (determined without regard to any extensions) filed within one year from the original due date of the return. The amending of Reg. 1.911-7 now provides a fourth time to make a valid election. If no federal tax is owed after taking into account the foreign earned income exclusion or housing cost amount an election may be made at anytime later than the times provided above whether or not the IRS has discovered the failure to make the election. The change applies to taxable years beginning after December 31, 1981.

Once you choose to exclude your foreign earned income, that choice remains in effect for that year and all later years unless you revoke it. If you revoke your choice for any tax year, you cannot claim the exclusion again for your next 5 tax years without the approval of the IRS. The government charges $375 for this request. **This provision had made it very important for missionaries to timely file their initial tax returns**. The $75,000/$80,000 exclusion in 1982 and 1983 was denied a taxpayer, an American citizen, who worked abroad and failed to file timely returns. (William J. Faltesek, Docket No. 48522-86, 6-6-89)

- *Foreign Housing Exclusion*

In addition to the foreign earned income exclusion, you can separately claim an exclusion or a deduction from gross income for your housing amount if your tax home is in a foreign country and you qualify under either the bona fide residence test or the physical presence test.

For missionaries who earn considerably less than the $70,000 foreign earned income exclusion, it isn't advisable for them to choose the foreign housing exclusion. In addition to a complex computation, **if chosen,** the foreign housing exclusion **must be used first** and fully before using the foreign earned income exclusion. In any year that a missionary earns over $70,000, he can initially choose and apply the foreign housing exclusion on a timely filed return by completing the appropriate section on Form 2555. The two exclusions available can be separately chosen and separately revoked. By attaching a statement to the return or an amended return for the first year that you do not wish to claim the exclusion(s), you can revoke either choice for any tax year.

Sec. 911 foreign housing exclusion is unique, and very different from Sec. 107 housing for ministers and Sec. 119 housing. Any year your income exceeds $70,000, take the time to study IRS Publication 54, page 5. Being able to use the foreign earned income exclusion first makes your Form 2555 less complicated.

- *Vacation Computation*

According to Rev. Ruling 76-191, while home in the U. S., (unless on vacation ONLY), income earned is usually taxable on your federal return. Vacation time earned during the last year preceding your leave can be considered eligible for the above exclusion. If your mission gives you 6 months vacation (without work) for a four year term, one-fourth, or 45 days is eligible for the exclusion. If you are working and traveling on deputation all of your furlough, all of your leave would be taxable.

To determine the amount of U. S. income you should count the number of days in the U.S., subtract the vacation days, divide the result by 365 days, then multiply that percentage times the annual salary. For a missionary, who usually works a 7 day week, you would count 7 days for each week.

Example:

	Days in U.S.	75 days
	Less vacation	(21 days)
		54 days
	54 ÷ 365 =	14.79%
Taxable income for U.S. −	14.79% X $35,500 =	**$5,250.45**

Moving Expense—Overseas

- ***Foreign Moves - Form 3903F***

If you move to a new principal place of work outside the United States and its possessions, it is a "foreign move." If all or part of the income that you earn at the new foreign location is excluded under the foreign earned income exclusion, the part of the moving expense that is allocable to the excluded income is not deductible. The following modified moving rules apply to Form 3903F:
  1. The period for deducting the costs of occupying temporary quarters is increased from 30 to 90 days after obtaining employment.
  2. The limitation on the expense of pre-move househunting trips, occupying temporary quarters, and expenses of selling or purchasing your residence is increased from $3,000 to $6,000, and the $1,500 limitation on househunting trips and occupancy of temporary quarters is increased to $4,500. Meals while enroute, during house hunting trips, and temporary living period, must be reduced by 20%.
  3. The costs of moving household goods is expanded to include the reasonable expenses of moving household goods and personal effects to and from storage, and of storing the goods and effects for part or all of the period that your new place of work abroad continues to be your principal place of work.

- ***Non-Foreign Move—Form 3903***

A move from a foreign country to the U.S. isn't a foreign move. The regular moving limits and requirements discussed in Chapter Three will apply. If you permanently retire and your principal place of work and former home were outside the U.S. and its possessions, you do not have to satisfy the 39 work week requirement. You may deduct the move back to the U.S., subject to all of the other requirements and limitations of Form 3903.

When and Where To File As An Overseas Missionary

There is an automatic extension of two months to June 15th for any U.S. citizen with **both their tax home and their abode** outside the U.S. on April 15th. This is an extension of time to file only, tax liability has to be paid by April 15th. If you take advantage of the automatic extension, you are required to attach a statement to your return showing you were residing outside the U.S. on the due date of your return. If additional time is required the regular automatic 4 month extension, Form 4868 can be filed by June 15th for an extra two months of extension.

File Form 2555 with Form 1040 and send to:

**INTERNAL REVENUE SERVICE CENTER
Philadelphia, PA 19255**

- **Special Extensions Of Time For Filing**
  A new missionary arriving in an overseas country anytime during the year cannot file Form 2555 the first year and claim the foreign earned income exclusion. However, after he has established his bona fide residence or met the physical presence test, all of his income is eligible for the special tax treatment from the **date of his arrival**. There are two ways to handle the problem of filing:
  1. **File Form 2350**, requesting an extension of filing your return until after establishing foreign residence. It is necessary to pay any anticipated tax on U.S. income with Form 2350. Then, within 30 days after meeting the residency requirements, file your return along with a copy of the approved Form 2350.
     A. An earlier first year return can often be filed by satisfying the physical presence rules.
     B. After satisfying the bona fide residency rules, it is best to switch to bona fide resident because it doesn't have to be re-established after a furlough or vacation back in the U.S.
  2. (Not the best choice!) File the current year's return and pay tax on all income, including income earned abroad. After meeting the residency requirements, file Form 1040X and Form 2555 within one year of the due date of the original return to claim a refund of taxes on earnings while overseas.

Independent Missionaries

If a missionary has a sponsoring mission or church, it is incorrect for that organization to treat the missionary as an "Independent Contractor". Under the "common law rules" you are the employer and penalties for not preparing information returns and withholding required taxes will apply. Missionaries who perform ministerial duties and are employed by a foreign mission board or an integral agency of a church are entitled to dual-status treatment. Missionaries who do secular jobs (carpenters, physicians, mechanics, etc.) are regular employees subject to withholding and matching of social security and medicare tax.

When a missionary does not have a sponsoring mission or church, it becomes very difficult to properly prepare his tax return. Several independent missionaries have been audited, and the IRS personnel in foreign countries are often less knowledgeable than those in the States. The communication between the missionary and the IRS agent can be difficult, frustrating and time consuming.

We have included further instructions and recommendations for handling independent religious workers in Chapter Six.

Religious Orders — Two Types

Protestant Religious Orders Described in Sec. 1402(c)(4)

The idea of non-integral agency protestant ministries adopting the status of "religious order" was popular in the late 70's and early 80's. Some were advised, change your by-laws and declare your organization to be a "religious order." The Social Security Amendments Act of 1983, and the mandatory application of social security coverage to employees of not-for-profit organizations made the idea flourish. In order to avoid the cost of withholding and matching social security, several non-integral agency protestant ministries began claiming the status of "religious order." So many requests for determination were received by IRS that they put a freeze on responding to them. During 1985 the IRS responded with letters stating that the question of what constitutes a religious order was under intensive study by the Service and that they would not be able to respond to the requests until their study was completed.

During 1991, IRS issued **Revenue Procedure 91-20, IRB 1991-10**. It sets forth guidelines that will be used by IRS in determining whether an organization is a religious

order for federal employment tax purposes. IRS has identified from previous court cases the following characteristics:
1. The organization is described in Sec. 501(c)(3) of the Code.
2. The members of the organization vow to live under a strict set of rules requiring moral and spiritual self-sacrifice and dedication to the goals of the organization at the expense of their material well-being.
3. The members of the organization, after successful completion of the organization's training program and probationary period, make a long-term commitment to the organization (normally more than two years).
4. The organization is, directly or indirectly, under the control and supervision of a church or convention or association of churches, or is significantly funded by a church or convention or association of churches.
5. The members of the organization normally live together as part of a community and are held to a significantly stricter level of moral and religious discipline than that required of lay church members.
6. The members of the organization work or serve full-time on behalf of the religious, educational, or charitable goals of the organization.
7. The members of the organization participate regularly in activities such as public or private prayer, religious study, teaching, care of the aging, missionary work, or church reform or renewal.

Being a 501(c)(3) organization is required. If all of the above characteristics are true, the organization will be treated as a religious order. Considering all the facts and circumstances about an organization it is not necessary that all of the above characteristics be true. In the absence of one or more of the above characteristics, Rev. Proc. 91-20 says, that the IRS will contact the organization and carefully consider their views about their status.

We are aware of and have read the IRS's favorable private letter rulings granting Sec. 1402(c)(4) status of religious order to two different organizations during 1992.

If a non-integral agency ministry wrongly claims the status of a "religious order," the underpayment of payroll taxes could be so overwhelming that the ministry could find it hard to survive. IRS indicates by publishing Rev. Proc. 91-20, that they have a new awareness of this area of tax law.

- *Information Returns and Proper Tax Treatment for Sec. 1402(c)(4) Religious Orders*

The proper form to report the income paid to a member of a "religious order" is Form W-2. **The practice of issuing Form 1099 to employee-members is not correct.** To qualify as an "independent contractor" or a "non-employee" of a religious order would be impossible, due to the amount of control a religious order has over its members.
1. Member, ordained or "the equivalent thereof," doing duties of the ministry. Tax treatment is the same as a dual-status minister, eligible for parsonage allowance, self-employed for social security purposes and **must timely file Form 4361 to be exempt from social security.** Withholding of income tax is optional, Form W-2 is the proper form to show taxable salary.
2. Member, lay employee of order, performing services required by the order are not eligible for parsonage allowance. Earnings are treated as self-employment for social security purposes, **must timely file Form 4361 to be exempt from social security.** Withholding of income tax is optional, Form W-2 is the proper form to show taxable salary.
3. Non-member lay employees are automatically covered by social security, cannot become exempt and are to receive a regular Form W-2 with income tax withholding.

Religious Orders Described in Sec. 1402(g)

Sec. 1402(g) describes Religous Orders that are opposed to insurance and have taken a "vow of Poverty." Examples of such orders are the Amish, Quakers and Catholic Monastic

OVERSEAS MISSIONARIES and RELIGIOUS ORDERS

Orders. The term "religious order" is not well defined in IRS Code or regulations. In a 1969 tax court case, Eighth Street Baptist Church, Inc. v. U.S., 295 F.Supp. 1400 (D.Kan. 1969), the judge cited Webster's dictionary as his best source of a definition to determine that Eighth Street Baptist Church was not a religious order. Sec. 1402(g)(1)(E) gives the fact that a religious order or sect has to have been in existence at all times since December 31, 1950. In a court case for the year of 1976, a taxpayer argued that this provision was unconstitutional under the first amendment since it discriminates against religious sects not established prior to December 31, 1950. The judge stated that Congress has great latitude in limiting the exemptions by any general standards, (TC Memo 1980-284, Glen A. Ross, Docket No. 3593-79). Sec. 1402(g)(1)(D) states that a religious order must have for a substantial period of time been making reasonable provisions for its dependent members.

- *Information Returns and Proper Tax Treatment for Sec. 1402(g) Religious Orders*
  1. Member, employee working for order, doing duties required by the order, receives no salary, and has no income tax or social security tax liability, does not have to file any forms.
  2. Member, working outside of the order, earnings are given to the order, and duties are the kind that are ordinarily performed by members of the order and they are required to be exercised on the behalf of the religious order as its agent. Examples in Publication 517 indicate that being instructed to be a secretary qualified and being instructed to be a lawyer did not.
     A. If duties qualify, the earnings are not taxable to member and there are no tax liabilities.
     B. If duties do not qualify, even though the order receives the salary, the earnings are taxable to member and subject to federal income tax withholding and social security tax withholding and matching.
  3. Member, working outside of the order, self employed doing secular work, profits are subject to regular income tax and self-employment tax. An exemption is available from self-employment tax by filing **Form 4029 at any time.** To be able to file for this exemption, the member must be conscientiously opposed to accepting benefits of **any private or public insurance and waive all rights to ever receive any social security benefits.**
  4. Since 1988, members or member partnerships who have filed Form 4029 and are exempt from social security, can employ other members who have also filed Form 4029 and be exempt from withholding and matching social security tax on their wages. An exempt employer will be required to withhold income tax and prepare Form W-2 for exempt employees.
  5. Non-member lay employees are automatically covered by social security, cannot become exempt and are to receive a regular Form W-2 with income tax and social security tax withholding and matching.

CHAPTER SIX

COMPLETED PAYROLL REPORTS

Now we are ready for the practical application of all the information presented in the preceding chapters! Even though the tax laws are complex, the examples shown in this Chapter are for the purpose of teaching the simplest approach to designing the best compensation package. **Regardless of what creative label the employer might call money or property "paid" to an employee, it is taxable if a section of the Internal Revenue Code does not exclude it.** Generally, the employee will be taxed on all remuneration that is not a qualified fringe benefit (Chapter One), parsonage allowance (Chapter Two), or an accountable reimbursement plan for professional expenses (Chapter Three). Tax law excludes these categories of a compensation package from federal income tax. Fringe benefits and an accountable reimbursement plan for professional expenses are also excluded from social security and medicare tax.

Our payroll sheets are designed with an extra column for parsonage allowance and a section to keep a record of an accountable reimbursement plan. This is a tell and show chapter. You will benefit greatly by studying the filled out sample payroll sheets and reports at the end of the chapter.

Steps in Establishing a Compensation Package

1. **Establish the fringe benefits that will be provided.** The cost of medical insurance, contributions to a qualified pension plan, premiums for up to $50,000 group term life insurance, etc., generally are to be paid by the employer directly to the companies providing the plans. The employee does not personally receive the money and the amounts are not to be included on the payroll record, quarterly reports or in the W-2 at year end.

2. **Establish an accountable reimbursement plan for auto and professional employee business expenses.** Establish a written reimbursement plan for each employee using the suggested wordings in Chapter Three. Employees must "adequately account" their professional expenses to the employer.

    The tax benefits to be gained by establishing an accountable reimbursement plan should convince employers to bear the burden of the "cost of doing ministry business." An employer should be willing to reimburse their employees for all auto and professional expenses over and above their salary. In the first year of establishing an accountable plan the employer can initially adjust the salary to fund the plan.

    If the employer provides an auto for an employee, they must have a written plan and follow the IRS regulations to determine how much to include in the employee's income for personal use.

3. **Determine the amount of the cash salary.** You may wish to obtain a copy of "compensation guidelines" provided by denominational handbooks or other organizations.

4. **Designate an adequate parsonage allowance in advance for the dual-status minister.** When a church or integral agency of a church owns the house in which the minister lives, they must designate a portion of his cash compensation as parsonage allowance for the additional home expenses he personally incurs. When

a church or integral agency of a church does not provide the home and the minister owns his own home, they must designate a portion of his cash compensation as parsonage allowance for the whole cost of providing the home. Use the "Suggested Wordings" in Chapter Two. The amount of **designated housing allowance**, divided by the number of pay periods is shown on the payroll record as a subtraction, and **is not to be shown on the 941 quarterly reports or W-2 at year end**. The minister is responsible to show any unused portion as income.

When an employer provides housing and utilities for a lay employee that satisfies all three conditions of Sec. 119, the value is not to be shown on the payroll report, 941 quarterly reports or W-2 at year end. It is free from federal income tax, social security and medicare tax. When one of the tests is not satisfied, the value of housing and utilities provided is subject to income tax, social security and medicare tax and is to be shown as taxable compensation on the payroll reports. In our payroll example below we illustrate the janitor, Joseph Mop, being provided Sec. 119 housing.

Dual-Status Minister - Rev. Snodgrass' Compensation Package

Fringe Benefits Provided:
    Hospital Insurance Premiums $5,520
    Group Term Life Insurance Premiums . $ 420
Total Cash Compensation $32,400
    *Parsonage Allowance Designated . . . . ($18,000)
    Contributions to Salary Reduction 403(b) Retirement ($ 2,400)
Taxable Salary on W-2 . . . . **$12,000**

* Rev. Snodgrass owns his own home. **The $18,000 parsonage allowance is not to be shown in Box 1 of his W-2.** As we illustrate on his tax return in Chapter 7, he is responsible to show the unused portion of $1,517 as income on Form 1040, line 22. (When the parsonage is owned by the church employer, don't include it's value in Box 1 of his W-2.) Rev. Snodgrass will include the $18,000 parsonage allowance on his Schedule SE for social security purposes, unless he had an approved Form 4361 exemption.

Mission Community Church adopted an unlimited professional expense reimbursement plan. Upon submitting adequate records to his employer, he received separate checks each month in the amount of his auto and professional expenses of $9,265.

Calculation for Amount of Paycheck: The contributions to the 403(b) retirement will be paid directly to a mutual fund or insurance company by the employer. $32,400 less $2,400 = $30,000 divided by the number of paydays in the year. Our sample payroll sheet illustrates semimonthly pay periods:
    $30,000 ÷ 24 = **$1,250.00** per pay check.

Lay Employee - Joseph Mop's Compensation Package

Value of Home & Utilities Provided (Sec. 119) . . $5,700
Fringe Benefits Provided:
    Hospital Insurance Premiums $3,970
    Group Term Life Insurance Premiums . $ 276
Total Cash Compensation $21,600
    Contributions to Salary Reduction 403(b) Retirement ($ 1,200)
Taxable Salary on W-2 . . . . **$20,400**

Mission Community Church adopted an unlimited professional expense reimbursement policy for Joseph Mop. Upon submitting adequate records to his employer, he received separate checks each month in the amount of his actual auto and professional expenses, total of $947 for the year.

Calculation for Amount of Paycheck: The contributions to the 403(b) retirement will be paid directly to a mutual fund or insurance company by the employer. $21,600 less $1,200 = $20,400 divided by the number of paydays in the year. Our sample payroll sheet illustrates semimonthly pay periods:

$$\$20,400 \div 24 = \$ 850.00 \text{ per pay check.}$$

Organizations Must File Information Returns!

Gone are the days when an employer can get by with handing the minister a piece of paper stating the amount of money paid for his services during the year. The following quotes and facts are provided with the hope that not-for-profit employers will take heed, do what the law requires and avoid the frustration of penalties and problems with the IRS.

Who is An Employer?

It is very important that a not-for-profit organization practice responsible payroll accounting in a business-like manner. IRS Publication 15, "Employer's Tax Guide", page 3, defines who is an employer:

"Generally, an employer is a person or organization for whom a worker performs a service as an employee. The employer usually gives the worker the tools and place to work and has the right to fire the worker. A person or organization paying wages to a former employee after the work ends is also considered an employer. For income tax withholding purposes, the term employer includes organizations that are exempt from income, social security, medicare, and FUTA taxes."

In Chapter One, we discussed the "common law rules" that are to be used to determine if an individual who has been paid for services rendered is an employee or an independent contractor. According to **Sec. 3509**, employers **are liable** for income tax and the employee's portion of social security if they don't deduct and withhold these taxes because they wrongly treat an employee as a nonemployee.

Who Is An Employee?

When janitors, secretaries, paid babysitters, musicians, etc. are paid for the services they do, and according to the common law rules they cannot be considered an independent contractor, you are the employer. **Payment of $108 or more in a year** to an employee is subject to withholding and matching of social security and medicare tax. You must carefully study federal employment tax rules and timely file payroll reports and Form W-2's. We have prepared sample payroll reports in this chapter to help you.

Who Is An Independent Contractor?

Musicians, evangelists, contractors, and others who provide occasional services are examples of non-employees or independent contractors. Have each person prepare a Form W-9 and prepare a **Form 1099** for each individual non-employee that you paid **$600** or more during the year. Form 1099's do not have to be prepared for payments to corporations.

A dual-status evangelist can have you designate parsonage allowance for him and adequately account travel expenses to you. At the time of the engagement, have the evangelist prepare a Form W-9 and a parsonage allowance designation. If the **net honorarium is $600** or more for the year, prepare a **Form 1099**. If an evangelist or musical group is employed by a corporation, a Form 1099 is not required.

If you wish to avoid payroll calculations and taxes for janitorial and lawn work, look in the yellow pages or the want ads, and hire a service to do the type of work you need to have done.

COMPLETED PAYROLL REPORTS

Informational Return Penalties

IRS emphasis on informational reporting in recent years affects everyone, not just not-for-profit corporations. **Computer cross-matching of all informational returns with individuals' tax returns** gives the IRS the ability to detect unreported income. Since 1982, there have been penalties for failure to submit W-2's and 1099's to the IRS. Information return penalties include failure to file an information return, failure to file information returns correctly and on time, failure to file paper forms that are machine readable (must be typed with black ink), and failure to file on magnetic media if filing more than 250 Form W-2's or 50 Form 1099's. For your reading pleasure, the IRS has 123 different tax codes dealing with penalties they can assess various taxpayers! Their current emphasis is on **correct and timely information**. The penalty for failure to file information returns is provided for in **Sec. 6652**.

Sec. **6721** imposes a penalty for any failure to file an information return on time, any failure to include all information required to be shown on the return, or for the inclusion of incorrect information. The amount of the penalty is based on how late the return is filed or when the failure is corrected. If corrected by the 30th day after the due date, the penalty is $15 a return, maximum of $75,000 a year. If filed or corrected more than 30 days late but by August 1, the penalty is $30 a return, maximum of $150,000 a year. If filed after August 1st of any year, the penalty is $50 a return, maximum of $250,000 a year.

Willful Or Intentional Disregard

Willful or intentional disregard causes very severe penalties. An example of a longstanding penalty for intentional disregard of doing payroll taxes from **Sec. 6672, is the 100% penalty.**

*"Any person required to collect, truthfully account for, and pay over any tax imposed by this title who willfully fails to collect such tax, or truthfully account for and pay over such tax, or willfully attempts in any manner to evade or defeat any such tax or the payment thereof, shall, in addition to other penalties provided by law, be liable to a penalty **equal to the total** amount of the tax evaded, or not collected, or not accounted for and paid over."*

Late payment penalties and interest are in addition to the above penalties. **Trustees or treasurers** of not-for-profit organizations, whether paid or volunteer, **can be held responsible when** the organization fails to pay the taxes.

It is unfortunate that such severe penalties exist. **It is very important** for an employer to **fulfill the informational return filing requirements,** rather than having to go before the board or congregation and ask for funds to be raised to pay penalties and interest that could have been avoided by filing timely returns.

Attitude Towards the IRS Should Be One of Cooperation

We recommend that the attitude of any organization towards the IRS or its agents should be one of cooperation. If your organization was not aware of your obligation to withhold income tax and withhold and match social security and medicare tax, it is our position that for all wages paid within the three year statute of limitations, late reports should be filed and taxes paid. It is possible to write a letter and claim "reasonable cause" and lack of knowledge, rather than unwillingness, and have the IRS forgive some or all of the penalties. There will always be interest assessed on the late payments.

To be uncooperative would cause the IRS to suspect your church to be a fraudulent one. Avoid being considered as a "tax protest" church. There are those who are not religious or not actually ministers, but become "ordained" by mail and establish not-for-profit churches in their homes for the purpose of "tax avoidance" or "tax protest." As in District Court Case No. 82-3675, Freedom Church of Revelation v. USA, the IRS has been successful in revoking the exempt status of "tax protest" churches because they can not prove that they operate exclusively for charity and fail to establish that no part of their earnings inure (becomes useful) to the benefit of private individuals. If you are aware of anyone involved in this type of "tax protest," ask the IRS for Form 211, report them and be eligible for up to 10% of tax collected as a reward from the IRS!

The employer is responsible for filing informational reports, not the employee. However, **we recommend that the minister take an active part** in helping the treasurer prepare and timely file required reports. Treasurers hold a very responsible position; consider paying them wages for carrying out their duties. When a new person assumes the responsibility, be sure they are properly informed and taught the importance of timely and correctly filed payroll reports.

Do not hesitate to seek professional accounting help in preparing the informational returns. **The staff at Worth Tax & Financial Service is available** to prepare payroll reports and W-2's for churches.

How To Prepare Information Returns

We would encourage the careful reading and study of the **IRS Publication 15,** "Employer's Tax Guide," and **IRS Publication 393,** "1993 Federal Employment Tax Forms," which provide line by line instructions for preparing Forms W-2 and W-3. These employer publications are automatically sent to you each year. They are sent to all new organizations that file for an identification number. Preprinted 941's and Federal Tax Deposit coupons are also automatically sent to employers. Anytime you need forms you can call the IRS toll-free number listed in your phone book and ask for them to be sent to you.

We will teach you how to prepare the proper payroll forms by example. Rev. Snodgrass and Joseph Mop are employed by Mission Community Church. We have used their sample "compensation packages," shown earlier in this chapter, to prepare the reports. Refer to them often as we give you step by step instructions.

Obtain A Federal Identification Number

Does your organization or church have one? The bank where you have your organization's checking account has required you to furnish them with a Federal Identification Number. It looks like this: 00-0000000, nine digits. It is a Federal Identification Number for federal reports, and is not your state incorporation number or sales tax exempt number.

New churches and existing churches without a number should request one by filing Form SS-4. Send the request to your IRS Service Center and they will assign your church a number in a short period of time. It is now possible to phone a special IRS phone number and be assigned an identification number. Call the IRS toll-free number listed for your state and ask for the non-toll-free number for your state. If you need to file payroll reports before your number is assigned, enter "Applied For" on the reports.

Withhold Required Taxes

It is important to understand that dual-status ministers and lay employees are treated differently for withholding purposes. The charts in **IRS Publication 15** tell us the following:

Lay Employees

Their income **IS** subject to income tax withholding and each lay employee should be asked to fill out a Form W-4. The status and number of allowances claimed will determine how much income tax is to be withheld. **Publication 15** contains the tables showing how much is required to be withheld. Joseph Mop's W-4 shows he is married and wishes to claim "0" allowance. Turn to page 38 of Publication 15 (1993) and find his semimonthly pay of $850.00 on the left-hand column. Under the "0" allowance column we see the proper amount to withhold is **$89.00**.

Their income **IS** subject to social security and medicare tax withholding and matching. 1993 combined rate to be withheld for employees was 7.65%. Employers pay an additional 7.65% when they file Form 941. The rate for 1994 remains the same. **The 7.65% combined rate is made up of 6.2% rate for social security tax and 1.45% rate for medicare.**

The only exception to the above paragraph is for **electing churches**, who have filed **Form 8274** and are exempt **because of religious reasons**, Sec. 3121(w). The election merely **transfers** the social security liability **from the church to the employee**. Churches who desire to be an electing church must file two copies of Form 8274 after they hire employees, but before the first date on which a quarterly employment tax return is due. (See more detailed discussion in Chapter Four.) Lay employees of churches that have filed Form 8274 are subject to paying social security at the 1993 self-employed rate of 15.3% (less adjustments) on their personal return.

Dual-Status Ministers

Their income **IS NOT** subject to withholding income tax according to Sec. 3401(a)(9). The dual-status minister is to "prepay" his taxes by filing Form 1040ES, Estimated Tax for Individuals. When a dual-status minister files Form 1040ES, we recommend that he does not prepare Form W-4 for the employer.

Their income **IS NOT** subject to withholding and matching for social security and medicare tax purposes. Sec. 1402(a)(8), is an **exception** to the normal employer/employee common law rules, and states that the dual-status minister is to be treated as self-employed for social security purposes. The dual-status minister does have an individual choice during the early part of his ministry to remain in social security or to become exempt by filing Form 4361. This is discussed fully in Chapter Four. When the employer is a church or integral agency of a church, **it is NEVER correct** to treat a dual-status minister, doing the duties of a minister, **as an employee** for social security and medicare tax purposes.

- *Optional Withholding*

If the employer and the dual-status minister make a written agreement, the employer can withhold "income tax" and pay it to the IRS on Form 941, "Employer's Quarterly Federal Tax Return." This option would take the place of the dual-status minister pre-paying his taxes on Form 1040ES. The dual-status minister should "estimate" his total tax liability—income tax and social security and medicare tax; divide it by the number of pay periods (24 if paid semimonthly) and have the employer "withhold" that amount each payday as income tax withholding. A Form W-4 can be used as the written agreement with the amount to be withheld entered on line 6. (Status and number of allowances should be omitted.) The amount withheld will be shown as credit in Box 2 of Form W-2. Rev. Snodgrass estimated he needed $3,840.00 prepaid and had $160.00 withheld each payday.

$$3,840.00 \div 24 = \$160.00$$

His other choice would have been to personally pay 4 estimated tax payments of $960.00 on **Form 1040ES**.

Independent Religious Workers

If a religious worker has a sponsoring mission or church, it is incorrect for that organization to treat them as an "independent contractor" and issue a Form 1099. Under the "common law rules" the organization is considered the employer and penalties for not preparing information returns and withholding required taxes will apply. If a religious worker does not qualify for dual-status treatment, the sponsoring organization is liable for withholding both income tax and social security tax.

When an independent religious worker does not have a sponsoring mission or church, it becomes very difficult to properly prepare his tax return. Often independent religious workers experience the time consuming trauma of an IRS audit. Communication between the religious worker and an IRS agent can be difficult and frustrating. When the religious worker personally receives his support from individual contributions, the donors cannot use their gifts as contributions on their Schedule A. To be deductible as contributions, their gifts must be to a U.S. charitable organization. When a religious worker receives, in addition to his personal support, large amounts of money for work projects, it becomes necessary to show these large amounts on Schedule C and to deduct the "work" expenses. To prove that the "work projects" are legitimate ordinary and necessary business expenses to the IRS is difficult. When building or equipment projects are donated to a foreign church or ministry they are not allowable Sch A contribution deductions either. **The ideal solution to the Sch C problem for the independent religious worker is to establish an employer/employee relationship with a church in the U.S.**

Every independent religious worker or missionary needs a supporting organization or church to be willing to function as his/her employer. It involves setting up a checking account with the religious worker having signature privileges and allowing the support monies to be receipted as contributions to the church. As the religious worker pays for "work projects" and employee business expenses, they become legitimate church ministry expenses of the organization. Copies of all of the financial transactions and detailed receipts should be submitted to the sponsoring church. The income the religious worker receives for his personal salary is recorded on a payroll record and included on the church's quarterly Form 941 and a **Form W-2 at year end**. The religious worker's uncomplicated Form 1040 will reflect only his true personal earnings.

If the religious worker qualifies for dual-status treatment, he will be responsible for his own social security on Schedule SE, the same as any dual-status minister employed by a church or integral agency of a church. If he does not qualify for dual-status treatment, the support received can be used to provide the necessary social security and medicare tax withholding and matching.

Prepare a Payroll Sheet for each Employee

Employers are responsible for accurate recording of the salary, deductions and net pay for each individual employee. We have created and have available "Payroll Sheets" that contain the extra column needed to show parsonage allowance and provides a section to keep a record of the professional business expense reimbursements.

1. Begin entering a paycheck on the "Payroll Sheet" by entering the total cash salary (including parsonage allowance) in the "total" column in the middle.
2. The columns to the right of the "total" column allow you to show income tax, social security tax, medicare tax, state income tax, and local income tax deductions. A dual-status minister who "prepays" his taxes on Form 1040ES will not use these columns.
3. The columns to the left of the "total" column allow you to subtract the parsonage allowance for the dual-status minister. The parsonage allowance of $18,000 for Rev. Snodgrass is divided by 24 to arrive at the semimonthly amount of $750.00.
4. Use the right hand section to record the checks written to reimburse all employees for adequately accounted employee business expenses. Study Chapter Three and **be sure you have adopted a written reimbursement plan** that satisfies the IRS Regulation 1.62-2 that **became effective 1-1-91**.
5. Contributions to a Tax Sheltered Account are subject to social security and medicare tax withholding and matching for the lay employee. They are not subject to social security on Schedule SE for the dual-status employee. Therefore, we recommend

COMPLETED PAYROLL REPORTS 89

that the "parsonage" column be relabeled "TSA" and used for TSA contributions by a lay employee. We recommend that "TSA contributions for the dual-status minister not be shown on the payroll sheet, due to lack of columns and that they are not subject to social security.

Chart of Where to Show Income

Study of our **"Chart of Where to Show Income"**, shown in this chapter will guide you as to what portions of the compensation package you are required to include and what portions you are not required to include on the payroll reports. The payroll sheet's "total" column, for each employee, should include any item from the chart with a "yes" in the "taxable income" column.

- *Use A Blank "Payroll Sheet" As A Summary*

Use a blank "Payroll Sheet" as a summary of monthly or quarterly totals if you have several employees. **It is important** that your "payroll sheets," Form 941's (all four quarters), and the W-2's at year end **reconcile or balance.** IRS's computer will automatically bill additional tax or inquire as to the reason if there are errors. It is our experience that it takes **a LONG TIME to correct payroll report problems.**

Make Payroll Tax Deposits as Required

The amount of payroll taxes you owe determines the frequency of deposits. You owe these taxes when you pay the wages. There are penalties for making late deposits. When you make a payroll tax deposit with Form 8109, the bank electronically transmits your payment to the IRS Service Center that day.

To simplify federal tax deposits, the IRS has amended the deposit rules applicable to employment taxes for payments made after December 31, 1992. An employer is either a monthly depositor or a semi-weekly depositor. This determination is made based on the aggregate amount of employment taxes reported during a "lookback" period. The regulations define a lookback period as the twelve-month period ending on the preceding June 30th. The determination is made by the IRS prior to the beginning of each calendar year and **employers are advised which deposit rules to follow.**

Combine federal income tax withheld with total amount of social security and medicare tax to be paid (15.3%) to determine total liability for each period.

- *Monthly Rule*

An employer is a monthly depositor if the aggregage amount of employment taxes reported for the lookback period is $50,000 or less. A monthly depositor must deposit employment taxes for payments made during a calendar month by the 15th day of the following month.

- *Semi-weekly Rule*

An employer is a semi-weekly depositor if the aggregate amount of employment taxes reported for the lookback period is more than $50,000. Under the semi-weekly deposit rule, those paying wages on Wednesday, Thursday, and/or Friday must deposit employment taxes by the next Wednesday, while those paying wages on Saturday, Sunday, Monday, and/or Tuesday are required to deposit employment taxes on the following Friday.

- *How To Make A Deposit*

Use the Federal Tax Deposit Coupons, Form 8109, to make the deposits. Write the amount due on the coupon, indicate it is 941 tax liability and which quarter is being paid. Write the check, paid to the order of your bank, and take it to the bank and ask for a receipt.

Mission Community Church's Form 941 for the 4th quarter shows the monthly liabilities in the "ROFT" or Record of Federal Tax Liability section. **We computed the monthly liabilities as follows:**

Joseph's Social Security tax - $1,800.00 X 12.4%=	$ 223.20
Joseph's Medicare Tax - $1,800.00 X 2.9% =	52.20
Rev. Snodgrass' Federal Tax	320.00
Joseph's Federal Tax	178.00
October Total	**$ 773.40**
Joseph's taxable wage - $1,800.00 X 12.4% =	$ 223.20
Joseph's Medicare Tax - $961.54 X 2.9% =	52.20
Rev. Snodgrass' Federal Tax	320.00
Joseph's Federal Tax	178.00
November Total	**$ 773.40**
Joseph's taxable wage - $961.54 X 12.4	$ 223.20
Joseph's Medicare Tax - $961.54 X 2.9% =	52.20
Rev. Snodgrass' Federal Tax	320.00
Joseph's Federal Tax	178.00
December Total	**$ 773.40**

Prepare Quarterly Reports

- **Form 941**

Form 941 is the correct quarterly report to be filed for all not-for-profit organizations that have not filed Form 8274.

LINE 2 will include taxable salaries of both dual-status ministers and lay employees from the extreme left-hand column of the "Payroll Sheets".

LINE 6a will only include taxable salaries (including TSA contributions) of lay employees. In our 1993 example, the employee's withheld social security tax of 6.2% and the employer's matching portion 6.2% is combined for a total tax of 12.4%. The 1994 rate will be the same.

LINE 7 will only include taxable salaries (including TSA contributions) of lay employees. In our 1993 example, the employee's withheld medicare tax of 1.45% and the employer's matching portion 1.45% is combined for a total tax of 2.9%. The 1994 rate will be the same.

LINE 18 undeposited taxes due must be less than $500 or you will be billed up to a 10% penalty for not making a payroll tax deposit at your local bank.

- **Form 941E**

If an existing church filed Form 8274 by October 31, 1984 (a new church by the first date on which a quarterly tax return would be due) and for religious reasons became exempt from withholding and matching social security, they should use Form 941E. Their employees will be liable for paying social security and medicare tax at the combined rate of 15.3% (less adjustments) on their personal Schedule SE for 1993.

LINE 2 will include taxable salaries of both dual-status ministers and lay employees from the extreme left-hand column of the "Payroll Sheet".

LINE 6 does not apply to electing churches. If IRS sends you a bill for medicare tax in error—**Do not pay**! Request that the bill be canceled. (Publication 15, page 21)

LINE 16 undeposited taxes due must be less than $500 or you will be billed up to a 10% penalty for not making a deposit at your local bank.

- **Due Dates for Quarterly Reports**

January, February and March	due on April 30th
April, May and June	due on July 31st
July, August and September	due on October 31st
October, November and December	due on January 31st.

COMPLETED PAYROLL REPORTS 91

- **What To Do If IRS Says 941 Reports Are Not Necessary**
  When a church has only one dual-status employee, there is often no tax liability. When there is no tax liability, there will not be a penalty for not filing the 941 or 941E. IRS computers seem programmed to look at Form 941, line 3, and send a letter to churches without a tax liability. The letter says "since you have no employees, you do not have to file returns" or "since you have no liability, you do not have to file returns." The IRS then stops sending the pre-printed 941's or 941E's. We strongly recommend ignoring the notices, getting blank Form 941's or 941E's and filing them every quarter anyway. Because, we feel that **it is important** that your 941 quarterly reports and the W-2's at year end **reconcile or balance.**

Prepare Year End Reports

The W-3 and Copy A of all the W-2's are to be sent to the Social Security Administration office address given on Form W-3. **They must be typed.** Specific line by line instructions are given in Publication 393 for the preparation of the W-3 and the W-2's. If a box **does not apply,** instructions say to **leave it blank.** A dual-status minister's W-2 **must not** have any entry in **Boxes 3, 4, 5, and 6.** If the figures on the W-3 do not reconcile with the figures that have been reported quarterly on the 941 or 941E, you will receive a computer print-out from the IRS asking why they are different and a billing of tax liability they think you owe.

     Form 941's, Line 2 wages should   = W-2's, Box 1
     Form 941's, Line 3 tax should   = W-2's, Box 2
     Form 941's, Line 6 wages should   = W-2's, Box 3
     Form 941's, Line 6 tax should   = W-2's, Box 4 X 2
     Form 941's, Line 7 wages should   = W-2's, Box 5
     Form 941's, Line 7 tax should   = W-2's, Box 6 X 2 (odd cents okay)

Year-end reports are to be prepared by January 31st. Employees are to be given their W-2 copies by January 31st. You have until February 28th to actually send Copy A of the W-2 to the Social Security Administration. Some employers have given a W-2 to their employee, then failed to send Copy A to the Social Security Administration. **Please send Copy A to the government** so they can cross match it with your employees' returns so failure to file penalties can be avoided!

Box by box instructions for completing Form W-2 are given in Publication 393. We encourage you to read them carefully. We feel it will be helpful to list a few of the entries that are typical for religious workers. Enter appropriate codes using capital letters, leave one space blank after the code and enter the dollar amount on the same line. Use decimal points but not dollar signs or commas.

- Box 13: C 230   ($230 premium for over $50,000 group term life insurance)
           E 1200 ($1,200 elective deferral to 403(b) plan.)
           L 2800 ($3,500 reimbursement for 10,000 miles @ 35¢, enter $700 in Box 1)
           No Entry ($2,800 reimbursement for 10,000 miles @ 28¢)
           No Entry (All reimbursements with accountable plan at IRS rates or actual)
- Box 14: You may use this box for any other information you want to give your employee. Please label each item. Examples are parsonage allowance designated, moving expenses paid, or reminder for employee of an electing church to pay S.S. on Form SE.
- Box 10: Show total amount of dependent care benefits paid or incurred by you for your employee.
- Box 12: Show total value of taxable fringe benefits that are also shown in Box 1 as taxable, such as value of personal use of employer owned auto.

Forms 1099 and Form 1096 for independent contractors whom you paid more than $600 are required to be given to the recipients by January 31 and sent to your IRS Service Center by February 28th.

State Tax Withholding

Call your State Department and ask for materials and instructions for withholding the proper amount of state tax for your employees. Some states require that you withhold state tax for the dual-status minister as well as the lay employee.

Unemployment Taxes

Not-for-profit employers are not subject to Federal Unemployment Taxes. Publication 15, page 21 states this fact. Most states do not require not-for-profit employers to pay state unemployment tax. Consult with your state unemployment office to be sure.

Workmen's Compensation Insurance

Most states require not-for-profit employers to provide Workmen's Compensation Insurance. Consult with an insurance professional in your state to be sure.

Form I-9 - Employment Eligibility Verification

The Immigration Reform and Control Act of 1986 requires all employers to examine the applicant's documents proving identity and eligibility to work in the United States and complete Form I-9 before hiring the applicant. The law says that we cannot hire an alien if we know that the alien is not authorized to work in the U.S. The Form I-9 is not an IRS form and can be obtained from the U.S. Department of Justice, Immigration and Naturalization Service (INS), Washington, D.C. 20402. Fines for non-compliance are from $100 to $1,000 per employee for failure to maintain the necessary paperwork. Fines for hiring illegal aliens are from $250 to $10,000 per individual illegally employed.

How To Correct Information Returns

The IRS provides Form W-2c, Form W-3c and Form 941C as the means of correcting previously filed information returns. It is important to correct returns when you discover a mistake.

Use the following procedure if you had been misinformed concerning the proper information return for the dual-status minister and **had planned to prepare Form 1099**: Employers who have correctly prepared payroll returns for the lay employees, but have omitted the dual-status ministers need to do the following: write **"AMENDED RETURN"** across the top of Form 941 for each quarter affected, include the taxable wages of the dual-status minister on line 2, and write a letter explaining that you failed to include the taxable wages of the dual-status minister on staff on the original returns. Your Form 941's, line 2, will then "balance" with Box 1 of your W-2's.

COMPLETED PAYROLL REPORTS

Chart of Where to Show Income

For a dual-status employee, leave Boxes 3 & 5, W-2 blank. If a dual-status employee is exempt because he has filed Form 4361, then he is to disregard the column for Social Security and write "Exempt—Form 4361" on the self-employment line of Form 1040, Page 2.

Source of Income	*Taxable Income Box 1, W-2	Lay Employee FICA & Medicare Box 3 & 5, W-2	Dual-Status Sch. SE Line 2	Show on Sch. C	Not to be shown anywhere	Deducted on Form 1040
Salary, Dual-status minister	Yes		Yes			
Salary, Lay employee	Yes	Yes				
Professional income				Yes		
Bonus or gift from employer	Yes	Yes	Yes			
Gift from relative, etc.	No	No	No			
Soc. Security paid by employer, dual-status	Yes		Yes			
Qualified moving expense reimbursement	Yes	No	No			Sch. A, Ln. 18
Employer qualified pension—401a, SEP, 403b	No	No	No		Yes	
Premium for $50,000 term life insurance	No	No	No		Yes	
Premium for over $50,000 term life ins.	Yes	Yes	Yes			
Permanent life, employee's beneficiary	Yes	Yes	Yes			
Medical insurance paid by employer	No	No	No		Yes	
Qualified medical reimbursement plan	No	No	No		Yes	
Employee TSA, 403(b) lay employee	No	Yes				
Employee TSA, 403(b) dual-status	No		No			
Employee payments to an IRA						1040, Ln. 24
Self-employed Keogh payments						1040, Ln. 27
Value of home provided, dual-status	No		Yes			
Parsonage Allowance, dual-status	No		Yes			
Value of home provided, lay employee (Sec.119 qualifications met)	No	No				
Value of home provided, lay employee (Sec. 119 qualifications not met)	Yes	Yes				
Auto reimbursement	No	No	No			
Employer provided auto, personal use	Yes	Yes	Yes			
Travel and professional reimbursement	No	No	No			
Expense allowance without adequate accounting to employer	Yes	Yes	Deduct			Sch. A, Ln. 19
Unreimbursed business expenses			Deduct			Sch. A, Ln. 19

*Amounts in this column are to be shown in left-hand column of payroll sheets, line 2 of Form 941/941E, and Box 1 of W-2.

EMPLOYEE'S EARNINGS RECORD

YEAR 199 3

STATUS: MARRIED X SINGLE ___ OTHER ___
NUMBER OF DEPENDENTS: N/A
FEDERAL – NUMBER EXEMPTIONS: N/A
STATE – AMOUNT OF EXEMPTIONS: N/A
DATE OF EMPLOYMENT: ___
DATE TERMINATED: ___

NAME: H. James Snodgrass
ADDRESS: 2309 E. Smith St.
CITY: South Bend **STATE:** IN **ZIP:** 46617
SOC. SEC. No. 423-12-0000

UNORDAINED ☐
ORDAINED ☒
PARSONAGE ___
DESIGNATED $18,000.00

FIRST QUARTER

PAYROLL PERIOD ENDING	*TAXABLE SALARY & ALLOWANCES	PARSONAGE	TOTAL	FEDERAL W/H TAX	SOCIAL SECURITY TAX	MEDICARE TAX	STATE W/H TAX	LOCAL W/H TAX	NET PAY
JAN 3	500.00	750.00	1250.00	160.00			30.00		1060.00
17	500.00	750.00	1250.00	160.00			30.00		1060.00
MO TOTAL	1000.00	1500.00	2500.00	320.00			60.00		2120.00
FEB 7	500.00	750.00	1250.00	160.00			30.00		1060.00
21	500.00	750.00	1250.00	160.00			30.00		1060.00
MO TOTAL	1000.00	1500.00	2500.00	320.00			60.00		2120.00
MAR 7	500.00	750.00	1250.00	160.00			30.00		1060.00
21	500.00	750.00	1250.00	160.00			30.00		1060.00
MO TOTAL	1000.00	1500.00	2500.00	320.00			60.00		2120.00
QUARTERLY TOTAL	3000.00	4500.00	7500.00	960.00			180.00		6360.00
TOTAL TO DATE	3000.00	4500.00	7500.00	960.00			180.00		6360.00

SECOND QUARTER

PAYROLL PERIOD ENDING	*TAXABLE SALARY & ALLOWANCES	PARSONAGE	TOTAL	FEDERAL W/H TAX	SOCIAL SECURITY TAX	MEDICARE TAX	STATE W/H TAX	LOCAL W/H TAX	NET PAY
APRIL 4	500.00	750.00	1250.00	160.00			30.00		1060.00
18	500.00	750.00	1250.00	160.00			30.00		1060.00
MO TOTAL	1000.00	1500.00	2500.00	320.00			60.00		2120.00
MAY 2	500.00	750.00	1250.00	160.00			30.00		1060.00
19	500.00	750.00	1250.00	160.00			30.00		1060.00
MO TOTAL	1000.00	1500.00	2500.00	320.00			60.00		2120.00
JUNE 6	500.00	750.00	1250.00	160.00			30.00		1060.00
19	500.00	750.00	1250.00	160.00			30.00		1060.00
MO TOTAL	1000.00	1500.00	2500.00	320.00			60.00		2120.00
QUARTERLY TOTAL	3000.00	4500.00	7500.00	960.00			180.00		6360.00
TOTAL TO DATE	6000.00	9000.00	15000.00	1920.00			360.00		12720.00

THIRD QUARTER

PAYROLL PERIOD ENDING	*TAXABLE SALARY & ALLOWANCES	PARSONAGE	TOTAL	FEDERAL W/H TAX	SOCIAL SECURITY TAX	MEDICARE TAX	STATE W/H TAX	LOCAL W/H TAX	NET PAY
JULY 4	500.00	750.00	1250.00	160.00			30.00		1060.00
18	500.00	750.00	1250.00	160.00			30.00		1060.00
MO TOTAL	1000.00	1500.00	2500.00	320.00			60.00		2120.00
AUG 8	500.00	750.00	1250.00	160.00			30.00		1060.00
22	500.00	750.00	1250.00	160.00			30.00		1060.00
MO TOTAL	1000.00	1500.00	2500.00	320.00			60.00		2120.00
SEPT 5	500.00	750.00	1250.00	160.00			30.00		1060.00
19	500.00	750.00	1250.00	160.00			30.00		1060.00
MO TOTAL	1000.00	1500.00	2500.00	320.00			60.00		2120.00
QUARTERLY TOTAL	3000.00	4500.00	7500.00	960.00			180.00		6360.00
TOTAL TO DATE	9000.00	13500.00	22500.00	2880.00			540.00		19080.00

FOURTH QUARTER

PAYROLL PERIOD ENDING	*TAXABLE SALARY & ALLOWANCES	PARSONAGE	TOTAL	FEDERAL W/H TAX	SOCIAL SECURITY TAX	MEDICARE TAX	STATE W/H TAX	LOCAL W/H TAX	NET PAY
OCT 3	500.00	750.00	1250.00	160.00			30.00		1060.00
17	500.00	750.00	1250.00	160.00			30.00		1060.00
MO TOTAL	1000.00	1500.00	2500.00	320.00			60.00		2120.00
NOV 7	500.00	750.00	1250.00	160.00			30.00		1060.00
21	500.00	750.00	1250.00	160.00			30.00		1060.00
MO TOTAL	1000.00	1500.00	2500.00	320.00			60.00		2120.00
DEC 5	500.00	750.00	1250.00	160.00			30.00		1060.00
19	500.00	750.00	1250.00	160.00			30.00		1060.00
MO TOTAL	1000.00	1500.00	2500.00	320.00			60.00		2120.00
QUARTERLY TOTAL	3000.00	4500.00	7500.00	960.00			180.00		6360.00
TOTAL TO DATE	12000.00	18000.00	30000.00	3840.00			720.00		25440.00

*Amount to be shown on 941 or W-2. Carefully study chapter six in *Income and Tax Guide for Ministers and Religious Workers*

RECORD OF EMPLOYEE BUSINESS EXPENSE REIMBURSEMENT

Effective 1-1-91

Regulation 1.62-2 (T.D. 8324) requires many employers to modify their reimbursement policies. See Chapter 3 of "Income Tax Guide for Ministers and Religious Workers", 1992 Edition.

DATE PAID	CHECK #	AMOUNT	# OF MILES INCLUDED
2-1	1075	450.02	1342
3-1	1080	564.55	1231
4-1	1085	1328.81	1765
5-1	1093	831.50	1982
6-1	1097	408.17	1638
7-1	1104	430.81	2173
8-1	1110	836.02	2052
9-1	1116	1355.83	2652
10-1	1123	501.17	1227
11-1	1130	676.54	1333
12-1	1137	676.80	2028
1-1	1143	504.75	1317

TOTAL Taxes 04120315

COMPLETED PAYROLL REPORTS

EMPLOYEE'S EARNINGS RECORD
YEAR 199 **3**

STATUS: MARRIED ○ / SINGLE ● / OTHER —
NUMBER OF DEPENDENTS: 0
FEDERAL — NUMBER EXEMPTIONS: 00
STATE — AMOUNT OF EXEMPTIONS: 0
DATE OF EMPLOYMENT: —
DATE TERMINATED: —

NAME: Joseph E. James Mop
ADDRESS: 1621
CITY: South Bend STATE: IN ZIP: 46617
SOC. SEC. No. 403-19-0000

UNORDAINED: X
ORDAINED: —
PARSONAGE: —
DESIGNATED: $ —

FIRST QUARTER

PAYROLL PERIOD ENDING	TAXABLE SALARY & ALLOWANCES	TSA PARSONAGE	TOTAL	FEDERAL W/H TAX	SOCIAL SECURITY TAX	MEDICARE TAX	STATE W/H TAX	LOCAL W/H TAX	NET PAY
JAN 3	850.00	50.00	900.00	89.00	55.80	13.05	30.60		661.55
17	850.00	50.00	900.00	89.00	55.80	13.05	30.60		661.55
MO TOTAL	1700.00	100.00	1800.00	178.00	111.60	26.10	61.20		1323.10
FEB 7	850.00	50.00	900.00	89.00	55.80	13.05	30.60		661.55
21	850.00	50.00	900.00	89.00	55.80	13.05	30.60		661.55
MO TOTAL	1700.00	100.00	1800.00	178.00	111.60	26.10	61.20		1323.10
MAR 7	850.00	50.00	900.00	89.00	55.80	13.05	30.60		661.55
21	850.00	50.00	900.00	89.00	55.80	13.05	30.60		661.55
MO TOTAL	1700.00	100.00	1800.00	178.00	111.60	26.10	61.20		1323.10
QUARTERLY TOTAL TO DATE	5100.00	300.00	5400.00	534.00	334.80	78.30	183.60		3969.30

SECOND QUARTER

PAYROLL PERIOD ENDING	TAXABLE SALARY & ALLOWANCES	TSA	TOTAL	FEDERAL W/H TAX	SOCIAL SECURITY TAX	MEDICARE TAX	STATE W/H TAX	LOCAL W/H TAX	NET PAY
APRIL 4	850.00	50.00	900.00	89.00	55.80	13.05	30.60		661.55
18	850.00	50.00	900.00	89.00	55.80	13.05	30.60		661.55
MO TOTAL	1700.00	100.00	1800.00	178.00	111.60	26.10	61.20		1323.10
MAY 2	850.00	50.00	900.00	89.00	55.80	13.05	30.60		661.55
16	850.00	50.00	900.00	89.00	55.80	13.05	30.60		661.55
MO TOTAL	1700.00	100.00	1800.00	178.00	111.60	26.10	61.20		1323.10
JUNE 9	850.00	50.00	900.00	89.00	55.80	13.05	30.60		661.55
20	850.00	50.00	900.00	89.00	55.80	13.05	30.60		661.55
MO TOTAL	1700.00	100.00	1800.00	178.00	111.60	26.10	61.20		1323.10
QUARTERLY TOTAL	5100.00	300.00	5400.00	534.00	334.80	78.30	183.60		3969.30
TOTAL TO DATE	10200.00	600.00	10800.00	1068.00	669.60	156.60	367.20		7938.60

THIRD QUARTER

PAYROLL PERIOD ENDING	TAXABLE SALARY & ALLOWANCES	TSA	TOTAL	FEDERAL W/H TAX	SOCIAL SECURITY TAX	MEDICARE TAX	STATE W/H TAX	LOCAL W/H TAX	NET PAY
JULY 4	850.00	50.00	900.00	89.00	55.80	13.05	30.60		661.55
18	850.00	50.00	900.00	89.00	55.80	13.05	30.60		661.55
MO TOTAL	1700.00	100.00	1800.00	178.00	111.60	26.10	61.20		1323.10
AUG 22	850.00	50.00	900.00	89.00	55.80	13.05	30.60		661.55
	850.00	50.00	900.00	89.00	55.80	13.05	30.60		661.55
MO TOTAL	1700.00	100.00	1800.00	178.00	111.60	26.10	61.20		1323.10
SEPT 5	850.00	50.00	900.00	89.00	55.80	13.05	30.60		661.55
19	850.00	50.00	900.00	89.00	55.80	13.05	30.60		661.55
MO TOTAL	1700.00	100.00	1800.00	178.00	111.60	26.10	61.20		1323.10
QUARTERLY TOTAL	5100.00	300.00	5400.00	534.00	334.80	78.30	183.60		3969.30
TOTAL TO DATE	15300.00	900.00	16200.00	1602.00	1004.40	234.90	550.80		11907.90

FOURTH QUARTER

PAYROLL PERIOD ENDING	TAXABLE SALARY & ALLOWANCES	TSA	TOTAL	FEDERAL W/H TAX	SOCIAL SECURITY TAX	MEDICARE TAX	STATE W/H TAX	LOCAL W/H TAX	NET PAY
OCT 3	850.00	50.00	900.00	89.00	55.80	13.05	30.60		661.55
17	850.00	50.00	900.00	89.00	55.80	13.05	30.60		661.55
MO TOTAL	1700.00	100.00	1800.00	178.00	111.60	26.10	61.20		1323.10
NOV 7	850.00	50.00	900.00	89.00	55.80	13.05	30.60		661.55
21	850.00	50.00	900.00	89.00	55.80	13.05	30.60		661.55
MO TOTAL	1700.00	100.00	1800.00	178.00	111.60	26.10	61.20		1323.10
DEC 5	850.00	50.00	900.00	89.00	55.80	13.05	30.60		661.55
19	850.00	50.00	900.00	89.00	55.80	13.05	30.60		661.55
MO TOTAL	1700.00	100.00	1800.00	178.00	111.60	26.10	61.20		1323.10
QUARTERLY TOTAL	5100.00	300.00	5400.00	534.00	334.80	78.30	183.60		3969.30
TOTAL TO DATE	20400.00	1200.00	21600.00	2136.00	1339.20	313.20	734.40		15877.20

RECORD OF EMPLOYEE BUSINESS EXPENSE REIMBURSEMENT
Effective 1-1-91

Regulation 1.62-2 (T.D. 8324) requires many employers to modify their reimbursement policies. See Chapter 3 of "Income Tax Guide for Ministers and Religious Workers", 1992 Edition.

DATE PAID	CHECK #	AMOUNT	# OF MILES INCLUDED
2-1	1076	89.46	210
3-1	1081	84.12	229
4-1	1088	87.88	199
5-1	1094	68.12	174
6-1	1098	90.84	254
7-1	1105	103.44	298
8-1	1111	97.71	254
9-1	1117	53.60	120
10-1	1124	71.52	184
11-1	1131	77.16	145
12-1	1138	65.54	139
1-1	1144	58.12	139
TOTAL		**947.00**	**2125**

Form 941 — Employer's Quarterly Federal Tax Return

USE THIS FORM IF YOU DID NOT FILE FORM 8274

Form **941** (Rev. January 1993)
Department of the Treasury — Internal Revenue Service

► See separate instructions for information on completing this form.
Please type or print.

Enter state code for state in which deposits made ► **IN** (see page 2 of instructions).

Name: **Mission Community Church**
Date quarter ended: **12-31-93**
Employer identification number: **35-2938279**
Address: **1620 E. Jones St.**
City, state, ZIP: **South Bend, IN 46617**

OMB No. 1545-0029 Expires 1-31-96

1. Number of employees (except household) employed in the pay period that includes March 12th ► **2**
2. Total wages and tips subject to withholding, plus other compensation ... **8,100.00**
3. Total income tax withheld from wages, tips, pensions, annuities, sick pay, gambling, etc. ... **1,494.00**
4. Adjustment of withheld income tax for preceding quarters of calendar year (see instructions) ...
5. Adjusted total of income tax withheld (line 3 as adjusted by line 4—see instructions) ... **1,494.00**
6a. Taxable social security wages ... $ **5,400.00** × 12.4% (.124) = **669.60**
6b. Taxable social security tips ... $ × 12.4% (.124) =
7. Taxable Medicare wages and tips ... $ **5,400.00** × 2.9% (.029) = **156.60**
8. Total social security and Medicare taxes (add lines 6a, 6b, and 7) ... **826.20**
9. Adjustment of social security and Medicare taxes (see instructions for required explanation) ...
10. Adjusted total of social security and Medicare taxes (line 8 as adjusted by line 9—see instructions) ... **826.60**
11. Backup withholding (see instructions) ...
12. Adjustment of backup withholding tax for preceding quarters of calendar year ...
13. Adjusted total of backup withholding (line 11 as adjusted by line 12) ...
14. **Total taxes** (add lines 5, 10, and 13) ... **2,320.20**
15. Advance earned income credit (EIC) payments made to employees, if any ...
16. Net taxes (subtract line 15 from line 14). This should equal line 20, col. (d), below or line D of Schedule B (plus line D of Schedule A if you treated backup withholding as a separate liability) ... **2,320.20**
17. Total deposits for quarter, including overpayment applied from a prior quarter, from your records ... **2,320.20**
18. Balance due (subtract line 17 from line 16). This should be less than $500. Pay to the Internal Revenue Service ... **0**
19. Overpayment, if line 17 is more than line 16, enter excess here ► $ _____ and check if to be: ☐ Applied to next return OR ☐ Refunded.
20. **Monthly Summary of Federal Tax Liability.** If line 16 is less than $500, you need not complete line 20. If you are a monthly depositor, summarize your monthly tax liability below. If you are a semiweekly depositor or have accumulated a tax liability of $100,000 or more on any day, attach Schedule B (Form 941) and check here (see instructions) ... ►☐

	(a) First month	(b) Second month	(c) Third month	(d) Total for quarter
Liability for month	773.40	773.40	773.40	2,320.20

Sign Here — Under penalties of perjury, I declare that I have examined this return, including accompanying schedules and statements, and to the best of my knowledge and belief, it is true, correct, and complete.

Signature ► _____ Print Your Name and Title ► _____ Date ► _____

For Paperwork Reduction Act Notice, see page 1 of separate instructions. Cat. No. 17001Z Form **941** (Rev. 1-93)

Form W-3 Transmittal of Wage and Tax Statements 1993

DO NOT STAPLE

a. Control number: **33333** For Official Use Only ► OMB No. 1545-0008

b. Kind of Payer: 941/941E ☒ Military ☐ 943 ☐ CT-1 ☐ 942 ☐ Medicare govt. emp. ☐

c. Total number of statements: _____
d. Establishment number: _____
e. Employer's identification number: **35-2938279**
f. Employer's name: **Mission Community Church**
g. Employer's address and ZIP code: **1620 E Jones St, South Bend, IN 46617**
h. Other EIN used this year: _____
i. Employer's state I.D. No.: _____

1. Wages, tips, other compensation: **32,400.00**
2. Federal income tax withheld: **5,976.00**
3. Social security wages: **21,600.00**
4. Social security tax withheld: **1,339.20**
5. Medicare wages and tips: **21,600.00**
6. Medicare tax withheld: **313.20**
7. Social security tips:
8. Allocated tips:
9. Advance EIC payments:
10. Dependent care benefits:
11. Nonqualified plans:
12. Deferred compensation: **3,600.00**
13. Adjusted total social security wages and tips:
14. Adjusted total Medicare wages and tips:
15. Income tax withheld by third-party payer:

Under penalties of perjury, I declare that I have examined this return and accompanying documents, and, to the best of my knowledge and belief, they are true, correct, and complete.

Signature ► _____ Title ► _____ Date ► _____
Telephone number ( ) _____

Form **W-3 Transmittal of Wage and Tax Statements 1993**
Department of the Treasury — Internal Revenue Service

COMPLETED PAYROLL REPORTS

W-2 Wage and Tax Statement 1993 (Copy A For Social Security Administration)

Box	Field	Value
a	Control number	22222
b	Employer's identification number	35-2938279
c	Employer's name, address, and ZIP code	Mission Community Church, 1620 E. Jones St., South Bend, IN 46617
d	Employee's social security number	483-12-0000
e	Employee's name	H. James Snodgrass
	Address	2309 E. Smith St., South Bend, IN 46617
1	Wages, tips, other compensation	12,000.00
2	Federal income tax withheld	3,840.00
13	See Instrs. for Box 13	E 2,400.00
14	Other	Ordained - Not included above $18,000 Parsonage Allowance
15	Pension plan	X
	Deferred compensation	X
16	Employer's state I.D. No.	IN
17	State wages, tips, etc.	12,000.00
18	State income tax	720.00
19	Locality name	St. Joe
20	Local wages, tips, etc.	12,000.00

Cat. No. 10134D — Department of the Treasury—Internal Revenue Service
OMB No. 1545-0008

Do NOT Cut or Separate Forms on This Page

W-2 Wage and Tax Statement 1993 (Copy A For Social Security Administration)

Box	Field	Value
a	Control number	22222
b	Employer's identification number	35-2928279
c	Employer's name, address, and ZIP code	Mission Community Church, 1620 E. Jones St., South Bend, IN 46617
d	Employee's social security number	403-19-0000
e	Employee's name	Joseph Mop
	Address	1621 E. Jones St., South Bend, IN 46617
1	Wages, tips, other compensation	20,400.00
2	Federal income tax withheld	2,136.00
3	Social security wages	21,600.00
4	Social security tax withheld	1,339.20
5	Medicare wages and tips	21,600.00
6	Medicare tax withheld	313.20
13	See Instrs. for Box 13	E 1,200.00
15	Pension plan	X
	Deferred compensation	X
16	Employer's state I.D. No.	IN
17	State wages, tips, etc.	20,400.00
18	State income tax	734.40
19	Locality name	St. Joe
20	Local wages, tips, etc.	20,400.00

Cat. No. 10134D — Department of the Treasury—Internal Revenue Service
OMB No. 1545-0008

Chapter Six

375 2-93

Form 941E
(Rev. January 1993)
Department of the Treasury
Internal Revenue Service

USE THIS FORM IF YOU HAVE FILED FORM 8274
Quarterly Return of Withheld Federal Income Tax and Medicare Tax
► See Circular E for more information concerning employment tax returns.

OMB No. 1545-0029
Expires 1-31-96

Enter state code for state in which deposits made. ► T N (see page 4 of instructions).

Name: Mission Community Church
Address (number and street): 1620 E. Jones St.
City, state, and ZIP code: South Bend, IN 46617
Date quarter ended: 12-31-93
Employer identification number: 35-2938279

T	
FF	
FD	
FP	
I	
T	

If address is different from prior return, check here ►

IRS Use

1 1 1 1 1 1 1 1 2 3 3 3 3 3 3 4
5 5 5 6 7 8 8 8 8 8 8 9 9 10 10 10 10 10 10 10 10

If you do not have to file returns in the future, check here ► ☐ Date final wages paid ►
If you are an intermittent filer, see **Intermittent filers** on page 2 and check here ► ☐

Complete for First Quarter Only

1 Number of employees (except household) employed in the pay period that includes March 12th .... ► | 1 | |

			2	
2	Total wages and tips subject to withholding, plus other compensation		2	8,100 00
3	Total income tax withheld from wages, tips, pensions, annuities, sick pay, gambling, etc.		3	1,494 00
4	Adjustment of withheld income tax for preceding quarters of calendar year (see instructions)		4	
5	Adjusted total of income tax withheld (line 3 as adjusted by line 4)		5	1,494 00
6	Taxable Medicare wages paid .... $ _____ × 2.9% (.029)		6	
7	Adjustment of Medicare tax		7	
8	Adjusted total of Medicare tax (line 6 as adjusted by line 7)		8	
9	Backup withholding		9	
10	Adjustment of backup withholding for preceding quarters of calendar year		10	
11	Adjusted total of backup withholding (line 9 as adjusted by line 10)		11	
12	**Total taxes** (add lines 5, 8, and 11)		12	1,494 00
13	Advance earned income credit (EIC) payments made to employees, if any (see instructions)		13	
14	Net taxes (subtract line 13 from line 12). **This should equal line 18, column (d), below or line D of Schedule B (Form 941)** (plus line D of Schedule A (Form 941) if you have treated backup withholding as a separate liability)		14	1,494 00
15	**Total deposits** for quarter, including overpayment applied from prior quarter, from your records		15	1,494 00
16	**Balance due** (subtract line 15 from line 14). This should be less than $500. Pay to Internal Revenue Service		16	0 00
17	**Overpayment**, if line 15 is more than line 14, enter excess here ► $ _____ and check if to be: ☐ Applied to next return OR ☐ Refunded			

18 **Monthly Summary of Federal Tax Liability.** If line 14 is less than $500, you need not complete line 18. If you are a monthly depositor, summarize your monthly tax liability below. If you are a semiweekly depositor or have accumulated a tax liability of $100,000 or more on any day, attach Schedule B (Form 941) and check here (see instructions) .... ► ☐

Liability for month	(a) First month	(b) Second month	(c) Third month	(d) Total for quarter
	498.00	498.00	498.00	1,494.00

Sign Here
Under penalties of perjury, I declare that I have examined this return, including accompanying schedules and statements, and to the best of my knowledge and belief, it is true, correct, and complete.
Signature ►   Print Name and Title ►   Date ►

For Paperwork Reduction Act Notice, see page 2.   Cat. No. 17011V   Form **941E** (Rev. 1-93)

DO NOT STAPLE

a Control number	33333	For Official Use Only ► OMB No. 1545-0008		
b Kind of Payer	941/941E [X] Military ☐ 943 ☐ CT-1 ☐ 942 ☐ Medicare govt. emp. ☐		1 Wages, tips, other compensation 32,400.00	2 Federal income tax withheld 5,976.00
			3 Social security wages	4 Social security tax withheld
c Total number of statements 2	**d** Establishment number		5 Medicare wages and tips	6 Medicare tax withheld
	e Employer's identification number 35-2938279		7 Social security tips	8 Allocated tips
f Employer's name Mission Community Church 1620 E. Jones St. South Bend, IN 46617			9 Advance EIC payments	10 Dependent care benefits
			11 Nonqualified plans	12 Deferred compensation E 3,600.00
			13 Adjusted total social security wages and tips	
			14 Adjusted total Medicare wages and tips	
g Employer's address and ZIP code				
h Other EIN used this year			15 Income tax withheld by third-party payer	
i Employer's state I.D. No.				

Under penalties of perjury, I declare that I have examined this return and accompanying documents, and, to the best of my knowledge and belief, they are true, correct, and complete.

Signature ►   Title ►   Date ►
Telephone number ( )

Form **W-3 Transmittal of Wage and Tax Statements 1993**   Department of the Treasury Internal Revenue Service

COMPLETED PAYROLL REPORTS

Form W-2 Wage and Tax Statement 1993 — Copy A For Social Security Administration

Box	Field	Value
a	Control number	22222
	Void / For Official Use Only	□
b	Employer's identification number	35-2938279
c	Employer's name, address, and ZIP code	Mission Community Church, 1620 E. Jones St., South Bend, IN 46617
d	Employee's social security number	483-12-0000
e	Employee's name (first, middle initial, last)	H. James Snodgrass
	Employee address	2309 E. Smith St., South Bend, IN 46617
1	Wages, tips, other compensation	12,000.00
2	Federal income tax withheld	3,840.00
3	Social security wages	
4	Social security tax withheld	
5	Medicare wages and tips	
6	Medicare tax withheld	
7	Social security tips	
8	Allocated tips	
9	Advance EIC payment	
10	Dependent care benefits	
11	Nonqualified plans	
12	Benefits included in Box 1	
13	See Instrs. for Box 13	E 2,400.00
14	Other	Ordained - Not included above $18,000 Parsonage Allowance
15	Statutory employee / Deceased / Pension plan / Legal rep / 942 emp / Subtotal / Deferred compensation	Pension plan: X; Deferred compensation: X
16	State	IN
	Employer's state I.D. No.	
17	State wages, tips, etc.	12,000.00
18	State income tax	720.00
19	Locality name	St. Joe
20	Local wages, tips, etc.	12,000.00
21	Local income tax	

Cat. No. 10134D — Department of the Treasury—Internal Revenue Service

For Paperwork Reduction Act Notice, see separate instructions.
OMB No. 1545-0008

Do NOT Cut or Separate Forms on This Page

Form W-2 Wage and Tax Statement 1993 — Copy A For Social Security Administration

Box	Field	Value
a	Control number	22222
	Void / For Official Use Only	□
b	Employer's identification number	35-2938279
c	Employer's name, address, and ZIP code	Mission Community Church, 1620 E. Jones St., South Bend, IN 46617
d	Employee's social security number	403-19-0000
e	Employee's name (first, middle initial, last)	Joseph Mop
	Employee address	1621 E. Jones St., South Bend, IN 46617
1	Wages, tips, other compensation	20,400.00
2	Federal income tax withheld	2,136.00
3	Social security wages	
4	Social security tax withheld	
5	Medicare wages and tips	
6	Medicare tax withheld	
7	Social security tips	
8	Allocated tips	
9	Advance EIC payment	
10	Dependent care benefits	
11	Nonqualified plans	
12	Benefits included in Box 1	
13	See Instrs. for Box 13	E 1,200.00
14	Other	Electing Church employee to pay S.S. on S.E.
15	Statutory employee / Deceased / Pension plan / Legal rep / 942 emp / Subtotal / Deferred compensation	Pension plan: X; Deferred compensation: X
16	State	IN
	Employer's state I.D. No.	
17	State wages, tips, etc.	20,400.00
18	State income tax	734.40
19	Locality name	St. Joe
20	Local wages, tips, etc.	20,400.00
21	Local income tax	

Cat. No. 10134D — Department of the Treasury—Internal Revenue Service

For Paperwork Reduction Act Notice, see separate instructions.
OMB No. 1545-0008

CHAPTER SEVEN

COMPLETED INCOME TAX RETURN

A typical problem with the actual tax forms filled out seems to be the most practical way to further explain the tax law as it applies to the minister. So study the following information about Rev. Snodgrass and how it is to be shown on the tax forms.

To illustrate that $739.00 difference in tax liability resulted from Rev. Snodgrass having an accountable reimbursment plan, we have prepared his return both ways. The proration of unreimbursed employee business expenses, according to the Dalan Case is also illustrated. His W-2 would show $21,264 without reimbursement, and as shown in Chapter Six, $12,000 with reimbursement.

Facts of the Problem

Rev. H. James Snodgrass and Mary T., live at 2309 E. Smith St., South Bend, Indiana 46617. Rev. Snodgrass' S.S.# is 483-12-0000; Mary's S.S.# is 483-15-0000. They have three children, Ruth, Thomas and Samuel.

Rev. Snodgrass is pastor of Mission Community Church and Mrs. Snodgrass is a nurse at a local hospital. Mary's wage on her W-2 is $35,278 with $4,008 federal tax withheld, $2,187 social security tax, $512 medicare tax and $728 State tax withheld. Combine his salary of $12,000/$21,264 and her salary of $35,278 on line 7, Form 1040.

During the year Rev. Snodgrass received $690 professional income from weddings and funerals. In earning this income, Rev. Snodgrass spent $115 for booklets & $10 for Sch C tax prep fee.

The Snodgrasses own their own home (purchased 6-10-86) and they make payments of $743 a month. Their interest was $8,081 and principal payments were $835. Real estate taxes were $1,182. Insurance was $340, and repairs were $793. They bought a new couch & chair for $849, and a new TV & VCR for $560. Decorator items (oval rug for living room) cost $463. Utilities and personal phone were $2,738. Miscellaneous household expenses Mary kept a record of came to $642.

Professional expenses are as follows: Tuition for class at seminary $345, Office Supplies $86, Religious Materials $327, Subscriptions $132, Home entertainment meals $381. He purchased $649 worth of books this year and also bought a fax machine for $529. Rev. Snodgrass was reimbursed for the depreciation factor ($236) for prior year purchases and chose Sec. 179 expensing for this year's purchases. Travel expenses are as follows: Lodging $363, Meals away from home $256, Tips for meals $48, Cleaning while away from home $22. Local transportation expenses are as follows: Parking $11, Tolls $34. The total year's reimbursement for professional and travel expenses was $3,419 as shown on the payroll sheet.

Business auto mileage from his log book was 20,879 miles. Total miles driven for the year was 26,945. The church reimbursed mileage allowance of 28¢ a mile during the year for a total of $5,846. Actual expenses amount to less than 28¢ per mile for reimbursement. The return showing non-reimbursed expenses shows the actual expenses for each auto on "Worksheet for Form 2106." Without reimbursement, vehicle #1 is computed by actual method as required, and vehicle #2 is computed by optional which is slightly better. Details of their auto trade are shown on the "Auto Basis Worksheets."

Itemized deductions are as follows: Medical expenses were not greater than 7.5% of AGI. Additional State tax last spring of $152, Real Estate Tax is used again $1,182, personal property tax on the family auto of $78, personal property tax of $456 on vehicle #2 must be deducted on Sch A as taxes. He can no longer use auto interest of $639 on Sch A (vehicle #1 $158 & vehicle #2 $481). Interest on home is used again $8,081. Personal interest of $753 can not be used. Contributions were to Mission Community Church $5,308, Central Bible College $200. Tax Return preparation fee $185 (in addition to $10 for Sch C above), Nursing license $135, Uniforms, shoes, nylons and cost of cleaning them $375.

Due to the fact a minister is self-employed for social security purposes, we are able to use the business % of personal property tax, auto interest and business portion of tax preparation fee as a reduction of S.S. base.

Study the completed forms on the following pages to see how the Snodgrass return is prepared.

COMPLETED INCOME TAX RETURN

Form 1040 — U.S. Individual Income Tax Return 1993

Label: H. James Snodgrass / Mary T. Snodgrass
2309 E. Smith St.
South Bend, IN 46617

Your social security number: 483 12 0000
Spouse's social security number: 483 15 0000

Presidential Election Campaign: Do you want $3 to go to this fund? — Yes (X for you, X for spouse)

Filing Status
2. [X] Married filing joint return

Exemptions
6a. [X] Yourself
6b. [X] Spouse
6c. Dependents:
- Ruth A. Snodgrass — Daughter — 483 13 0000 — age under 1 — 12 months
- Thomas A. Snodgrass — Son — 485 14 0000 — 12
- Samuel A. Snodgrass — Son — 486 15 0000 — 12

No. of children on 6c who lived with you: 3
Total number of exemptions claimed: 5

Income
7. Wages, salaries, tips, etc. (W-2): 21,264. + 35,278 = 56,542
8a. Taxable interest income: 9
10. Taxable refunds: 565
22. **Total income**: 58,624

Adjustments to Income
28. Alimony paid. Recipient's SSN ▶ xxxxx Parsonale, A.: 2,125
30. Add lines 24a through 29: 2,125
31. **Adjusted Gross Income**: 56,499

Page 2

32. Amount from line 31 (adjusted gross income): 56,499
34. Itemized / standard deduction: 21,591
35. Subtract line 34 from line 32: 34,908
36. Exemptions: 11,750
37. Taxable income. Subtract line 36 from line 35: 23,158
38. Tax: 3,476
40. Add lines 38 and 39: 3,476
45. Total credits: 0
46. Subtract line 45 from line 40: 3,476
47. Self-employment tax. Attach Schedule SE: 4,250
53. Add lines 46 through 52. This is your **total tax**: 7,726
54. Federal income tax withheld from Forms W-2 and 1099: 7,848
60. Add lines 54 through 59. These are your **total payments**: 7,848
61. If line 60 is more than line 53, subtract line 53 from line 60. This is the amount you **OVERPAID**: 122
62. Amount of line 61 you want **REFUNDED TO YOU**: 122

Sign Here
Your occupation: Minister
Spouse's occupation: Nurse

Schedule C-EZ (Form 1040) — Net Profit From Business

WITHOUT REIMBURSEMENT

Name of proprietor: H. James Snodgrass
Social security number (SSN): 483 12 0000
B Enter principal business code: 8 1 7 1 1
D Employer ID number (EIN): none

Part I — General Information

You May Use This Form If You:
- Had gross receipts from your business of $25,000 or less.
- Had business expenses of $2,000 or less.
- Use the cash method of accounting.
- Did not have an inventory at any time during the year.
- Did not have a net loss from your business.
- Had only one business as a sole proprietor.

And You:
- Had no employees during the year.
- Are not required to file Form 4562, Depreciation and Amortization, for this business. See the instructions for Schedule C, line 13, on page C-3 to find out if you must file.
- Do not deduct expenses for business use of your home.
- Do not have prior year unallowed passive activity losses from this business.

A Principal business or profession, including product or service: Honorariums
C Business name. If no separate business name, leave blank.
E Business address (including suite or room no.). Address not required if same as on Form 1040, page 1.
City, town or post office, state, and ZIP code

Part II — Figure Your Net Profit

1 Gross receipts. 1 690
2 Total expenses. 2 125
3 Net profit. Subtract line 2 from line 1. .... 3 565

Part III — Information on Your Vehicle.

4 When did you place your vehicle in service for business purposes? (month, day, year)
5 Of the total number of miles you drove your vehicle during 1993, enter the number of miles you used your vehicle for:
a Business ____ b Commuting ____ c Other ____
6 Do you (or your spouse) have another vehicle available for personal use? ☐ Yes ☐ No
7 Was your vehicle available for use during off-duty hours? ☐ Yes ☐ No
8a Do you have evidence to support your deduction? ☐ Yes ☐ No
b If "Yes," is the evidence written? ☐ Yes ☐ No

Schedules A&B (Form 1040) — Schedule A — Itemized Deductions

WITHOUT REIMBURSEMENT

Name(s) shown on Form 1040: H. James & Mary T. Snodgrass
Your social security number: 483 12 0000

Medical and Dental Expenses	1	Medical and dental expenses		
	2	Enter amount from Form 1040, line 32: L 2		
	3	Multiply line 2 above by 7.5% (.075)		0
	4	Subtract line 3 from line 1		
Taxes You Paid	5	State and local income taxes 728+152+720	1,600	
	6	Real estate taxes	1,182	
	7	Other taxes — personal property taxes Auto P.P. 78 + 456	534	
	8	Add lines 5 through 7		3,316
Interest You Paid	9a	Home mortgage interest and points reported on Form 1098	8,081	
	9b	Home mortgage interest not reported on Form 1098		
	10	Points not reported to you on Form 1098		
	11	Investment interest. Attach Form 4952		
	12	Add lines 9a through 11		8,081
Gifts to Charity	13	Contributions by cash or check	5,508	
	14	Other than by cash or check. If over $500, attach Form 8283		
	15	Carryover from prior year		
	16	Add lines 13 through 15		5,508
Casualty and Theft Losses	17	Casualty or theft loss(es). Attach Form 4684		
Moving Expenses	18	Moving expenses. Attach Form 3903 or 3903-F		
Job Expenses and Most Other Miscellaneous Deductions	19	Unreimbursed employee expenses — job travel, union dues, job education, etc. MUST attach Form 2106.	8,826	
	20	Other expenses — investment, tax preparation, safe deposit box, etc. List type and amount. See explanation at bottom	(3,010)	
	21	Add lines 19 and 20	5,816	
	22	Enter amount from Form 1040, line 32: [22] 56,492		
	23	Multiply line 22 above by 2% (.02)	1,130	
	24	Subtract line 23 from line 21		4,686
Other Miscellaneous Deductions	25	Other — from list on page A-5		
Total Itemized Deductions	26	Is the amount on Form 1040, line 32, more than $108,450		21,591

Ln. 20 — Tax Prep-185;(W)Nusing License & Uniforms-510
IRC 265 Limitation-(3,705)

COMPLETED INCOME TAX RETURN

Form 2106 (1993) — Page 2

Part II — Vehicle Expenses (See instructions to find out which sections to complete.)

Section A.—General Information

		(a) Vehicle 1	(b) Vehicle 2
12	Enter the date vehicle was placed in service	1/06/90	3/10/93
13	Total miles vehicle was driven during 1993	6,630 miles	20,315 miles
14	Business miles included on line 13	5,320 miles	15,559 miles
15	Percent of business use. Divide line 14 by line 13	80.24 %	76.59 %
16	Average daily round trip commuting distance	8 miles	8 miles
17	Commuting miles included on line 13	320 miles	2,176 miles
18	Other personal miles. Add lines 14 and 17 and subtract the total from line 13	990 miles	2,580 miles
19	Do you (or your spouse) have another vehicle available for personal purposes?	☒ Yes ☐ No	☒ Yes ☐ No
20	If your employer provided you with a vehicle, is personal use during off duty hours permitted? ☐ Yes ☐ No ☒ Not applicable		
21a	Do you have evidence to support your deduction?	☒ Yes ☐ No	☒ Yes ☐ No
21b	If "Yes," is the evidence written?	☒ Yes ☐ No	☒ Yes ☐ No

Section B.—Standard Mileage Rate (Use this section only if you own the vehicle.)

22	Multiply line 14 by 28¢ (.28). Enter the result here and on line 1. (Rural mail carriers, see instructions.)	22 4,357

Section C.—Actual Expenses

		(a) Vehicle 1	(b) Vehicle 2
23	Gasoline, oil, repairs, vehicle insurance, etc.	799	
24a	Vehicle rentals	0	
24b	Inclusion amount (see instructions)	0	
24c	Subtract line 24b from line 24a		
25	Value of employer-provided vehicle (applies only if 100% of annual lease value was included on Form W-2—see instructions)	799	
26	Add lines 23, 24c, and 25	641	
27	Multiply line 26 by the percentage on line 15	546	
28	Depreciation. Enter amount from line 38 below		
29	Add lines 27 and 28. Enter total here and on line 1.	1,187	

Section D.—Depreciation of Vehicles (Use this section only if you own the vehicle.)

		(a) Vehicle 1	(b) Vehicle 2
30	Enter cost or other basis (see instructions)	* 11,821	
31	Enter amount of section 179 deduction (see instructions)	0	
32	Multiply line 30 by line 15 (see instructions) If you elected the section 179 deduction	9,485	
33	Enter depreciation method and percentage (see instructions)	DDB 11.52	
34	Multiply line 32 by the percentage on line 33 (see instructions)	546	
35	Add lines 31 and 34	546	
36	Enter the limitation amount from the table in the line 36 instructions	1,475	
37	Multiply line 36 by the percentage on line 15		** 592
38	Enter the smaller of line 35 or line 37. Also, enter this amount on line 28 above	546	

* Line 30-Basis is determined by using line G from Auto Worksheet 9485 ÷ 80.2%
** Line 37 - 1184 ÷ ½ = 592 Year of sale limitation

Form 2106 — Department of the Treasury, Internal Revenue Service
OMB No. 1545-0139
Attachment Sequence No. 54
1993

Employee Business Expenses
► Attach to Form 1040.
► See separate instructions.

Your name: **H. James Snodgrass**
Social security number: **483:12:0000**
Occupation in which expenses were incurred: **Minister**

Part I — Employee Business Expenses and Reimbursements

STEP 1 — Enter Your Expenses

		Column A — Other Than Meals and Entertainment	Column B — Meals and Entertainment
1	Vehicle expense from line 22 or line 29	5,544	
2	Parking fees, tolls, and transportation, including train, bus, etc., that did not involve overnight travel	45	
3	Travel expense while away from home overnight, including lodging, airplane, car rental, etc. Do not include meals and entertainment	385	
4	Business expenses not included on lines 1 through 3. Do not include meals and entertainment	2,304	
5	Meals and entertainment expenses (see instructions)		685
6	Total expenses. In Column A, add lines 1 through 4 and enter the result. In Column B, enter the amount from line 5	8,278	685

Note: *If you were not reimbursed for any expenses in Step 1, skip line 7 and enter the amount from line 6 on line 8.*

STEP 2 — Enter Amounts Your Employer Gave You for Expenses Listed in STEP 1

7	Enter amounts your employer gave you that were not reported to you in box 1 of Form W-2. Include any amount reported under code "L" in box 13 of your Form W-2 (see instructions)		

STEP 3 — Figure Expenses To Deduct on Schedule A (Form 1040)

8	Subtract line 7 from line 6	8,278	685
	Note: *If both columns of line 8 are zero, stop here. If Column A is less than zero, report the amount as income on Form 1040, line 7, and enter -0- on line 10, Column A.*		
9	Enter 20% (.20) of line 8, Column B		137
10	In Column A, enter the amount from line 8. In Column B, subtract line 9 from line 8	8,278	548
11	Add the amounts on line 10 of both columns and enter the total here. Also, enter the total on Schedule A (Form 1040), line 19. (Qualified performing artists and individuals with disabilities, see the instructions for special rules on where to enter the total.) ►		8,826

For Paperwork Reduction Act Notice, see instructions. Cat. No. 11700N Form **2106** (1993)

WORKSHEET TO BE USED WITH FORM 2106
WITHOUT REIMBURSEMENT

Taxable Year: 1993

Your Name: H. James Snodgrass
Social Security Number: 483-12-0000
Occupation in which expenses were incurred: Minister

[X] Ordained [ ] Licensed [ ] Commissioned [ ] Other   Filed Form 4361? [ ] Yes [X] No

ACTUAL AUTO EXPENSES
(Complete Form 2106, Part II, Sec. A & B first)

	Vehicle 1	Vehicle 2
1. Garage rent		
2. Gas	300	1,339
3. Oil & lubrication	30	76
4. Repairs	200	242
5. Tires & batteries	84	
6. Insurance & auto club	161	389
7. License		13
8. Washing and polishing	24	120
9. Other		
10. TOTAL	799	2,179

(enter on Form 2106, Part II Section C, Line 23)

LOCAL TRAVEL EXPENSES

11. Parking 11
12. Tolls 34
13. Fares ....
14. **TOTAL** 45

(enter on Form 2106, Part I, line 2)

OVERNIGHT TRAVEL EXPENSES

15. Auto rental, taxi, etc. ....
16. Fares (air, train, bus) ....
17. Parking & tolls ....
18. Laundry & cleaning 22
19. Lodging 363
20. Telephone, telegraph, postage ..
21. Tips other than meals ....
22. **TOTAL** 385

(enter on Form 2106, Part I, line 3)

PROFESSIONAL EXPENSES (UNREIMBURSED)

23. Business-in-home (see attached) ..
24. Education expense 345
25. Equipment depreciation (see attached) .. 1,414
26. Office supplies and postage 86
27. Religious materials 327
28. Sales aids ....
29. Seminars and dues ....
30. Subscriptions and paperbacks .. 132
31. Telephone ....
32. Other ....
33. **TOTAL** 2,304

(enter on Form 2106, Part I, line 4)

MEALS AND ENTERTAINMENT

1. Meals while away from home 256
   [ ] Actual [ ] Optional
2. Entertainment, meals 381
3. Entertainment, other ....
4. Tips for meals 48
5. **TOTAL** 685

(enter on Form 2106, Part I, line 5)

COMPUTATION OF PARSONAGE ALLOWANCE

Date of purchase: 6/10/86
FMV of home you own: $115,000

	A PROVIDED BY CHURCH	B PAID BY MINISTER
1. Value of parsonage provided by church		
2. Rent or principal payments		835
3. Taxes		1,182
4. Interest		8,081
5. Insurance		340
6. Repairs & upkeep		793
7. Furniture, appliances, etc.		1,409
8. Decorator items		463
9. Utilities		2,738
10. Miscellaneous supplies		642
11. **TOTALS**		16,483
12. *Fair Rental Value Computation		22,143

*Compute in year of purchase and in any year of major expense. (Homeowners only)

FRV of Home 13,800
FRV of Furniture ... 4,500
Decorator items ... 463
Utilities 2,738
Miscellaneous 642
Total to line 12 ... 22,143

13. Lesser of Column B, line 11 or line 12 16,483
14. Amount designated 18,000
15a. If line 14 is greater than line 13, enter the difference and as income on Form 1040, line 22; or
15b. If amount designated is included in error on W-2, enter the lesser of line 13 or 14 as a deduction on Form 1040, line 22. 1,517

COMPUTATION OF SOCIAL SECURITY BASE

If exempt, you may omit this section, write "Exempt-Form 4361" on the self-employed line, Form 1040, page 2.

1. Salary from W-2 21,264
2. Parsonage provided, column A, line 11 ..
3. Parsonage allowance, column B, line 14 18,000
4. Recapture of auto depreciation ....
5. Less moving expense reimbursement in W-2 ..
6. Less business % of auto interest + P.P. tax ... (924)
7. Less unreimbursed employee business expense (8,826)
   (enter from Form 2106, line 11)
8. **TOTAL** (enter on Schedule SE, Sec. A, line 2) 29,514

Auto #1: $158 interest X 80.24% business % = $ 127
Auto #2: ($481 interest + $456 personal property tax) X 76.57% business % = $ 718
Business portion of tax preparation fee = $ 79
Total (to line 6 of Computation of Social Security Base, above) = $ 924

COMPLETED INCOME TAX RETURN

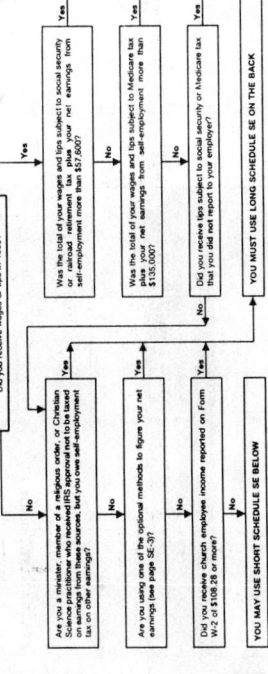

SCHEDULE SE (Form 1040)
WITHOUT REIMBURSEMENT
Self-Employment Tax
► See Instructions for Schedule SE (Form 1040).
► Attach to Form 1040.

OMB No. 1545-0074
1993
Attachment Sequence No. 17

Name of person with self-employment income (as shown on Form 1040): H. James Snodgrass
Social security number of person with self-employment income ► 483 12 0000

Who Must File Schedule SE
You must file Schedule SE if:
- Your wages (and tips) subject to social security AND Medicare tax (or railroad retirement tax) were less than $135,000, AND
- Your net earnings from self-employment from other than church employee income (line 4 of Short Schedule SE or line 4c of Long Schedule SE) were $400 or more, OR
- You had church employee income of $108.28 or more. Income from services you performed as a minister or a member of a religious order is not church employee income. See page SE-1.

Note: Even if you have a loss or a small amount of income from self-employment, it may be to your benefit to file Schedule SE and use either "optional method" in Part II of Long Schedule SE. See page SE-3.

Exception. If your only self-employment income was from earnings as a minister, member of a religious order or Christian Science practitioner, AND you filed Form 4361 and received IRS approval not to be taxed on those earnings, DO NOT file Schedule SE. Instead, write "Exempt-Form 4361" on Form 1040, line 47.

May I Use Short Schedule SE or MUST I Use Long Schedule SE?

Did you receive wages or tips in 1993?
- No → Are you a minister, member of a religious order, or Christian Science practitioner who received IRS approval not to be taxed on earnings from these sources, but you owe self-employment tax on other earnings?
  - No → Are you using one of the optional methods to figure your net earnings (see page SE-3)?
    - No → Did you receive church employee income reported on Form W-2 of $108.28 or more?
      - No → **YOU MAY USE SHORT SCHEDULE SE BELOW**
      - Yes → YOU MUST USE LONG SCHEDULE SE ON THE BACK
    - Yes → YOU MUST USE LONG SCHEDULE SE ON THE BACK
  - Yes → YOU MUST USE LONG SCHEDULE SE ON THE BACK
- Yes → Was the total of your wages and tips subject to social security or railroad retirement tax plus your net earnings from self-employment more than $57,600?
  - No → Was the total of your wages and tips subject to social security or railroad retirement tax plus your net earnings from self-employment more than $135,000?
    - No → Did you receive tips subject to social security or Medicare tax that you did not report to your employer?
      - No → **YOU MAY USE SHORT SCHEDULE SE BELOW**
      - Yes → YOU MUST USE LONG SCHEDULE SE ON THE BACK
    - Yes → YOU MUST USE LONG SCHEDULE SE ON THE BACK
  - Yes → YOU MUST USE LONG SCHEDULE SE ON THE BACK

Section A—Short Schedule SE. Caution: *Read above to see if you can use Short Schedule SE.*

1	Net farm profit or (loss) from Schedule F, line 36, and farm partnerships, Schedule K-1 (Form 1065), line 15a	
2	Net profit or (loss) from Schedule C, line 31; Schedule C-EZ, line 3; and Schedule K-1 (Form 1065), line 15a (other than farming). Ministers and members of religious orders see page SE-1 for amounts to report on this line. See page SE-2 for other income to report.	30,079
3	Combine lines 1 and 2	30,079
4	Net earnings from self-employment. Multiply line 3 by 92.35% (.9235). If less than $400, do not file this schedule; you do not owe self-employment tax	27,778
5	• $57,600 or less, multiply line 4 by 15.3% (.153) and enter the result. • More than $57,600 but less than $135,000, multiply the amount in excess of $57,600 by 2.9% (.029). Then, add $8,812.80 to the result and enter the total. • $135,000 or more, enter $11,057.40. Also, enter on Form 1040, line 47. (Important: You are allowed a deduction for one-half of this amount. Multiply line 5 by 50% (.5) and enter the result on Form 1040, line 25.)	4,250

For Paperwork Reduction Act Notice, see Form 1040 Instructions.   Cat. No. 113582   Schedule SE (Form 1040) 1993

2046

Schedule SE (Form 1040) 1993
Name of person with self-employment income (as shown on Form 1040)
Social security number of person with self-employment income ►

Section B—Long Schedule SE

Part I   Self-Employment Tax

Note: *If your only income subject to self-employment tax is church employee income, skip lines 1 through 4b. Enter -0- on line 4c and go to line 5a. Income from services you performed as a minister or a member of a religious order is not church employee income. See page SE-1.*

A	If you are a minister, member of a religious order, or Christian Science practitioner AND you filed Form 4361, but you had $400 or more of other net earnings from self-employment, check here and continue with Part I. ► ☐	
1	Net farm profit or (loss) from Schedule F, line 36, and farm partnerships, Schedule K-1 (Form 1065), line 15a. **Note:** *Skip this line if you use the farm optional method. See page SE-3*	
2	Net profit or (loss) from Schedule C, line 31; Schedule C-EZ, line 3; and Schedule K-1 (Form 1065), line 15a (other than farming). Ministers and members of religious orders see page SE-1 for amounts to report on this line. See page SE-2 for other income to report. **Note:** *Skip this line if you use the nonfarm optional method. See page SE-3*	
3	Combine lines 1 and 2	
4a	If not required to file Sch. SE, enter amount from line 3 (see page SE-3)	
b	If you elected one or both of the optional methods, enter the total of lines 17 and 19 here	
c	Combine lines 4a and 4b. If less than $400, do not file this schedule; you do not owe self-employment tax. **Exception.** *If less than $400 and you had church employee income, enter -0- and continue.* ►	
5a	Enter your church employee income from Form W-2. Caution: *See page SE-1 for definition of church employee income.*	
b	Multiply line 5a by 92.35% (.9235). If less than $100, enter -0-	
6	Net earnings from self-employment. Add lines 4c and 5b	57,600 00
7	Maximum amount of combined wages and self-employment earnings subject to social security tax or the 6.2% portion of the 7.65% railroad retirement (tier 1) tax for 1993	
8a	Total social security wages and tips (from Form(s) W-2) and railroad retirement (tier 1) compensation	
b	Unreported tips subject to social security tax (from Form 4137, line 9)	
c	Add lines 8a and 8b	
9	Subtract line 8c from line 7. If zero or less, enter -0- here and on line 10 and go to line 12a ►	
10	Multiply the smaller of line 6 or line 9 by 12.4% (.124)	
11	Maximum amount of combined wages and self-employment earnings subject to Medicare tax or the 1.45% portion of the 7.65% railroad retirement (tier 1) tax for 1993	135,000 00
12a	Total Medicare wages and tips (from Form(s) W-2) and railroad retirement (tier 1) compensation	
b	Unreported tips subject to Medicare tax (from Form 4137, line 14)	
c	Add lines 12a and 12b	
13	Subtract line 12c from line 11. If zero or less, enter -0- here and on line 14 and go to line 15 ►	
14	Multiply the smaller of line 6 or line 13 by 2.9% (.029)	
15	**Self-employment tax.** Add lines 10 and 14. Enter here and on Form 1040, line 47. (Important: You are allowed a deduction for one-half of this amount. Multiply line 15 by 50% (.5) and enter the result on Form 1040, line 25.)	

Part II   Optional Methods To Figure Net Earnings (See page SE-3.)

16	**Farm Optional Method.** You may use this method only if (a) Your gross farm income was not more than $2,400 or (b) Your gross farm income was more than $2,400 and your net farm profits were less than $1,733. Maximum income for optional methods	1,600 00
17	Enter the smaller of: two-thirds (2/3) of gross farm income (not less than zero) or $1,600. Also, include this amount on line 4b above	
18	**Nonfarm Optional Method.** You may use this method only if (a) Your net nonfarm profits were less than $1,733 and also less than 72.189% of your gross nonfarm income, and (b) You had net earnings from self-employment of at least $400 in 2 of the prior 3 years. **Caution:** *You may use this method no more than five times.* Subtract line 17 from line 16	
19	Enter the smaller of: two-thirds (2/3) of gross nonfarm income (not less than zero) or the amount on line 18. Also, include this amount on line 4b above	

From Schedule F, line 11 and Schedule K-1 (Form 1065), line 15b   From Schedule C, line 31; Schedule C-EZ, line 3; and Schedule K-1 (Form 1065), line 15a
From Schedule F, line 36 and Schedule K-1 (Form 1065), line 15a   From Schedule C, line 7; Schedule C-EZ, line 1; and Schedule K-1 (Form 1065), line 15c

Chapter Seven

STATEMENT OF UNREIMBURSED EXPENSE ALLOCATION - SEC. 265

Taxpayer's Name	Social Security Number	Year
H. James Snodgrass	483-12-0000	1993

TAXABLE COMPENSATION

W-2 SALARY .... $ 21,264
PLUS
UNUSED PARSONAGE ALLOW .. $ 1,517 = TOTAL $ 22,781
PLUS
RECAPTURE OF AUTO DEPR ... $

DIVIDED BY

GROSS COMPENSATION
(from Worksheet to be Used with Form 2106 - Social Security Base × Lines 1 thru 4)

W-2 SALARY .... $ 21,264
PLUS
PARSONAGE PROVIDED ...... $ 18,000 = TOTAL $ 39,264
PLUS
PARSONAGE ALLOWANCE .... $
PLUS
RECAPTURE OF AUTO DEPR ... $

INCLUSION RATIO

TAXABLE COMPENSATION DIVIDED BY GROSS COMPENSATION

= 58.02 %

COMPUTATION OF DEDUCTIBLE EMPLOYEE BUSINESS EXPENSE

1. TOTAL UNREIMBURSED CLERGY BUSINESS EXPENSE (FORM 2106, LINE 11) ...... $ 8,826
2. INCLUSION RATIO (FROM ABOVE) .... 58.02 %
3. ALLOWABLE DEDUCTIBLE EXPENSES TO SCHEDULE A (LINE 1 × LINE 2) ...... $ 5,121
4. EXPENSES DISALLOWED (LINE 1 - LINE 3) .... $ 3,705

Form **8824**
Department of the Treasury — Internal Revenue Service

Like-Kind Exchanges
(and nonrecognition of gain from conflict-of-interest sales)
▶ See separate instructions.
▶ Attach to your tax return.
▶ Use a separate form for each like-kind exchange.

OMB No. 1545-1190
1993
Attachment Sequence No. 49

Name(s) shown on tax return: H. James Snodgrass
Identifying number: 483-12-0000

Part I — Information on the Like-Kind Exchange

Note: *If the property described on line 1 or line 2 is real property located outside the United States, indicate the country.*

1 Description of like-kind property given up ▶ 1989 Oldsmobile
2 Description of like-kind property received ▶ 1993 Mazda 626
3 Date like-kind property given up was originally acquired (month, day, year) ... 3 / 1 / 06 / 90
4 Date you actually transferred your property to other party (month, day, year) . 4 3 / 10 / 93
5 Date the like-kind property you received was identified (month, day, year). See instructions 5 3 / 10 / 93
6 Date you actually received the like-kind property from other party (month, day, year) . 6 3 / 10 / 93
7 Was the exchange made with a related party? If "Yes," complete Part II. If "No," go to Part III. See instructions.
  a ☐ Yes, in this tax year b ☐ Yes, in a prior tax year c ☒ No

Part II — Related Party Exchange Information

8 Name of related party
Address (no., street, and apt., room, or suite no.)
City or town, state, and ZIP code
Related party's identifying number
Relationship to you

9 During this tax year (and before the date that is 2 years after the last transfer of property that was part of the exchange), did the related party sell or dispose of the like-kind property received from you in the exchange? ☐ Yes ☐ No
10 During this tax year (and before the date that is 2 years after the last transfer of property that you received), did you sell or dispose of the like-kind property you received? ☐ Yes ☐ No

If both lines 9 and 10 are "No" and this is the year of the exchange, go to Part III. If either line 9 or line 10 is "Yes," the deferred gain or (loss) from line 24 must be reported on your return this tax year, unless one of the exceptions on line 11 applies. See Related Party Exchanges in the instructions.

11 If one of the exceptions below applies to the disposition, check the applicable box.
  a ☐ The disposition was after the death of either of the related parties.
  b ☐ The disposition was an involuntary conversion, and the threat of conversion occurred after the exchange.
  c ☐ You can establish to the satisfaction of the IRS that neither the exchange nor the disposition had tax avoidance as its principal purpose. If this box is checked, attach an explanation. See instructions.

Part III — Realized Gain or (Loss), Recognized Gain, and Basis of Like-Kind Property Received

Caution: *If you transferred and received (a) more than one group of like-kind property, or (b) cash or other (not like-kind) property, see instructions under Multi-Asset Exchanges.*

Note: *Complete lines 12 through 14 ONLY if you gave up property that was not like-kind. Otherwise, go to line 15.*

12 Fair market value (FMV) of other property given up 12
13 Adjusted basis of other property given up 13
14 Gain or (loss) recognized on other property given up. Subtract line 13 from line 12. Report the gain or (loss) in the same manner as if the exchange had been a sale 14

15 Cash received, FMV of other property received, plus net liabilities assumed by other party, reduced (but not below zero) by any exchange expenses you incurred. See instructions .... 15 | 0
16 FMV of like-kind property you received .... 16 | 14,498
17 Add lines 15 and 16 .... 17 | 14,498
18 Adjusted basis of like-kind property you gave up, net amounts paid to other party, plus any exchange expenses not used on line 15. See instructions .... 18 | 13,095
19 Realized gain or (loss). Subtract line 18 from line 17 .... 19 | 1,403
20 Enter the smaller of line 15 or line 19, but not less than zero .... 20 | 0
21 Ordinary income under recapture rules. Enter here and on Form 4797, line 17. See instructions .... 21 | 0
22 Subtract line 21 from line 20. If zero or less, enter -0-. If more than zero, enter here and on Schedule D or Form 4797, unless the installment method applies. See instructions .... 22 | 0
23 Recognized gain. Add lines 21 and 22 .... 23 | 0
24 Deferred gain or (loss). Subtract line 23 from line 19. If a related party exchange, see instructions .... 24 | 1,403
25 Basis of like-kind property received. Subtract line 15 from the sum of lines 18 and 23 .... 25 | 13,095

For Paperwork Reduction Act Notice, see separate instructions. Cat. No. 12311A Form **8824** (1993)

COMPLETED INCOME TAX RETURN

WITHOUT REIMBURSEMENT
STATEMENT OF DEPRECIATION AND COST RECOVERY

Attach to Schedule _____ A

Description Of Property	N Or U	Date Acq.	Cost Or Other Basis	Bus. %	Business Basis	20% Bonus Expensing	Salvage Land / ITC Adj.	Adj. Basis	Prior Dpr. Or Recovery	ACRS Or MACRS Class	Method Used	Life Or Rec. Per.	Year 19 _93_	%	Year 19 ___	%	Year 19 ___	%
Total Amount Expensed for Each Year (After 12/31/81)													1,178					
Library		1-89	533		533			533	366	7	DDB½		48	8.93				
Equipment		1-89	538		538			538	370	7	DDB½		48	8.93				
Library		1-90	400		400			400	225	7	DDB½		50	12.49				
Library		1-92	366		366			366	52	7	DDB½		90	24.49				
Fax Machine		2-10-93	529		529	529		0					0					
Library		1-93	649		649	649		0					0					

TOTAL 3,015   TOTAL 1,414

Form **4562** (Rev. 10-93)
Department of the Treasury — Internal Revenue Service

WITHOUT REIMBURSEMENT
Depreciation and Amortization
(Including Information on Listed Property)

▶ See separate instructions. ▶ Attach this form to your return.

OMB No. 1545-0172
1993
Attachment Sequence No. 67

Name(s) shown on return: **H. James Snodgrass**
Business or activity to which this form relates: **Form 2106**
Identifying number: **483-12-0000**

Part I — Election To Expense Certain Tangible Property (Section 179) (Note: If you have any "Listed Property," complete Part V before you complete Part I.)

1. Maximum dollar limitation (If an enterprise zone business, see instructions) **1** $17,500
2. Total cost of section 179 property placed in service during the tax year (see instructions) **2** 14,273
3. Threshold cost of section 179 property before reduction in limitation **3** $200,000
4. Reduction in limitation. Subtract line 3 from line 2, but do not enter less than -0- **4** 0
5. Dollar limitation for tax year. Subtract line 4 from line 1, but do not enter less than -0-. (If married filing separately, see instructions.) **5** 17,500

	(a) Description of property	(b) Cost	(c) Elected cost
6	Fax Machine	529	529
	Library	649	649

7. Listed property. Enter amount from line 26 .... **7**
8. Total elected cost of section 179 property. Add amounts in column (c), lines 6 and 7 .... **8** 1,178
9. Tentative deduction. Enter the smaller of line 5 or line 8 .... **9** 1,178
10. Carryover of disallowed deduction from 1992 (see instructions) **10** 0
11. Taxable income limitation. Enter the smaller of taxable income or line 5 (see instructions) **11** 17,500
12. Section 179 expense deduction. Add lines 9 and 10, but do not enter more than line 11 ▶ **12** 1,178
13. Carryover of disallowed deduction to 1994. Add lines 9 and 10, less line 12 ▶ **13**

Note: Do not use Part II or Part III below for listed property (automobiles, certain other vehicles, cellular telephones, certain computers, or property used for entertainment, recreation, or amusement). Instead, use Part V for listed property.

Part II — MACRS Depreciation For Assets Placed In Service ONLY During Your 1993 Tax Year (Do Not Include Listed Property)

14 (a) Classification of property	(b) Month and year placed in service	(c) Basis for depreciation (business/investment use only—see instructions)	(d) Recovery period	(e) Convention	(f) Method	(g) Depreciation deduction
a 3-year property						
b 5-year property						
c 7-year property						
d 10-year property						
e 15-year property						
f 20-year property						
g Residential rental property			27.5 yrs.	MM	S/L	
			27.5 yrs.	MM	S/L	
h Nonresidential real property				MM	S/L	
				MM	S/L	

15 Alternative Depreciation System (ADS) (see instructions):

a Class life					S/L	
b 12-year			12 yrs.		S/L	
c 40-year			40 yrs.	MM	S/L	

Part III — Other Depreciation (Do Not Include Listed Property)

16. GDS and ADS deductions for assets placed in service in tax years beginning before 1993 (see instructions) **16** 236
17. Property subject to section 168(f)(1) election (see instructions) **17**
18. ACRS and other depreciation (see instructions) **18**

Part IV — Summary

19. Listed property. Enter amount from line 25 .... **19** 0
20. Total. Add deductions on line 12, lines 14 and 15 in column (g), and lines 16 through 19. Enter here and on the appropriate lines of your return. (Partnerships and S corporations—see instructions) **20** 1,414
21. For assets shown above and placed in service during the current year, enter the portion of the basis attributable to section 263A costs (see instructions) **21**

For Paperwork Reduction Act Notice, see page 1 of the separate instructions. Cat. No. 12906N Form **4562** (1993)

3231-13

108

Chapter Seven

WORKSHEET TO COMPUTE AUTO BASIS
WITHOUT REIMBURSEMENT — WHEN USE IS PART BUSINESS AND PART PERSONAL

FORMULA FOR COMPUTING GAIN OR LOSS WHEN USE IS PART BUSINESS AND PART PERSONAL:

		DESCRIPTION OF AUTO
1. Odometer reading when traded (old car)	86,206 Miles	DATE ACQUIRED 1/06/90
2. Odometer reading when acquired (old car)	3,280 Miles	YEAR 1989
3. Total miles driven while owned (line 1 less line 2)	82,926 Miles	MAKE Oldsmobile
4. Business miles driven while owned (line D)	67,286 Miles	(NEW) OR USED (circle one)
5. Average business % while owned (line 4 divided by line 3)	81.14 %	
6. Purchase price of old car (list price)	$ 7,890	
7. Trade-in allowance towards new car or Sales price	$(3,000)	
8. **Difference** (line 6 less line 7)	$ 4,890	
9. Business portion (line 8 times line 5)	$ 3,968	
10. Gain or loss on previous trade-in (if none, enter zero)	$ 0	
11. Balance of lines 9 and 10 (subtract gain or add loss)	$ 3,968	
12. Depreciation and expensing allowed or allowable (use worksheet below)	$ 3,423	Sales Tax
(Gain when line 12 is greater than line 11)		
(Loss when line 11 is greater than line 12)	$ 545	Gain or (Loss) (circle one) = $ 11,141
14. Purchase price of new car	$ 10,610	+ $ 531 = Total
	List price	

Year	(H) Basis From G	(I) Expensing Sec. 179	(J) Remaining Basis	(K) Adjusted Basis	(L) ITC ADJ	(L) Class Life	(M) Method Used	(N) Life or RP	(O) Act Opt	(P) Deprec. Computed	(Q) Deprec. Limit	(R) Deprec. Allowed	(S) Deprec. Recapture
19 90 1st Year	29,260		29,260	10,217		5	DDB½	20	A	2,043	2,309	2,043	
19 91 2nd Year	29,260		29,260	10,257		5	DDB½	32	A	3,282	3,661	3,282	
19 92 3rd Year	33,060		33,060	10,036		5	DDB½	19.20A		1,926	2,172	1,926	
19 93 4th Year	25,400		28,820	9,485		5	DDB½	11.52A		546	592	546	
19													

A. Odometer reading end of year 10,217
B. Odometer reading beginning of year 10,257
C. Total miles driven during year (A minus B) 10,036
D. Business miles from log 9,485
E. Business % (D divided by C) .... 86.81% | 87.17% | 85.19% | 80.24%
F. Multiply line 14 by E .... $ 9,672 | $ 9,712 | 9,491 | 10,036
G. Basis for depreciation:
 Subtract gain. Add (loss) .... 10,217 | 10,257 | 10,036 | 9,485

General Instructions:

Lines 1 through 11: Enter information from previous auto's worksheet if there has been a trade. Leave blank if newly acquired auto is the result of an outright purchase.

Line 12: Depreciation allowed or allowable is computed as follows:
 Actual Depreciation and optional or optional "factor" [see ¶ (P)] .... $ 3,423
 Plus Expensing - Code Sec. 179 ....
 Less ½ Investment Credit (ITC) downward Basis Adjustment ....
 Plus ½ Recapture of Credit (ITC) upward Basis Adjustment ....
 Total to be taken to line 12 .... $ 3,423

Line 13: If auto is sold, take Gain or Loss to Form 4797. If trade, complete form 8824.

(H) An election in year of purchase, reduce basis each year by amount claimed in year of purchase. Since 6-18-84, luxury auto rules severely limit the use of Code Sec. 179 expensing for autos.

(I) In the year of purchase, use this basis for investment credit. (Before 12-31-85)
 If optional method is used, "non-recovery" rates must be used:
  3 years but less than 5 .... 33⅓%
  5 years but less than 7 .... 66%
  7 or more years 100%

WITHOUT REIMBURSEMENT

(J) Investment credit recapture is to be computed if you took the investment credit for an auto and in a later year the percentage of business use falls to a lower percentage of the total use for the year. Autos purchased after 6-18-84: if business use falls to 50% or less in any year, you are treated as having disposed of the auto for investment credit recapture purposes. Subtract ⅔ of ITC recaptured from Column J when applicable.
 Tax Reform Act of 1986 ended the credit. Since 12-31-85, investment credit is no longer available.
(K) Adjusted basis - Column G minus H & J + K. (Basis used for depreciation computation.)
(L) When actual expenses are used, enter "3" for autos purchased before 1-1-87; "5" for autos purchased after 12-31-86.
 When optional method is used, leave blank.
(M) Indicate MACRS percentage method by using "DDB".
 Indicate conventions by "½" or "¼". If 40% of purchases are after 9-30, you must use mid-quarter convention.
 Indicate ACRS Section 179 percentage method by "SLY-PRE".
 Indicate Straight Line method by "SL".
(N) When ACRS or MACRS percentage method is chosen, enter % used.
 When ACRS straight line method is chosen, indicate choice of 3, 5, or 12 years. When MACRS straight line is chosen, enter 5 years.
 When optional method was chosen in 1st year and you have switched to actual, enter the life chosen according to useful life.
 8, 10, 10%, or 11¢ rate is used. ("O-10½" or "O-11").
(O) Indicate whether depreciation computation in Column (P) is actual method "A" or optional method "O". If optional, indicate whether 7, 7½,
(P) **COMPUTE ACTUAL DEPRECIATION AS FOLLOWS:**
 MACRS percentage method: Before 1-1-87 - Column K multiplied by 25% 1st year, 38% 2nd year, 37% 3rd year.
 MACRS percentage method: After 12-31-86 - Column K multiplied by:

Year	Mid-year	Mid-quarter (1st)	Mid-quarter (2nd)	Mid-quarter (3rd)	Mid-quarter (4th)
1	20%	35%	25%	15%	5%
2	32%	26%	30%	34%	38%
3	19.20%	15.60%	18%	20.40%	22.80%
4	11.52%	11.01%	11.37%	12.24%	13.68%
5	11.52%	11.01%	11.37%	11.30%	10.94%
6	5.76%	1.38%	4.26%	7.06%	9.58%

ACRS percentage method: Column K divided by choice of 3, 5, or 12 year. First year is only ½ year only.
MACRS straight line method: Column K divided by 5 years. First year is either ½ year or mid-quarter convention.
When business use is 50% or less, only 5 year straight line can be computed for autos purchased since 6-18-84.
No depreciation is allowed in year of trade or sale for autos purchased after 1-1-81 and before 1-1-87. (ACRS)
 If Code Sec. 179 expensing has been elected, add Column H to actual depreciation.
 Since 1-1-81, if you choose actual depreciation in year of purchase, you must continue to use actual as long as you own that car.
COMPUTE OPTIONAL DEPRECIATION FACTOR AS FOLLOWS:
 1980 thru 1989: Business miles up to but no more than 15,000 per year or 60,000 per auto, multiplied by 7¢ in 1980 and 1981; 7½¢ in 1982, 8¢ in 1983, 1984, and 1985; 9¢ in 1986; 10¢ in 1987; 10½¢ in 1988; 11¢ in 1989.
 1990 thru 1992: All business miles multiplied by 11¢ in 1990 and 1991; 11½¢ in 1992.
 1993: All business miles multiplied by 11½¢.
 If optional method is elected in the 1st year, the election to exclude the auto from the ACRS or MACRS methods of depreciation is required to be computed as straight line over the useful life in any year election is changed to actual method. As "non-recovery" property, you may choose actual or optional method each year.
(Q) Luxury auto limitations for depreciation:

Date Auto Placed in Service 1/06/90

	Date Auto Placed in Service			Date Auto Placed in Service				Amount from Table	Bus. %	Depr. Limit
# of Years Owned	1-1-87 thru 12-31-87	1-1-88 thru 12-31-88	1-1-89 thru 12-31-89	1-1-90 thru 12-31-90	1-1-91 thru 12-31-91	1-1-92 thru 12-31-92	after 12-31-92			
1st year	$2,560	$4,100	$2,660	$2,660	$2,660	$2,760	$2,860	1st year: $2,660	× 86.81%	= $2,309
2nd year	$4,100	$4,200	$4,300	$4,200	$4,400	$4,600	2nd year: $4,200	× 87.17%	= $3,661
3rd year	$2,450	$2,550	$2,550	$2,550	$2,650	$2,750	3rd year: $2,550	× 85.19%	= $2,172
4th - 6th	$1,475	$1,475	$1,475	$1,575	$1,575	$1,675	4th year: $1,475	× 80.24%	= $1,184
5th year							5th year:	×	=
6th year							6th year:	×	=

divided by 2 = 592

(R) Enter the smallest of Column P or Q. Also, enter this amount on Form 2106.
(S) Autos purchased after 6-18-84. Depreciation Recapture or "pay back" is to be computed if an auto was more than 50% business use in year of purchase, but drops below 50% business use in any future year when a method of accelerated depreciation was used. You must recompute at the 5 year straight line method. You must continue using 5 year straight line even if business use rises back above 50%. The rest of the useful life. "Non-recovery" property, depreciation is required to be computed as straight line over the useful life of the auto. If this happens, get another worksheet, figure the 5 year SL on it and use it for the rest of the useful life. The recapture amount is shown as an income on Form 4797. Employees enter the income on Form 1040, line 22; Ministers also include in computation for Social Security; Self employed taxpayers on Sch. C, line 6; Farmers on Sch. F, line 10.

COMPLETED INCOME TAX RETURN

WORKSHEET TO COMPUTE AUTO BASIS

WITHOUT REIMBURSEMENT

FORMULA FOR COMPUTING GAIN OR LOSS WHEN USE IS PART BUSINESS AND PART PERSONAL:

1. Odometer reading when traded *(old car)*	101,020	Miles
2. Odometer reading when acquired *(old car)*	0	Miles
3. Total miles driven while owned *(line 1 less line 2)*	101,020	Miles
4. Business miles driven while owned *(line D)*	86,860	Miles
5. Average business % while owned *(line 4 divided by line 3)*	85.98	%
6. Purchase price of old car *(list price)*	$ 11,141	
7. Trade-in allowance towards new car or Sales price	$ 4,338	
8. **Difference** *(line 6 less line 7)*	$ 6,803	
9. Business portion *(line 8 times line 5)*	$ 5,849	
10. Gain or loss on previous trade-in *(if none, enter zero)*	$ 545	
11. Balance of lines 9 and 10 *(subtract gain or add loss)*	$ 6,394	
12. Depreciation and expensing allowed or allowable *(use worksheet below)*	$ 7,797	
13. Gain or loss on business portion	$ 1,403	
(Gain when line 12 is greater than line 11)		
(Loss when line 11 is greater than line 12)		
14. Multiply line 14 by E	$ 695 + $ 18,235 – $ 18,930 = **(Gain)** or Loss *(circle one)*

DESCRIPTION OF AUTO
DATE ACQUIRED: 3/10/93
YEAR: 1993
MAKE: Mazda 626
NEW or USED *(circle one)*

Year	19 93 1st Year	19 2nd Year	19 3rd Year	19 4th Year	19 5th Year	19 6th Year
List price	18,235					
Sales tax						
Total						

Year	(H) Basis From G	(I) ITC ADJ	(J) Remaining Sec. 179	(K) Adjusted Basis	(L) Class Life	(M) Method Used	(N) Life or RP	(O) Act Opt	(P) Depreciation Computed	(Q) Depreciation Limit	(R) Depreciation Allowed	(S) Recapture
1993	13,095		13,095	13,095	5	DDB½	20	A	1789	(15,559 × 11¢) 2,619	2,190	2,190
19												
19												
19												
19												

Note: Actual depreciation would have been $ 7,797

A. Odometer reading end of year: 20,315
B. Odometer reading beginning of year: 0
C. Total miles driven during year *(A minus B)*: 20,315
D. Business miles from log: 15,559
E. Business % *(D divided by C)*: 76.59 %
F. Multiply line 14 by E: $14,498
G. Basis for depreciation
 *(Balance of line 13 and F;
 Subtract gain, Add loss)*: $13,095

General Instructions:

Lines 1 through 11: Enter information from previous auto's worksheet if there has been a trade. Leave blank if newly acquired auto is the result of an outright purchase.

Line 12: Depreciation allowed or allowable is computed as follows:
 Actual Depreciation or optional "factor" [see 1 (P)] ... $ 7,797
 Plus Expensing - Code Sec. 179 ... $
 Plus ½ Investment Credit (ITC) downward Basis Adjustment ... $
 Less ½ Recapture of Credit (ITC) upward Basis Adjustment ... $
 Total to be taken to line 12 ... $ 7,797

Line 13: If auto is sold, take Gain or Loss to Form 4797. If trade, complete form 8824.

(H) An election in year of purchase, reduce basis each year by amount claimed in year of purchase. Since 6-18-84, luxury auto rules severely limit the use of Code Sec. 179 expensing for autos.

(I) In the year of purchase, use this basis for investment credit. (Before 12-31-85)
 If optional method is used, "non-recovery" rates must be used:
  3 years but less than 5 ... 33⅓%
  5 years but less than 7 ... 66⅔%
  7 or more years ... 100%

WITHOUT REIMBURSEMENT

(J) Investment credit recapture is to be computed if you took the investment credit for an auto and in a later year the percentage of business use falls to a lower percentage of the total use for the year. Autos purchased after 6-18-84, if business use falls to 50% or less in any year, you are treated as having disposed of the auto for investment credit recapture purposes. Subtract ½ of ITC recaptured from Column J when applicable.

Tax Reform Act of 1986 ended the credit. Since 12-31-85, investment credit is no longer available.

(K) Adjusted basis - Column G minus H & J = K. (Basis used for depreciation computation.)
(L) When actual expenses are used, enter "3" for autos purchased before 1-1-87; "5" for autos purchased after 12-31-86.
 When optional method is used, leave blank.
(M) Indicate MACRS percentage method by using "DDB".
 Indicate conventions by "½" or "¼". If 40% of purchases are after 9-30, you must use mid-quarter convention.
 Indicate ACRS percentage method by "PRE".
 Indicate Straight Line method by "SL".
(N) Indicate whether ACRS or MACRS percentage method is chosen, enter "%" used.
 When ACRS straight line method is chosen, indicate choice of 3, 5, or 12 years. When MACRS straight line is chosen, enter 5 years.
 When optional method was chosen in 1st year and you have switched to actual, enter the life chosen according to useful life.
(O) Indicate whether depreciation computation in Column (P) is actual method "A" or optional method "O". If optional, indicate whether 7, 7½, 8, 10, 10%, or 11¢ rate is used. ("O-10½" or "O-11").
(P) **COMPUTE ACTUAL DEPRECIATION AS FOLLOWS:**

ACRS percentage method: Before 1-1-87 - Column K multiplied by 25% 1st year, 38% 2nd year, 37% 3rd year.
MACRS percentage method: After 12-31-86 - Column K multiplied by:

Year	Mid-year	Mid-quarter (1st)	Mid-quarter (2nd)	Mid-quarter (3rd)	Mid-quarter (4th)
1	20%	35%	25%	15%	5%
2	32%	26%	30%	34%	38%
3	19.20%	15.60%	18%	20.40%	22.80%
4	11.52%	11.01%	11.37%	12.24%	13.68%
5	11.52%	11.01%	11.37%	11.30%	10.94%
6	5.76%	1.38%	4.26%	7.06%	9.58%

ACRS straight line method: Column K divided by choice of 3, 5, or 12 years. First year is only ½ year only.
MACRS straight line method: Column K divided by 5 years. First year is either ½ year or mid-quarter convention.
When business use is 50% or less, only 5 year straight line can be computed for autos purchased after 6-18-84.
No depreciation is allowed in year of trade or sale for autos purchased after 1-1-87 and before 1-1-87. (ACRS)
If Code Sec. 179 expensing has been elected, add Column H to actual depreciation.
Since 1-1-81, if you choose actual depreciation in year of purchase, you must continue to use actual as long as you own that car.

COMPUTE OPTIONAL DEPRECIATION FACTOR AS FOLLOWS:

1980 thru 1989: Business miles up to no more than 15,000 per year or 60,000 per auto, multiplied by 7¢ in 1980 and 1981; 7½¢ in 1982; 8¢ in 1983, 1984, and 1985; 9¢ in 1986; 10¢ in 1987; 10½¢ in 1988; 11¢ in 1989.
1990 thru 1992: All business miles multiplied by 11¢ in 1990 and 1991; 11½¢ in 1992.
1993: All business miles multiplied by 11½¢.

If optional method is elected in the 1st year, it carries with it the election to exclude the auto from the ACRS or MACRS methods of depreciation. As "non-recovery" property, depreciation is required to be computed as straight line over the useful life in any year election is changed to actual method. As "non-recovery" property, you may choose actual or optional method each year.

(Q) Luxury auto limitations for depreciation:

Date Auto Placed in Service 3/10/93

	Amount from Table		Bus. %		Depr. Limit
1st year:	$ 2,860	×	76.59 %	=	$ 2,190
2nd year:		×	%	=	
3rd year:		×	%	=	
4th year:		×	%	=	
5th year:		×	%	=	
6th year:		×	%	=	

Date Auto Placed in Service

# of Years Owned	1-1-87 thru 12-31-88	1-1-89 thru 12-31-89	1-1-90 thru 12-31-90	1-1-91 thru 12-31-91	1-1-92 thru 12-31-92	after 12-31-92
1st year	$2,560	$2,660	$2,660	$2,660	$2,760	$2,860
2nd year	$4,100	$4,200	$4,200	$4,300	$4,400	$4,600
3rd year	$2,450	$2,550	$2,550	$2,550	$2,650	$2,750
4th - 6th	$1,475	$1,475	$1,475	$1,575	$1,575	$1,675

(R) Enter the smallest of Column P or Q. Also, enter this amount on Form 2106.
(S) Autos purchased after 6-18-84: Depreciation Recapture or "pay back" is to be computed when a method of accelerated depreciation was used. You must recapture the excess of depreciation claimed in any future year when business use in any future year drops to 50% or less. The amount of depreciation recaptured at the 5 year straight line method. You must continue using 5 year straight line even if business use rises back above 50%. When this happens, get another worksheet, figure the income as follows: figure the income on Form 1040, line 22. Ministers also include in computation for Social Security. Self employed taxpayers on Sch. C, line 6; Farmers on Sch. F, line 10.

109

Form 1040 — U.S. Individual Income Tax Return 1993

WITH ACCOUNTABLE REIMBURSEMENT POLICY

OMB No. 1545-0074

Label
- Your first name and initial: H. James
- Last name: Snodgrass
- Your social security number: 483:12:0000
- Spouse's first name and initial: Mary T.
- Last name: Snodgrass
- Spouse's social security number: 483:15:0000
- Home address: 2309 E. Smith St.
- City, town or post office, state, and ZIP code: South Bend, IN 46617

Presidential Election Campaign
- Do you want $3 to go to this fund? — Yes (You), Yes (Spouse) — "Checking 'Yes' will not change your tax or reduce your refund."

Filing Status
3. ☒ Married filing joint return

Exemptions
6a. ☒ Yourself
6b. ☒ Spouse — No. of boxes checked on 6a and 6b: 2
6c. Dependents:
 (1) Name / (2) Check if under age 1 / (3) dependent's social security number / (4) Dependent's relationship to you / (5) No. of months lived in home in 1993
  - Ruth A. Snodgrass — 483:13:0000 — Daughter — 12
  - Thomas A. Snodgrass — 485:14:0000 — Son — 12
  - Samuel A. Snodgrass — 486:15:0000 — Son — 12
- No. of your children on 6c who lived with you: 3
- Total number of exemptions claimed: 5

Income
7. Wages, salaries, tips, etc. (Attach Form(s) W-2): 12,000 + 35,278 = 47,278
8a. Taxable interest income: 565
22. Other income (list type and amount — see page 20): EXCESS Parsonage.A: 2,096
23. Add the amounts in the far right column for lines 7 through 22. This is your total income ▶ : 49,360

Adjustments to Income
30. Add lines 24a through 29. These are your total adjustments: 2,096

Adjusted Gross Income
31. Subtract line 30 from line 23: 47,264

Page 2

Tax Computation
32. Amount from line 31 (adjusted gross income): 47,264
33a. Check if: ☐ You were 65 or older, ☐ Blind; ☐ Spouse was 65 or older, ☐ Blind. Add the number of boxes checked and enter the total here.
34. Enter the larger of your: Itemized deductions from Schedule A, line 26, OR Standard deduction
 • Married filing jointly or Qualifying widow(er)—$6,200: 16,905
35. Subtract line 34 from line 32: 30,359
36. Multiply $2,350 by the total number of exemptions claimed: 11,750
37. Taxable income. Subtract line 36 from line 35: 18,609
38. Tax. Check if from: a ☒ Tax Table: 2,794
40. Add lines 38 and 39: 2,794

Credits
44. Add lines 41 through 44:

Other Taxes
45. Subtract line 44 from line 40: 2,794
47. Self-employment tax. Attach Schedule SE: 4,193
53. Add lines 46 through 52. This is your total tax: 6,987

Payments
54. Federal income tax withheld: 7,848
59. Add lines 54 through 58. These are your total payments: 7,848

Refund or Amount You Owe
60. If line 59 is more than line 53, subtract line 53 from line 59. This is the amount you OVERPAID: 861
61. Amount of line 60 you want REFUNDED TO YOU: 861

Sign Here
- Your occupation: Minister
- Spouse's occupation: Nurse

COMPLETED INCOME TAX RETURN

SCHEDULE C-EZ (Form 1040) — Net Profit From Business (Sole Proprietorship) 1993

WITH ACCOUNTABLE REIMBURSEMENT POLICY

OMB No. 1545-0074
Attachment Sequence No. 09A
2045-3-5

▶ Partnerships, joint ventures, etc., must file Form 1065.
▶ Attach to Form 1040 or Form 1041. ▶ See instructions on back.

Name of proprietor: H. James Snodgrass
Social security number: 483 : 12 : 0000

Part I General Information

You May Use This Form If You:
- Had gross receipts from your business of $25,000 or less.
- Had business expenses of $2,000 or less.
- Use the cash method of accounting.
- Did not have an inventory at any time during the year.
- Did not have a net loss from your business.
- Had only one business as a sole proprietor.

And You:
- Had no employees during the year.
- Are not required to file Form 4562, Depreciation and Amortization, for this business. See the instructions for Schedule C, line 13, on page C-3 to find out if you must file.
- Do not deduct expenses for business use of your home.
- Do not have prior year unallowed passive activity losses from this business.

A Principal business or profession, including product or service: **Honorariums**
B Enter principal business code (see page C-6) ▶ **8 | 7 | 1 | 1**

C Business name. If no separate business name, leave blank.
D Employer ID number (EIN), if any

E Business address (including suite or room no.). Address not required if same as on Form 1040, page 1.
City, town or post office, state, and ZIP code

Part II Figure Your Net Profit

1 Gross receipts. If more than $25,000, you must use Schedule C. **Caution:** If this income was reported to you on Form W-2 and the "Statutory employee" box on that form was checked, see Statutory Employees in the instructions for Schedule C, line 1, on page C-2 and check here . . . ▶ ☐ **1** 690
2 Total expenses. If more than $2,000, you must use Schedule C. See instructions **2** 125
3 Net profit. Subtract line 2 from line 1. Enter on Form 1040, line 12, and ALSO on Schedule SE, line 2. (Statutory employees do not report this amount on Schedule SE, line 2. Fiduciaries, enter on Form 1041, line 3.) If less than zero, you must use Schedule C **3** 565

Part III Information on Your Vehicle. Complete this part ONLY if you are claiming car or truck expenses on line 2.

4 When did you place your vehicle in service for business purposes? (month, day, year) ▶ __ / __ / __
5 Of the total number of miles you drove your vehicle during 1993, enter the number of miles you used your vehicle for:
   a Business _____   b Commuting _____   c Other _____
6 Do you (or your spouse) have another vehicle available for personal use? .... ☐ Yes ☐ No
7 Was your vehicle available for use during off-duty hours? .... ☐ Yes ☐ No
8a Do you have evidence to support your deduction? .... ☐ Yes ☐ No
 b If "Yes," is the evidence written? .... ☐ Yes ☐ No

For Paperwork Reduction Act Notice, see Form 1040 instructions. Cat. No. 14374D Schedule C-EZ (Form 1040) 1993

SCHEDULES A&B (Form 1040) — Schedule A—Itemized Deductions 1993

WITH ACCOUNTABLE REIMBURSEMENT POLICY

OMB No. 1545-0074
Attachment Sequence No. 07
2045

(Schedule B is on back)
▶ Attach to Form 1040. ▶ See Instructions for Schedules A and B (Form 1040).

Name(s) shown on Form 1040: H. James & Mary T. Snodgrass
Your social security number: 483 : 12 : 0000

Section	Line	Description	Amount	Total
Medical and Dental Expenses	1	Medical and dental expenses (see page A-1)		
	2	Enter amount from Form 1040, line 32	2	
	3	Multiply line 2 above by 7.5% (.075)	3	
	4	Subtract line 3 from line 1. If zero or less, enter -0-		4 0
Taxes You Paid	5	State and local income taxes 728 + 152 + 720	5 1,600	
	6	Real estate taxes (see page A-2)	6 1,182	
	7	Other taxes. List—include personal property taxes ▶ Auto 78 + 456	7 534	
	8	Add lines 5 through 7		8 3,316
Interest You Paid	9a	Home mortgage interest and points reported to you on Form 1098	9a 8,081	
	9b	Home mortgage interest not reported to you on Form 1098. If paid to the person from whom you bought the home, see page A-3 and show that person's name, identifying no., and address ▶	9b	
	10	Points not reported to you on Form 1098. See page A-3 for special rules	10	
	11	Investment interest. If required, attach Form 4952. (See page A-3)	11	
	12	Add lines 9a through 11		12 8,081
Gifts to Charity	13	Contributions by cash or check	13 5,508	
	14	Other than by cash or check. If over $500, you MUST attach Form 8283	14	
	15	Carryover from prior year	15	
	16	Add lines 13 through 15		16 5,508
Casualty and Theft Losses	17	Casualty or theft loss(es). Attach Form 4684. (See page A-4)		17
Moving Expenses	18	Moving expenses. Attach Form 3903 or 3903-F. (See page A-4)		18
Job Expenses and Most Other Miscellaneous Deductions	19	Unreimbursed employee expenses—job travel, union dues, job education, etc. If required, you MUST attach Form 2106. (See page A-4) ▶	19	
	20	Other expenses—investment, tax preparation, safe deposit box, etc. List type and amount ▶ P. 185 W-Nursing Expenses - 510	20 695	
	21	Add lines 19 and 20	21 695	
	22	Multiply line 22 above by 2% (.02)	22 147,264	
	23	Subtract line 23 from line 21. If zero or less, enter -0-		23 945
Other Miscellaneous Deductions	24	Other—from list on page A-5. List type and amount ▶		24 0
Total Itemized Deductions	25	Is the amount on Form 1040, line 32, more than $108,450 (more than $54,225 if married filing separately)? • NO. Your deduction is not limited. Add lines 4, 8, 12, 16, 17, 18, 24, and 25 and enter the total here. Also enter on Form 1040, line 34, the larger of this amount or your standard deduction. • YES. Your deduction may be limited. See page A-5 for the amount to enter.		25 16,905

For Paperwork Reduction Act Notice, see Form 1040 instructions. Cat. No. 11330X Schedule A (Form 1040) 1993

112 Chapter Seven

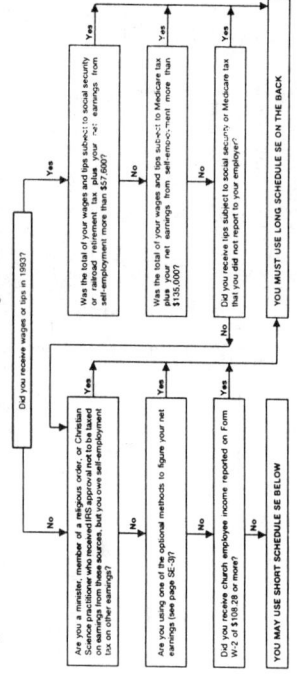

WITH ACCOUNTABLE REIMBURSEMENT POLICY
WORKSHEET TO BE USED WITH FORM 2106

Your Name: H. James Snodgrass
Social Security Number: 483 : 12 :0000
Occupation in which expenses were incurred: Minister
Taxable Year: 1993
☒ Ordained ☐ Licensed ☐ Commissioned ☐ Other Filed Form 4361? ☐ Yes ☒ No
Vehicle 1 Vehicle 2

ACTUAL AUTO EXPENSES (Complete Form 2106, Part II, Sec. A & B lists)

1. Garage rent
2. Gas
3. Oil & lubrication
4. Repairs
5. Tires & batteries
6. Insurance & auto club
7. License
8. Washing and polishing
9. Other
10. TOTAL
(enter on Form 2106, Part II, Section C, Line 23)

LOCAL TRAVEL EXPENSES
11. Parking
12. Tolls
13. Fares
14. TOTAL
(enter on Form 2106, Part I, line 2)

OVERNIGHT TRAVEL EXPENSES
15. Auto rental, taxi, etc.
16. Fares (air, train, bus)
17. Parking & tolls
18. Laundry & cleaning
19. Lodging
20. Telephone, telegraph, postage
21. Tips other than meals
22. TOTAL
(enter on Form 2106, Part I, line 3)

MEALS AND ENTERTAINMENT
1. Meals while away from home
   ☐ Actual ☐ Optional
2. Entertainment, meals
3. Entertainment, other
4. Tips for meals
5. TOTAL
(enter on Form 2106, Part I, line 5)

COMPUTATION OF PARSONAGE ALLOWANCE

Date of purchase: 6/10/86
FRV of home you own: $115,000

	A PROVIDED BY CHURCH	B PAID BY MINISTER
1. Value of parsonage provided by church	835	
2. Rent or principal payments		1,182
3. Taxes		8,081
4. Interest		340
5. Insurance		793
6. Repairs & upkeep		1,409
7. Furniture, appliances, etc.		463
8. Decorator items		2,738
9. Utilities		642
10. Miscellaneous supplies		
11. TOTALS		16,483
12. * Fair Rental Value Computation	22,143	

* Compute in year of purchase and in any year of major expense. (Homeowners only)

FRV of Home 13,800
FRV of Furniture 4,500
Decorator items 463
Utilities 2,738
Miscellaneous 642
Total to line 12 22,143

13. Lesser of Column B, line 11 or line 12 16,483
14. Amount designated 18,000
15a. If line 14 is greater than line 13, enter the difference and as income on Form 1040, line 22; or
15b. If amount designated is included in error on W-2, enter the lesser of line 13 on line 22; or as a deduction on Form 1040, line 22 1,517

COMPUTATION OF SOCIAL SECURITY BASE

If exempt, you may omit this section, write "Exempt-Form 4361" on the self-employed line, Form 1040, page 2.

1. Salary from W-2 12,000
2. Parsonage provided, column A, line 11 . . . .
3. Parsonage allowance, column B, line 14 18,000
4. Recapture of auto depreciation . . . .
5. Less moving expense reimbursement in W-2 . . . .
6. Less business % of auto interest + P.P. tax . . . .
7. Less unreimbursed employee business expense (enter from Form 2106, line 11) . . . . (893)
8. TOTAL (enter on Schedule SE, Sec. A, line 2) 29,107

PROFESSIONAL EXPENSES (UNREIMBURSED)
23. Business-in-home (see attached)
24. Education expense
25. Equipment depreciation (see attached)
26. Office supplies and postage
27. Religious materials
28. Sales aids
29. Seminars and dues
30. Subscriptions and paperbacks
31. Telephone
32. Other
33. TOTAL
(enter on Form 2106, Part I, line 4)

* Auto 1 ($158 int. X 80.24% bus. %) + Auto 2 ($481 int. + $456 P.P. tax) X 76.59 bus %) + $48 business portion of tax preparation fee = $ 893

Year _____

CHECKLIST
INCOME TAX DATA

THESE CHECKLISTS WILL SERVE AS A GUIDE IN ASSEMBLING YOUR TAX DATA AND HELP YOU TO TAKE ADVANTAGE OF ALL ALLOWABLE DEDUCTIONS. ROUND OFF ALL FIGURES TO THE NEAREST EVEN DOLLAR.

Last Name _____

TAXPAYER		SPOUSE	
First Name and Initial		First Name and Initial	
Occupation	Blind?	Occupation	Blind?
Soc. Sec. Number	Birth Date	Soc. Sec. Number	Birth Date

Address _____ Street (necessary for UPS) _____
         P.O. Box

City _____ State _____ Zip _____

County of Residence _____ Township or City _____

Telephone _____ _____
              (Home)   (Work)

Best time to reach _____

CHECK HOW YOU WANT TO PAY.   **CHECK HOW TO SEND:**
☐ Send complete returns C.O.D.   ☐ First Class Mail.
☐ Charge to my bankcard.   ☐ United Parcel Service.
☐ Send Invoice, hold returns
  until you receive payment.

☐ American Express ☐ Discover ☐ VISA ☐ MASTERCARD   Expiration Date
                                                              Month   Year

Charge this order to my Charge Account as I have indicated, to be paid according to the current terms of that Account.

Signature _____
              (Authorized credit card signature.)

Compliments of . . .

WORTH TAX & FINANCIAL SERVICE

	LOCATION:	**MAIL TO:**	**PHONE:**
Home Office	Just East of Bob Evans	P.O. Box 725	219•267•4687
Warsaw/Winona Lake, IN	3201 E. Center St.	Winona Lake, IN 46590	219•267•2870 Fax
Branch Office	Wawasee Village	804 S. Huntington St.	
Syracuse, IN	Highway 13 South	Syracuse, IN 46567	219•457•3044

© Copyright 1993 - Worth Tax & Financial Service

Dependents
Children living at home, if 1 year old, must have S.S. #.

FIRST, INITIAL, LAST	DATE OF BIRTH	S.S. #	RELATIONSHIP	MO. IN HOME

Estimated Tax Paid
Send copies of canceled checks

QUARTER	FEDERAL	DATE PAID	STATE	DATE PAID	LOCAL	DATE PAID
Prior Year Credit	$		$		$	
1st (4-15)	$		$		$	
2nd (6-15)	$		$		$	
3rd (9-15)	$		$		$	
4th (1-15)	$		$		$	
Paid with Extension	$		$		$	

Wages from W-2's
(Indicate H for husband or W for wife)

HW	EMPLOYER	FED TAX	WAGE	FICA	MEDICARE	STATE	LOCAL

Enclose all copies of W-2 wage statements.
IF CLERGY, SEND A COPY OF PAYROLL SHEET.

☐ Yes ☐ No Did you work two jobs in the same day?
_____ # of days; Give distance between jobs: _____ miles

Pensions, Annuities
Enclose all statements - 1099R and W-2P

HW	SOURCE & TYPE	FED TAX	TOTAL	TAXABLE

Unemployment			H	W
Social Security			H	W

CHECKLIST

Interest Income

Enclose all 1099 statements
(Indicate H for Husband, W for Wife or J for Joint)

HWJ	SOURCE (If seller-financed mortgage, list first)	*FORFEITURE	AMOUNT
	Municipal Bond Interest		

* Penalty on early withdrawal of savings

If seller-financed mortgage, give name, address and social security number: _____

Dividend Income

Enclose all 1099 statements

HWJ	NAME	# SHARES	*AMOUNT

*If mutual fund give the following

ORDINARY DIVIDENDS	CAPITAL GAIN	NON-TAXABLE

Other Income

HWJ	SOURCE	AMOUNT
	Alimony Received (bring copy of divorce decree)	
	Baby Sitting	
	Director's Fees	
	Hobbies	
	Jury Duty	
	Odd Jobs	
	Partnership/Estate/Corporation (enclose K-1s)	
	Prizes and Awards	
	Royalties	
	State Refund if you itemized last year	
	City or Local Refund if you itemized last year	
	Tips not reported to employer	
	Honorariums	
	Lottery, Gambling Sch. A Losses ( )	
	Other	

CHECKLIST

Itemized Deductions - Sch. A

Medical

TYPE OF EXPENSES	AMOUNT
Insurance Premiums	
Medicare Premiums	
Prescriptions	
Insulin	
Doctors	
Dentists	
Chiropractors	
Hospitals	
Ambulance	
Artificial Teeth	
Eye Glasses	
Hearing Aid	
Batteries	
Lab Fees	
Nursing Fees	
Special Shoes	
X-Rays	
Medical Supplies	
Nursing Home	
Air Conditioning	
Humidifier	
Electricity	
Auto Travel (miles)	
Transportation	
Lodging	
Other	

Taxes

KIND OF TAX	AMOUNT
Last year's paid in spring. State & Local Tax	
For a previous year, if you filed late, received a notice of change, or amended a return. State & Local Tax	
If you have purchased or sold home or personal use property, provide a copy of closing statement. Real Estate Tax #1	
Real Estate Tax #2	
Personal Property Tax	
Auto Excise	

NOTE: Sales Taxes are no longer deductible

Interest Paid

HOME INTEREST	AMOUNT
1st Mortgage	
2nd Mortgage	
Vacation Home	
Mortgage line of credit	
Points ☐ New ☐ Refinanced	
# of years of loan	

If home interest paid to individual, give name and address:

_____

_____

_____

INVESTMENT INTEREST	AMOUNT

NOTE: Personal Interest is no longer deductible.

Contributions

TO WHOM	AMOUNT
CASH: Church	
Church	
Red Cross/Scouts	
Salvation Army	
United Fund	
Missions	
Radio Broadcasts	
*Colleges	
Other	
**NON-CASH:	
Travel - Lodging & Meals	
Supplies	
Auto travel (miles)	
Transportation & fares	
FMV Clothing	
FMV Furniture	
FMV Real Estate	

* Indiana and Michigan residents, list name of college and date of contribution:

_____

** List name and address of organization to which items were donated to if $500 or more:

_____

_____

_____

CHECKLIST

Itemized Deductions (continued)

Miscellaneous

TYPE OF EXPENSES	AMOUNT
Tax Preparation	
Accounting Books	
Union Dues	
Professional Fees	
Professional Publications	
Supplies for Job	
Safety Equipment	
Safety Clothing	
Uniforms	
Cleaning of Uniforms	
Special shoes/Nylons	
Small Tools	
Equipment	
Telephone/Business	
Employment Agency Fee	
Other Job Expenses	

INVESTMENT EXPENSES	AMOUNT
Publications	
Broker Fees	
Safe Deposit Box	
Escrow Fees	
Other	

JOB HUNTING EXPENSES	AMOUNT
Meals	
Lodging	
Airfare, Auto Rental	
Auto Travel (miles)	
Postage, Typing	
Toll Calls	
Other	

CASUALTY OR THEFT	AMOUNT
Date property acquired	/ /
Date of casualty	/ /
Describe Property	
Cost of Property	
FMV before loss	
FMV after loss	
Insurance Reimbursed	

- ☐ Auto Accident
- ☐ Fire
- ☐ Wind
- ☐ Vandalism
- ☐ Theft
- ☐ Other_____

Casualties are limited by $100 floor and 10% of AGI.
Send complete details: Insurance reports, police reports, repair bills, etc. You must be owner of property damaged.

EDUCATIONAL EXPENSES	AMOUNT
Tuition and fees	
Books	
Supplies	
Auto travel (miles)	
Transportation	
Lodging	
Meals	
Name of School	
Date attended / / to / /	
Courses taken:	

Name of student:

Yes No
- ☐ ☐ Receive any reimbursement? How much? _____
- ☐ ☐ Are you currently employed?
- ☐ ☐ Did your employer require you to take courses?
- ☐ ☐ Were courses directly related to your profession?
- ☐ ☐ Have you already met minimum requirement of your profession?

Child and Dependent Care Credit

Persons or Organizations providing the care (nursery & kindergarten school expense may qualify for the credit):

NAME	ADDRESS	SSN or EIN	AMOUNT

NAME OF DEPENDENT	AGE	RELATIONSHIP

Employer-provided dependent care benefits received

Note: You are required to file payroll reports if amounts paid to persons working in your home is $50 or more in any calendar quarter.

Minister's Information

Position:	Duties:

Yes	No	
☐	☐	Ordained, Licensed or "the equivalent thereof?"
☐	☐	Are you exempt from paying Social Security (approved Form 4361)? *Send copy*
☐	☐	Does employer own and provide your parsonage?
		If yes, what is its rental value? $_____
☐	☐	Own your own home? Date of purchase: _____/_____/_____
		Purchase price: $_____
		Current FMV: $_____
☐	☐	Parsonage allowance officially designated in advance?
		Amount: $_____
☐	☐	Have you read the current "Income Tax Guide for Ministers"?
☐	☐	Is your W-2 prepared according to the chart in Chapter 6?
☐	☐	Have you adequately accounted to your employer and been reimbursed for your professional expenses?
		If no, show details of your expenses.
$_____		Amount you receive each payday? How often? _____
$_____		Amount you receive monthly?
		Please send a photocopy of your payroll sheet!! Thanks!

Parsonage Expenses (paid by you)

Parsonage allowance exclusion can apply to only one home at a time, the one that is your personal residence. If you have changed parsonages during the year, separate the expenses below.

Location:		Location:	
Date occupied: / /		Date Occupied: / /	
TYPE OF EXPENSES	**AMOUNT**	**TYPE OF EXPENSES**	**AMOUNT**
Rent paid		Rent paid	
Principal payments		Principal payments	
Taxes		Taxes	
Interest		Interest	
Insurance		Insurance	
Repairs and Upkeep		Repairs and Upkeep	
Furniture/appliances		Furniture/appliances	
Decorator items		Decorator items	
Utilities		Utilities	
Misc. Supplies/expenses		Misc. supplies/expenses	

Moving Expenses - Sch. A

Enclose Form 4782 from employer reimbursed moves. Is amount reimbursed in the W-2? ☐ Yes   ☐ No

Amount reimbursed by employer	( )
Distance between former residence and new job	
Distance between former residence and former job	
Date of departure: / / Date of arrival: / /	
Cost of moving furniture and personal effects	
Transportation of family: Auto travel (miles)	
Fares (air, bus, train, etc.)	
Cost of lodging enroute	
Cost of meals enroute	
Cost of pre-move househunting trips (after finding work) - Other than meals	
Temporary living expenses near new job (30 day period) - Other than meals	
Cost of pre-move househunting trips and temporary living expenses - Meals	
Expenses of sale of former home (Commissions, etc.)	
Other Expenses	

CHECKLIST

Auto Expenses   Amount Reimbursed $_____

If new client, send complete history of business use of auto. Send copies of invoice and complete details of purchase and/or trade for each business auto. Even if you have always used mileage allowance, you may have a taxable gain or deductible loss on the sale of a business auto that must be reported. If leasing, give beginning value.

AUTO INFORMATION	AUTO #1	AUTO #2	AUTO #3	AUTO #4	AUTO #5
Year					
Make					
Date of purchase					
Purchase price					
Odometer at purchase					
Total miles for the year					
* Business miles					
Daily roundtrip commuting					
Commuting miles for year					
Auto lease					
Garage rent					
Gas					
Oil & lube					
Repairs					
Tires & batteries					
Insurance & auto club					
License					
Washing and polishing					
Other					
** Interest					
** Personal property tax					
*** Sales tax					

* If you have used auto for more than one business activity, enter total business miles here and give us extra note stating how may miles were driven for each business activity.
** Employee's auto interest is no longer deductible; Employee's personal property tax is deductible on Sch. A only.
*** Sales tax can be used to increase cost basis.

Yes No N/A
☐ ☐   Do you (or your spouse) have another vehicle available for personal purposes?
☐ ☐ ☐   If your employer provided you with a vehicle, is personal use during off hours permitted?
☐ ☐   Do you have evidence to support your deduction?
☐ ☐   If yes, is the evidence written?

Travel & Professional Expenses   Amount Reimbursed $_____

TRAVEL - LOCAL	AMOUNT
Parking	
Tolls	
Fares	
TRAVEL - WHILE AWAY FROM HOME	
Auto rental/taxi/etc.	
Fares (air/train/bus)	
Parking & tolls	
Laundry & cleaning	
Lodging	
Telephone, postage	
Tips/other than meals	
MEALS AND ENTERTAINMENT	
Meals/away from home	
# days away from home	
Entertainment, meals	
Entertainment, other	
Tips for meals	

PROFESSIONAL EXPENSES	AMOUNT
Educational expenses	
Office Supplies	
Postage	
Religious Materials	
Sales aids	
Seminars and dues	
Subscriptions	
Paperbacks	
Business Telephone	
Other	

EQUIPMENT & LIBRARY:		
DATE	ITEM	AMOUNT

Business Income & Expense: Schedule C

Name of proprietor	
Principle activity/product or service	
Business name & address	
Employer ID number	
Inventory method	
Accounting method	

Yes No
- ☐ ☐ Was there any change in determining quantities, costs, or valuations between opening and closing inventory?
- ☐ ☐ Did you "materially participate" in operation of business?
- ☐ ☐ Were you a statutory employee with income reported on W-2?
- ☐ ☐ Was this business in operation at the end of the year?
- _____ How many months was this business in operation during the year?

RECEIPTS	AMOUNT
Services	
Sale of Merchandise	
Commissions	
Babysitting, odd jobs	
Honorariums	
Beginning acc'ts receivable	
Ending accounts receivable	

COST OF GOODS SOLD	AMOUNT
Beginning inventory	
Purchases	
Less personal use	
Contract Labor	
Supplies	
Freight/Receiving	
Ending Inventory	
Beginning accounts payable	
Ending accounts payable	

* BUILDING & EQUIPMENT		
DATE	ITEM	AMOUNT

BUSINESS-IN-HOME EXPENSE	
Total Sq. feet in home	
Sq. feet used/business	
Date of purchase	/ /
Cost of home	
Cost of improvements	
Rent	
Interest	
Taxes	
Insurance	
Heat & light	
Repairs - whole house	
Repairs - all business	

EXPENSES	AMOUNT
Advertising	
Bad debts from sales	
Bank service charges	
** Auto & truck expense	
Commissions	
Depletion	
Employee benefits	
Insurance	
Interest: Mortgage	
Interest: Other	
Legal & professional	
Office expense	
Pension plans	
Rent - Equipment	
Rent - Other business property	
Repairs & maintenance	
Supplies	
Real estate taxes	
Personal property tax	
Sales tax	
FICA & unemployment	
Travel	
Meals & entertainment	
Utilities	
Telephone	
Wages	
Wages paid spouse	
Wages paid children	
Miscellaneous	

* Bring in last years return, so that depreciation can be computed on prior owned items
** State details on page 7, Auto Expense

CHECKLIST

Sale of Property, Stock: Schedule D

HWJ	DESCRIPTION	# OF SHARES	DATE ACQUIRED	DATE SOLD	GROSS SALES PRICE	COST OR BASIS	EXPENSE OF SALE

Installment Sale

If contract began this year, send copies of contract, amortization schedule (list the principal and interest), original purchase closing statement, cost of all improvements. Enter interest on page 3.

DESCRIPTION	DATE ACQUIRED	DATE SOLD	GROSS PROFIT PERCENT	PRINCIPAL RECEIVED THIS YEAR	PRINCIPAL RECEIVED PRIOR YEARS

Sale of Personal Residence

Send copy of purchasing closing statement and selling closing statement.

		AMOUNT
Date old residence acquired:	/ /	
Original cost		
Purchasing closing costs		
Improvements:		
Less energy credits claimed		( )
Less GAIN postponed on previous sale		( )
Less depreciation for previous business use		( )
Less casualty losses previously allowed		( )

Fixing up expenses:	DATE DONE	DATE PAID	
	/ /	/ /	
	/ /	/ /	
	/ /	/ /	

Expenses of sale		
Sales price		
Purchase price of replacement home		
Improvements of replacement home (within 24 months)		
Date acquired		/ /
Date occupied		/ /
If home has not been replaced, will it be?	When?	/ /

CHECKLIST

Rental Income and Expense: Schedule E

KIND AND LOCATION OF PROPERTY

#1 _____
#2 _____
#3 _____
#4 _____
#5 _____

YES NO
☐ ☐ Did you or a member of your family use for personal purposes any of the properties for more than 14 days or 10% of the total days rented at fair rental value?
If yes, which property? #_____
☐ ☐ Did you actively participate in the management of your rentals?
If no, which property? #_____

REVENUES:	#1	#2	#3	#4	#5
Gross Rent Income					
Royalties					
Date Rental Activity Began	/ /	/ /	/ /	/ /	/ /
EXPENSES:					
Advertising					
Auto-travel					
Cleaning					
Commissions					
Insurance					
Legal & professional					
Management fees					
Mortgage interest					
Other interest					
Office supplies					
Repairs: General					
Plumbing					
Electrical					
Painting					
Supplies					
Taxes & licenses					
Utilities					
Wages & salaries					
Lot rent					
Other					

BUILDING, MAJOR IMPROVEMENTS, FURNITURE:

DATE	DESCRIPTION	PROPERTY #	AMOUNT

CHECKLIST 123

Farm Income and Expense: Schedule F

Location and size of farm:
Principle product:
Employer's ID number: Accounting method:

YES NO N/A
☐   ☐   Did you make an election in a prior year to include commodity credit loan proceeds as income in that year?
☐   ☐   Did you "materially participate" in the operation of this business during this year?
              If no, and you have a loss, loss will be limited.
☐   ☐   ☐   Do you elect, or did you previously elect, to currently deduct certain preproductive period expenses?

INCOME	AMOUNT	EXPENSES	AMOUNT
Cattle/raised/resale		Chemicals	
Cattle/purchased/resale		Conservation expenses	
Cost of cattle sold	( )	Custom machine hire	
Dairy/breeding cattle		Employee benefits	
Cost of dairy/breeding cattle sold	( )	Feed purchased	
Sheep/raised/resale		Fertilizers & lime	
Sheep/purchased/resale		Freight, trucking	
Cost of sheep sold	( )	Gasoline - # of gallons:	
Breeding sheep		Other fuel, oil	
Cost of breeding sheep sold	( )	Insurance	
Hogs/raised/resale		Interest: mortgage	
Hogs/purchased/resale		Interest: other	
Cost of hogs sold	( )	Labor hired	
Breeding hogs		Labor, spouse	
Cost of breeding hogs sold	( )	Pension plans	
Horses		Rent of machinery	
Poultry		Rent of land, animals	
Dairy products		Repairs/maintenance	
Eggs		Seeds & plants	
Wool		Storage/warehousing	
Cotton		Supplies	
Tobacco		Real estate taxes	
Vegetables		Personal property taxes	
Soybeans		FICA & unemployment	
Corn		Utilities	
Other grains		Telephone	
Hay & straw		Veterinary, medicine & breeding	
Fruit & nuts		Advertising/accounting	
Custom machine hire		Dues/subscriptions	
Patronage dividends		Meals for labor	
ASCS payments: cash		Office supplies	
Material & services		Travel	
C. C. loans		Meals & entertainment	
Federal gas tax credit		** Truck & auto expense	
State gas tax credit		Watchdog expense	
Crop insurance proceeds		Other	
Labor			
Other			

* BUILDINGS & EQUIPMENT		
DATE	ITEM	AMOUNT

  * Bring in last year's return so that depreciation can be
    computed on prior owned items.
 ** Show details on page 7, Auto Expense.

IRA and Keogh Transactions
Enclose all Form 5498s

HWJ	KIND	NAME OF INSTITUTION	DATE OF CONTRIBUTION	VALUE OF ACCOUNT (END OF YEAR)	AMOUNT

HWJ	KIND	NAME OF INSTITUTION	DATE OF WITHDRAWAL	VALUE OF ACCOUNT (END OF YEAR)	AMOUNT

YES NO
☐ ☐ Active participant in another plan?
☐ ☐ Spousal accounts?
☐ ☐ Over 59½?
☐ ☐ Rollover?

ALIMONY PAID (Bring copy of divorce decree) _____
TO WHOM: _____ S. S. # _____

Presidential Election Campaign Fund
YES NO
☐ ☐ Do you want $3 to go to this fund?
☐ ☐ If joint return, does spouse want $3 to go to this fund?

Questions, if yes explain below
☐ ☐ Any births, adoptions, marriages, divorces or deaths in your family during the past year?
☐ ☐ Does anyone owe you money that has become a bad debt?
☐ ☐ Have you used bartering to exchange any goods or services?
☐ ☐ Did you or your spouse receive any source of income that is not listed in this checklist?
☐ ☐ Did you sell an auto, equipment or any property? If yes, give details.
☐ ☐ Did you live in more than one state during the year? If yes, give date of move: ___/___/___

Non-Taxable Income

Child support	
Welfare payments	
Veterans benefits	
Workman's compensation	
Other (explain):	

State Information
Amount of rent paid $ _____ # of months rented _____ School district _____
Location of principal residence _____
Landlord's name _____ Address _____
(T) County of residence, Jan. 1? _____ County of work, Jan. 1? _____
(S) County of residence, Jan. 1? _____ County of work, Jan. 1? _____

How did you find out about our Tax Service?
☐ Recommendation   ☐ Paper   ☐ Book   ☐ Direct mail
☐ Sign   ☐ Radio   ☐ Yellow pages ☐ Prior client

Taxpayer's Statement
The information furnished herewith is to enable you to prepare my (our) income tax return for the above year. It is true and complete to the best of my (our) knowledge and belief, and is to be relied upon by you accordingly.

Signature _____   Date ___/___/___

Signature _____   Date ___/___/___

SERVICES

Professional Tax Record Book
- Business Mileage Diary
- Auto Expenses
- Travel Expenses
- Professional Expenses
- Entertainment Expenses
- Housing Expenses
- Professional Income
- Monthly Summary

There is room in the binder for you to add pages from "Day Runner", for Appointments, Calendars, etc.

Refill Pages & Tabs without Binder

1 to 4	$10.95
5 to 24	$ 9.85
25 to 99	$ 8.75
100 or more	$ 6.57

Vinyl Binder With Pockets, Looseleaf, 6 Rings, Page Size - 3¾ X 6¾

Complete Book with Binder

1 to 4	$14.95
5 to 24	$13.45
25 to 99	$12.00
100 or more	$ 8.97

Minister's Compensation Package Tax & Financial Planning
WITH B.J. WORTH

Minister's Audio Cassette

ONE HOUR AUDIO PRESENTATION of how to arrange a compensation package that promotes good stewardship and teaches how to legally lessen your tax burden. Financial planning for retirement has been neglected by many ministers. Today is the day to begin!

1 to 4	$8.95
5 to 24	$8.00
25 to 99	$7.10
100 or more	$5.37

Worksheet for Form 2106 for Ministers
Worksheet to Compute Auto Basis
Statement of Depreciation and Cost Recovery

1 Form	25¢
25 Forms	$3.00
50 Forms	$5.40
100 Forms	$9.00

Payroll Sheets for Employees of Not-For-Profit Organizations

1 Sheet	50¢
25 Sheets	$6.00
50 Sheets	$10.80
100 Sheets	$18.00

Income Tax Guide
For Ministers & Religious Workers
(Revised annually since 1973)

1 to 4	$9.99
5 to 24	$8.50
25 to 99	$8.00
100 to 999	$5.99
1000 or more	call

Send Order To:
WORTH TAX & FINANCIAL SERVICE
BOX 725, WINONA LAKE, IN 46590
Office: (219) 267-4687
Fax: (219) 267-2870

Postage & Handling Schedule:

$0.00 - $17.50	$4.00
$17.51 - $32.50	$5.00
$32.51 - $65.00	$6.00
$65.01 - $100.00	$7.25
$100.01 - $150.00	$8.50
Over $150.00	$10.00

(We Ship U.P.S.)

METHOD OF PAYMENT:

☐ Check enclosed. Make payable to Worth Tax & Financial Service.
☐ American Express ☐ Discover ☐ VISA ☐ MasterCard

Expiration Month / Year

Charge this order to my Charge Account as I have indicated, to be paid according to the current terms of that Account.

(Authorized credit card signature)   Phone

(Price Subject To Annual Change. Call For Current Prices.)

CONSULTATIONS

We encourage your reading "Income Tax Law For Ministers and Religious Workers" in its entirety. It will answer most of your questions.

We are available for consultation throughout the year and whether you are able to come to our office for an appointment or need to conduct the consultation by phone, or by letter, it is necessary for us to charge for our time. Our fee is $50.00 per hour for consultation.

We prefer phone consultations. Experience has shown us that requests for information and consultation by letter do not provide us with adequate facts. It is often necessary to call and ask for background and facts to give you the correct answer.

> Up to 12 minutes - $10.00
> 13 to 24 minutes - $20.00
> 25 to 36 minutes - $30.00
> 37 to 48 minutes - $40.00
> 49 to 60 minutes - $50.00

Please have your charge card number available or be prompt to send amount consultant requests.

For brief informational calls there will be no charge.

SEMINAR REGISTRATION INFORMATION

Those who attend seminars by Worth Tax & Financial Service are always enthusiastically thankful for the understandable presentation of how they can pay less tax legally. Call and ask for details on how you can sponsor a Seminar in your area.

Beverly J Worth will present seminars in person at the locations and times listed on the next page. **Registration** for this seminar is only **$69 per person** when pre-registered ($99.00 at the door.) **$10 off** seminar fee to spouse, or additional persons from same firm or organization. All seminar sessions are from 8:30 a.m. to 4:45 p.m.

* * * *

WORTH TAX & FINANCIAL SERVICE

Professional ... but affordable tax preparation service since 1973

- Specializes in tax preparation: Ministers and Payroll Reports (by mail or in person)
- Tax Consultations by phone or appointment (consultation fee based on the length of time)
- 403b's • IRA's • Mutual Funds • Investments • Lump Sum Distributions

Jack W. and Beverly J. Worth
Registered Representatives

Securities offered through H.D. Vest Investment Securities, Inc.
433 E. Las Colinas Blvd., Third Floor, Irving, Texas 75039 • (214) 566-1651
Member SIPC and NASD

WORTH TAX & FINANCIAL SERVICE • P.O. BOX 725 • WINONA LAKE, IN 46590
(219) 267-4687 • (219) 267-2870 (Fax)

SERVICES

TAX SEMINARS
For Clergy and Not-For-Profit Organizations

FALL 1993
DATES & LOCATIONS

Tuesday .... November 30
FORT WAYNE, INDIANA
Signature Inn
I-69 & St. Road 3, Exit #111B
(219) 489-5554

Saturday .... December 4
WINONA LAKE, INDIANA
Winona Lake Park Community Bldg.
1590 Park Avenue
Call Worth at (219) 267-4687

Monday .... December 6
CINCINNATI, OHIO
Signature Inn North
I-275 & I-75/Sharon Rd. Exit #15
(513) 772-7877

Friday .... December 10
SOUTH BEND, INDIANA
Signature Inn
U.S. 33/Bus. Rt. 31 & I-80/90, Exit #77
(219) 277-3211

Saturday .... December 11
CHICAGO, ILLINOIS
Best Western - Homewood
One block South of I-80 on Halsted Blvd.
(708) 957-1600

Monday .... December 13
GRAND RAPIDS, MICHIGAN
Days Inn - Airport
I-96 & 28th St, S.E., Exit #43B
(616) 949-8400

Tuesday .... December 14
DETROIT, MICHIGAN
Hampton Inn - Auburn Hills
I-75 & University Dr., Exit #79
(313) 370-0044

Friday .... December 17
LAFAYETTE, INDIANA
Signature Inn
I-65 & State Rd. 26, Exit #172
(317) 447-4142

Saturday .... December 18
INDIANAPOLIS, INDIANA
Signature Inn - South
I-65 and Southport Road, Exit #103
(317) 784-7006

> For Signature Inn room reservations call 1-800-822-5252.

SPRING 1994
DATES & LOCATIONS

Tuesday .... April 19
ST. LOUIS, MISSOURI
Holiday Inn - Airport (Oakland Park)
I-70, Exit 236 (4505 Woodson Road)
(314) 427-4700 or (800) 426-4700

Thursday .... April 21
KANSAS CITY, MISSOURI
Ramada Inn Southeast
6101 E. 87th Street (I-435 & 87th St.)
(816) 765-4331

Saturday .... May 7
WINSTON-SALEM, N.C.
Ramada Inn North Airport
531 Akron Drive
(919) 767-8240

Monday .... May 9
COLUMBIA, S.C.
Best Western Bradbury Suites
Exit 74 off I-20 (7525 Two Notch Road)
(803) 736-6666

Wednesday .... May 11
MADISON, GEORGIA
Ramada Inn Antebellum
U.S. 441 & I-20, Exit 51
(706) 342-2121

Friday .... May 13
CHATTANOOGA, TENNESSEE
Best Western Motor Inn - South
I-75 East Ridge, Exit 1 (6710 Ringgold Road)
(615) 894-6820

TAX PREPARATION BY MAIL

If you are a typical busy religious worker, you may want to let **Worth Tax & Financial Service** prepare your tax return by mail. We encourage you to take advantage of this special service. Our purpose is to be of service to you in any way possible to prevent a religious worker from being unnecessarily burdened by tax or financial problems.

WHAT YOU SHOULD SEND

1. If you are a minister - **Copy of your employer's PAYROLL RECORD for you.**
2. W-2's showing salaries, 1099's showing interest, dividends, etc., K-1's from partnerships, trusts, etc..
3. **COMPLETED CHECKLIST.** It is very important for you to carefully enter your income and deductions on the CHECKLIST provided in the back of this book. Enter an expense only once. For example, if you enter your home interest under "Parsonage expense", do not enter it again under Sch A. Keep your receipts and cancelled checks.
4. Detailed auto expense for each auto. Send copies of purchase invoices and complete history of auto use. Complete questions on page 12 of CHECKLIST.
5. If you have purchased or sold real estate, send us photocopies of closing statements, contracts and 1099B's.
6. Labels from your Federal and State form packets. We have forms for federal and all states, and you do not need to send your packets. If you need to have a city or local tax return prepared, send us these forms.
7. Copy of last year's tax return. If you feel your prior year's returns were not correctly prepared, it is possible to file Form 1040X and amend returns for 1990, 1991 and 1992. Corrections can result in substantial refunds, or additional liability.
8. Enter your work and home phone numbers on page 1 of the CHECKLIST and tell us when it is best to reach you. If we feel we need further explanation of your data or that you did not send complete information—**WE WILL CALL. Calls must be at your expense, we will include the phone cost on the invoice for your return.**
9. Your return will be closely checked for accuracy and completeness.

TAX PREP FEES AND PAYMENT

Our fees are very reasonable and are based on the complexity of your return. The cost for a minister's return will average between $75.00 to $200.00. Extra State returns and several auto transactions create a more complex return.

Tax Preparation, Consultation, and orders of books and supplies are all on a **CASH BASIS.** You may pay for our services as follows:

1. **AMERICAN EXPRESS, VISA, MASTERCARD and DISCOVER** convenience is available. Enter your number and expiration date on Page 1 of the Checklist.
2. Ask us to send invoice of fee, and we will hold your return until we receive your check.
3. We can send your completed returns by **COD United Parcel Service.** The extra fee is only $4.50 (subject to change). By request we can send **COD U.S. Mail**, we bill you for whatever the fee is.

SHIPPING INFORMATION

Our experience with United Parcel Service (UPS) has been good. Be sure and give us a **STREET ADDRESS** as they cannot deliver to a post office box.

WORTH TAX & FINANCIAL SERVICE • P.O. BOX 725 • WINONA LAKE, IN 46590
(219) 267-4687 • (219) 267-2870 (Fax)